Fodo

JAMAICA

1st Edition

Where to Stay and Eat
for All Budgets

Must-See Sights
and Local Secrets

Ratings You Can Trust

Fodor's Travel Publications New York, Toronto, London, Sydney, Auckland
www.fodors.com

FODOR'S JAMAICA

Series Editor: Douglas Stallings

Editor: Mark Sullivan

Editorial Production: Astrid deRidder

Editorial Contributors: John Bigley, Paris Permenter

Maps & Illustrations: Bob Blake and Rebecca Baer, *map editors*

Design: Fabrizio LaRocca, *creative director*; Guido Caroti, *art director*; Ann McBride, *designer*; Melanie Marin, *senior picture editor*

Cover Photo: (Sandals Negril Beach Resort): Ken Welsh/Alamy

Production/Manufacturing: Matthew Struble

COPYRIGHT

SPECIAL SALES

This book is available for special discounts for bulk purchases for sales promotions or premiums. Special editions, including personalized covers, excerpts of existing books, and corporate imprints, can be created in large quantities for special needs. For more information, write to Special Markets/Premium Sales, 1745 Broadway, MD 6-2, New York, New York, NY 10019, or e-mail specialmarkets@randomhouse.com.

AN IMPORTANT TIP & AN INVITATION

Although all prices, opening times, and other details in this book are based on information supplied to us at press time, changes occur all the time in the travel world, and Fodor's cannot accept responsibility for facts that become outdated or for inadvertent errors or omissions. **So always confirm information when it matters,** especially if you're making a detour to visit a specific place. Your experiences—positive and negative—matter to us. If we have missed or misstated something, **please write to us.** We follow up on all suggestions. Contact the Jamaica editor at editors@fodors.com or c/o Fodor's at 1745 Broadway, New York, NY 10019.

PRINTED IN THE UNITED STATES OF AMERICA

10 9 8 7 6 5 4 3 2 1

Be a Fodor's Correspondent

Your opinion matters. It matters to us. It matters to your fellow Fodor's travelers, too. And we'd like to hear it. In fact, we *need* to hear it. When you share your experiences and opinions, you become an active member of the Fodor's community. Here's how you can help improve Fodor's for all of us.

Tell us when we're right. We rely on local writers to give you an insider's perspective. But our writers and staff editors also depend on you. Your positive feedback is a vote to renew our recommendations for the next edition.

Tell us when we're wrong. We update most of our guides every year. But things change. If any of our descriptions are inaccurate or inadequate, we'll incorporate your changes in the next edition and will correct factual errors at fodors. com *immediately*.

Tell us what to include. You probably have had fantastic travel experiences that aren't yet in Fodor's. Why not share them with a community of like-minded travelers? Share your discoveries and experiences with everyone directly at fodors.com. Your input may lead us to add a new listing or a higher recommendation.

Give us your opinion instantly at our feedback center at www.fodors.com/feedback. You may also e-mail editors@fodors.com with the subject line "Jamaica Editor." Or send your nominations, comments, and complaints by mail to Jamaica Editor, Fodor's, 1745 Broadway, New York, NY 10019.

Happy Traveling!

Tim Jarrell, Publisher

CONTENTS

ABOUT THIS BOOK

Our Ratings

We wouldn't recommend a place that wasn't worth your time, but sometimes a place is so experiential that superlatives don't do it justice: you just have to be there to know. These sights, properties, and experiences get our highest rating, **Fodor's Choice** indicated by orange stars throughout this book. Black stars highlight sights and properties we deem **Highly Recommended** places that our writers, editors, and readers praise again and again for consistency and excellence.

Credit Cards

AE, D, DC, MC, V following restaurant and hotel listings indicate whether American Express, Discover, Diners Club, Master-Card, and Visa are accepted.

Restaurants

Unless we state otherwise, restaurants are open for lunch and dinner daily. We mention dress only when there's a specific requirement and reservations only when they're essential or not accepted.

Hotels

Unless we tell you otherwise, you can assume that the hotels have private bath, phone, TV, and air-conditioning. We always list facilities but not whether you'll be charged an extra fee to use them, so when pricing accommodations, find out what's included.

Many Listings

☆	Fodor's Choice
★	Highly recommended
✉	Physical address
⊕	Directions
✉	Mailing address
☎	Telephone
📠	Fax
⊕	On the Web
✉	E-mail
✆	Admission fee
☉	Open/closed times
Ⓜ	Metro stations
⊟	Credit cards

Hotels & Restaurants

🏨	Hotel
↵	Number of rooms
⚙	Facilities
⊙|	Meal plans
✗	Restaurant
⚐	Reservations
↘	Smoking
BYOB	BYOB
✗🏨	Hotel with restaurant that warrants a visit

Outdoors

⛳	Golf
⊿	Camping

Other

☺	Family-friendly
⇒	See also
✉	Branch address
☞	Take note

Jamaica

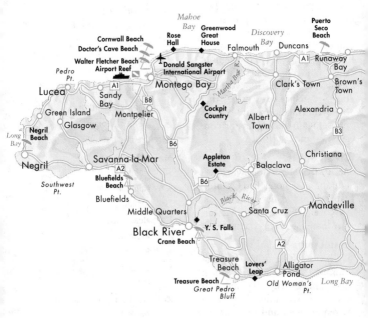

Puerto Seco Beach

Cornwall Beach
Doctor's Cave Beach
Rose Hall
Greenwood Great House
Falmouth
Discovery Bay
Duncans
A1
Runaway Bay

Walter Fletcher Beach
Airport Reef
Donald Sangster International Airport

Brown's Town

Pedro Pt.

Montego Bay

Martha Brae R.

Clark's Town

Lucea

A1

Sandy Bay

Cockpit Country

Green Island

B8

Montpelier

Albert Town

Alexandria

Glasgow

Negril Beach

B6

Appleton Estate

B3

Long Bay

Savanna-la-Mar

Christiana

Negril

A2

Balaclava

Southwest Pt.

Bluefields Beach

B6

Black River

Mandeville

Bluefields

Middle Quarters

Santa Cruz

Black River

Y. S. Falls

Crane Beach

A2

Treasure Beach

Lovers' Leap

Alligator Pond

Treasure Beach

Great Pedro Bluff

Old Woman's Pt.

Long Bay

Mahoe Bay

0   10 miles

0   15 km

Dunn's River
Falls
Mallard's
Beach
n's   Turtle   James Bond
y   Beach   Beach
                    Galina Pt.
              Oracabessa
Ocho Rios   Port Maria
                    Annotto
                    Bay
                         A4   St. Margaret's   Blue   San San
                              Bay   Lagoon   Beach
Walkerswood   Orange Bay   Northeast Pt.
Factory   Port Antonio   Boston Bay
                              Berridale   Rio   Priestman's
Ewarton   Troja   Grande   River
                    A3   BLUE   Moore
                         MOUNTAINS   Town
                                        Hectors River
                         Blue Mountains   Holland
                                                     Bay
Spanish   A1
Town   A1   Kingston
                              White   A4   Golden
Port Royal   Norman Manley   Horses   Grove
May Pen   International Airport
         Fort Clarence   Lyssons
         Beach   Morant   Beach
         B12   Port Royal   Bay
Portland   Polink Pt.   Sites
Bight
              Lime Cay
Portland Pt.

Caribbean Sea

KEY	
⟍	Beaches
⛴	Cruise Ship Terminal
◤	Dive Sites

WHEN TO GO

The high season in the Virgin Islands is traditionally winter—from December 15 to the week after the St. Thomas Carnival, usually the last week in April—when northern weather is at its worst. During this season, you're guaranteed the most entertainment at resorts and the most people with whom to enjoy it. It's also the most fashionable, the most expensive, and the most popular time to visit—and most hotels are heavily booked. You must make reservations at least two or three months in advance for the very best places (sometimes a year in advance for the most exclusive spots). Hotel prices drop 20% to 50% after April 15; airfares and cruise prices also fall. Saving money isn't the only reason to visit the Virgin Islands during the off-season. Summer is usually one of the prettiest times of the year; the sea is even calmer, and things move at a slower pace (except for the first two weeks of August on Tortola when the BVI celebrates Carnival). The water is clearer for snorkeling and smoother for sailing in the Virgin Islands in May, June, and July.

Climate

Weather in the Virgin Islands is a year-round wonder. The average daily temperature is about 80°F, and there isn't much variation from the coolest to the warmest months. Rainfall averages 40 to 44 inches per year. But in the tropics, rainstorms tend to be sudden and brief, often erupting early in the morning and at dusk.

In May and June what's known as the Sahara Dust sometimes moves through, making for hazy spring days and spectacular sunsets.

Toward the beginning of summer, of course, hurricane season begins in earnest, with the first tropical wave passing by in June. Islanders pay close attention to the tropical waves as they form and travel across the Atlantic from Africa. In an odd paradox, tropical storms passing by leave behind the sunniest and clearest days you'll ever see. (And that's saying something in the land of zero air pollution.)

Information **Weather Channel Connection** (☎900/932–8437 95¢ per minute from a Touch-Tone phone ⊕www.weather.com).

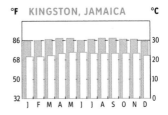

°F   KINGSTON, JAMAICA   °C

Montego Bay

WORD OF MOUTH

"Go to Rocklands Bird Sanctuary! It is amazing! You are given a little bottle of sugar water and instruction on how to hold your fingers out. Then hummingbirds zoom in and sit on your fingers to sip the sugar water."

—Tango

By Paris
Permenter
and John
Bigley

FOR MANY TRAVELERS, MONTEGO BAY is synonymous with Jamaica. This northern coast community is the capital of the island's tourism industry (although Ocho Rios is quickly moving up, having already taken over the top rank in terms of cruise-ship arrivals). Most visitors arrive in Montego Bay by air, but plenty of people get here by boat.

As home of the island's busiest international airport, Montego Bay (or MoBay, as it's locally known), is the first taste most visitors have of the island. Thanks to its numerous resorts, many travelers never venture any farther.

Today many explorations of MoBay are conducted from a reclining chair—frothy drink in hand—at Doctor's Cave Beach, the city's first tourist attraction, which attracted travelers who wanted to swim in what were called healing waters. Head out into the water off Doctor's Cave Beach, or any of the island's beautiful beaches, and you can find a world of undersea life awaiting exploration by snorkeling, diving, or even by venturing out in the belly of a small submarine or under your own power with the help of a high-tech dive helmet.

If you can pull yourself away from the water's edge and brush the sand off your toes, you can find some interesting colonial sights in the surrounding area. Because sugarcane plantations were an important part of the local economy for centuries, Montego Bay is home to some of the island's most famous greathouses, many open for public tours that give you a peek back at colonial days.

EXPLORING MONTEGO BAY

Montego Bay has the advantage of being the closest resort area to the island's main airport—an important consideration for travelers with a short vacation (or with restless children who don't want to spend another two hours in a bus after their flight). Three-night stays in Montego Bay aren't unusual and many travelers are willing to ignore jet noise to book a resort near the airport and maximize their vacation on the beach rather than on the bus to more distant towns.

Touring Jamaica can be both thrilling and frustrating. Rugged (albeit beautiful) terrain and winding (often potholed) roads make for slow going. Before you set off to explore

1

the island by car, *always* check conditions prior to heading out, but especially in the rainy season from May through October, when roads can easily be washed out. Primary roads that loop around and across the island have been recently improved between Montego Bay and Negril and MoBay and Ocho Rios; nonetheless, the roads are not particularly well marked. Numbered addresses are seldom used outside major townships (or, for that matter, even within towns), locals drive aggressively, and people and animals seem to have a knack for appearing on the street out of nowhere. That said, Jamaica's scenery shouldn't be missed. To be safe and avoid frustration, stick to guided tours and licensed taxis.

You can find at least three days' worth of activity right along MoBay's boundaries; you should also consider a trip to Cockpit Country in the island's interior or the lush resort area of Ocho Rios if you have the time. Day trips from Montego Bay to Negril also give you the opportunity to experience that community's 7-mi- (11-km-) long beach and watch the sunset from the island's westernmost point.

ABOUT THE RESTAURANTS

As Jamaica's second-largest city, Montego Bay has its fair share of fast-food joints. Don't worry—it is home to plenty of authentic eateries as well. Restaurants range from elegant dining rooms with white-glove service to casual beach bars a stone's throw from the surf. Reservations are required at a few of the top eateries (especially during high season from mid-December through mid-April) but generally are not necessary. Many all-inclusive resorts offer evening passes for nonguests who would like to eat at one of their restaurants. They often don't include all a resort's restaurants, so ask before you buy.

ABOUT THE HOTELS

As the first of the developed resort areas in Jamaica, Montego Bay is home many older (and now less-expensive) properties, most in the hills above the city with fine views of the sea. The beachfront is home to the area's largest and nicest resorts; the grandest of these are east of Montego Bay in the Rose Hall area and west of the city near Hopewell. Although Ocho Rios was the birthplace of the all-inclusive resort, Montego Bay has taken the concept to a higher level. Sandals has more locations here than anywhere else; other all-inclusive resorts cater to the adults-only and family markets.

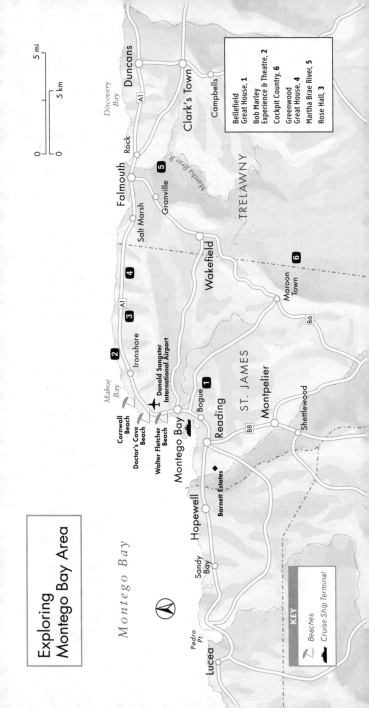

Exploring
Montego Bay Area

5 mi

5 km

0

0

Montego Bay

Pedro Pt.

Lucea

Sandy Bay

Hopewell

Barnett Estates

Reading

Montego Bay

Walter Fletcher Beach

Doctor's Cave Beach

Cornwall Beach

Maboe Bay

Donald Sangster International Airport

Bogue

A1

Ironshore

2

3

4

Salt Marsh

Granville

Falmouth

Rock

Discovery Bay

Duncans

A1

Clark's Town

Campbells

5

Martha Brae R.

ST. JAMES

Montpelier

B8

Shettlewood

Wakefield

Maroon Town

B6

6

TRELAWNY

KEY

Beaches

Cruise Ship Terminal

Bellefield Great House, **1**

Bob Marley Experience & Theatre, **2**

Cockpit Country, **6**

Greenwood Great House, **4**

Martha Brae River, **5**

Rose Hall, **3**

MONTEGO BAY TOP 5

Dancing the Night Away:
Montego Bay's "Hip Strip" has
a string of bars and clubs
that appeal to anyone waiting
to bust a move.

Pursuing Phantoms: The
haunted halls of the leg-
endary Rose Hall may be
enough to make you believe
in ghosts.

Riding the River: There's
nothing like gliding down the
smooth and gentle Martha

Brae River atop a traditional
bamboo raft.

Driving a Hard Bargain:
Perfect your haggling skills to
get the best possible price at
one of Montego Bay's lively
craft markets.

Getting Teed Off: The Tryall
Club, which is just south of
MoBay, has few rivals in the
Caribbean, which is why this
is a golfer's mecca.

The all-inclusive market is especially strong with couples
and honeymooners. To maintain a romantic atmosphere
(no Marco Polo games in the pool), some resorts have
minimum age requirements ranging from 14 to 18. Other
properties court families with tempting supervised kids'
programs, family-friendly entertainment, and in-room
amenities especially geared to young travelers.

WHAT IT COSTS IN DOLLARS				
$$$$	$$$	$$	$	¢
RESTAURANTS				
Over $30	$20–$30	$12–$20	$8–$12	under $8
HOTELS*				
Over $350	$250–$350	$150–$250	$80–$150	under $80
HOTELS**				
Over $450	$350–$450	$250–$350	$125–$250	under $125

*EP, BP, CP; **AI, FAP, MAP; Restaurant prices are per person for
a main course at dinner and do not include the 15% V.A.T. and
10% service charge. Hotel prices are per night for a double room
in high season, excluding 15% V.A.T. and 10% service charge.

TIMING

Like the rest of Jamaica, Montego Bay experiences high season from mid-December through mid-April, a time when the balmy breezes are a sharp contrast to the cold winds of the north. During that period, prices hit the roof at the end of the December and the beginning of January, dropping a bit after the holidays and rising again by late January as the pre-Valentine's crowds begin to arrive. Prices fall during the shoulder season that begins in mid-April then fall again in late summer as hurricane season reaches its peak. During mid-July, however, expect higher prices in Montego Bay as demand rises during the annual Reggae Sumfest, a weeklong music festival.

Spring break for college students, generally falling in late March and early April, can mean a busy time for properties along Gloucester Avenue (known as the "Hip Strip"). The higher rates of the all-inclusive resorts discourage that crowd. You will find a big demand for flights during those weeks, especially with charter air companies.

WHAT TO SEE

The name Montego is derived from *manteca* ("lard" in Spanish). The Spanish first named this Bahía de Manteca, or Lard Bay. Why? The Spanish once shipped hogs from this port city. When Columbus came along, he deemed this the Gulf of Good Weather, a description that remains true today.

Jamaican tourism began here in 1924, when the first resort opened at Doctor's Cave Beach so that health-seekers could "take the waters." Properties first built up near Doctor's Cave Beach and up on the Queen's Highway, a roadway high above the city that takes advantage of cooling breezes as well as excellent views.

With plenty of attractions and activities to fill a short vacation, Montego Bay makes a good home base for exploring the island. Day-trips can take you to interesting communities like Negril and Ocho Rios. Remember that although distances appear short on the map, heavy traffic, frequent road construction, and often poor road conditions can mean that destinations 50-mi (80-km) away easily take two hours to reach, however. The North Coast Highway–improvement project has improved access to both Ocho Rios and Negril, about 90 minutes to either community.

IF YOU LIKE

COLONIAL ARCHITECTURE

Rose Hall is undoubtedly Jamaica's most famous great-house, thanks to its scenic backdrop, titillating legend, and excellent renovation, but it's just one of many in the Montego Bay area. The area's longtime plantation history meant expansive farms were administered by greathouses, which once numbered 80 across the island.

GOLF

Jamaica is one of the Caribbean's top golf destinations and Montego Bay is the capital of the courses. The Tryall Club is one of the most prestigious, since the pros come here to play. East of town, Half Moon and the White Witch Course at the Ritz-Carlton vie for top honors. Neighboring Cinnamon Hill Ocean Course is on the grounds of a greathouse.

SOFT ADVENTURE

With its popular canopy tours and horseback rides, Montego Bay offers a wide selection of activities accessible to most travelers. From white-water rafting on the Great River to bouncy jeep tours across the countryside, you'll find plenty of half-day options for a little off-the-beach fun.

Numbers in the margin correspond to points of interest on the Montego Bay and Montego Bay Area maps.

1 Bellefield Great House. Since 1735 this imposing greathouse has stood on the Barnett Estate, a 3,000-acre plantation owned by the Kerr-Jarrett family for generations and still growing mangoes, sugarcane, and coconuts. Visitors on the 90-minute morning tour are greeted with a traditional Planter's Punch, then led on a tour that includes the sugar mill, boiler house, rum cellar, and jerk grill. Afternoon tours feature a four-course tea on the greathouse's spacious verandah. Transportation from Montego Bay hotels is included in the twice-weekly tour. ⊠ *Granville Main Rd.* ☎ *876/601–2382* ⊕ *www.bellefieldgreathouse.com* ☎ *$56 with lunch, transportation* ⊙ *Tours on Tues. and Fri.*

2 The Bob Marley Experience & Theatre. Although Montego Bay wasn't his home (you'll want to head to Kingston or Nine Mile near Ocho Rios to pick up that vibe), this theater is an interesting stop for fans of reggae pioneer Bob Marley. Along with some photos and displays, the facility's primary attraction is its theater, which shows a short film on the life and works of Robert Nesta Marley. There's also a large gift shop. ⊠*Half Moon Village, N. Coast Hwy.* ☎*876/953–3449* ⊒*Free* ⊗*Daily 10–6.*

❻ Cockpit Country. About 15 mi (24 km) inland from MoBay is one of the most untouched areas in the West Indies: a terrain of pitfalls and potholes carved by nature in limestone. For nearly a century after 1655 it was known as the Land of Look Behind, because British soldiers nervously rode their horses through here on the lookout for the guerrilla freedom fighters known as Maroons. Former slaves who refused to surrender to the invading English, the Maroons eventually won their independence. Today their descendants populate this area, untaxed and virtually ungoverned by island authorities. Most visitors to the area stop in Accompong, a small community in St. Elizabeth Parish. You can stroll through town, take in the historic structures, and learn more about the Maroons—considered Jamaica's greatest herbalists.

★ ❹ Greenwood Great House. Unlike Rose Hall, Greenwood has no spooky legend to titillate, but it's much better than Rose Hall at evoking life on a sugar plantation. The Barrett family, from whom the English poet Elizabeth Barrett Browning descended, once owned all the land from Rose Hall to Falmouth; on their vast holdings they built this and several other greathouses. (The poet's father, Edward Moulton Barrett, "the Tyrant of Wimpole Street," was born at nearby Cinnamon Hill, later the estate of country singer Johnny Cash.) Highlights of Greenwood include oil paintings of the Barretts, china made for the family by Wedgwood, a library filled with rare books from as early as 1697, fine antique furniture, and a collection of exotic musical instruments. There's a pub on-site as well. It's 15 mi (24 km) east of Montego Bay. ⊠*Greenwood* ☎*876/953–1077* ⊕*www.greenwoodgreathouse.com* ⊒*$12* ⊗*Daily 9–6.*

❺ Martha Brae River. This gentle waterway about 25 mi (40 km) southeast of Montego Bay takes its name from an Arawak Indian who killed herself because she refused to reveal the whereabouts of a local gold mine. According to legend, she agreed to take her Spanish inquisitors there and, on reaching the river, used magic to change its course, drowning herself and the greedy Spaniards with her. Her *duppy* (ghost) is said to guard the mine's entrance. Rafting on this river is a very popular activity.

NEED A BREAK? Grab a gelato—in island flavors such as passion fruit, guava, soursop, or papaya–or a free sample of the famous Tortuga Rum Cakes at **Calypso Gelato** (⊠ *N. Coast Hwy. [Reading Main Rd.]* ☎ *876/979-9381*). The facility houses a 10,000-square-foot baking facility for the famous cakes as well as an ample gift shop.

3 ★ FodorsChoice **Rose Hall.** In the 1700s Rose Hall may well have been the greatest of greathouses in the West Indies. Today it's popular less for its architecture than for the legend surrounding its second mistress, Annie Palmer. As the story goes, Annie was born in 1802 to an English mother and Irish father. When she was 10, Annie and her family moved from England to Haiti, where her parents promptly died of yellow fever. Annie was adopted by a Haitian voodoo priestess and soon became skilled in the practice of voodoo. Annie moved to Jamaica, married, and built Rose Hall, an enormous plantation spanning 6,600 acres that was served by more than 2,000 slaves. According to legend, Annie murdered several of her husbands and her slave lovers. To learn more about the tales of Rose Hall, read *The White Witch of Rose Hall,* a novel sold across the island. There's a pub on-site. It's across the highway from the Rose Hall Resort & Country Club. ⊠ *N. Coast Hwy.* ☎ *876/953–9982* ⊠ *$15* ☉ *Daily 9–6.*

WHERE TO EAT

As the birthplace of the island's tourism industry, Montego Bay is home to many restaurants. Reservations are often necessary during high season. Some restaurants require you get a bit dressed up, but you can also find plenty of casual eateries with a straight-from-the-beach dress code.

ECLECTIC

$$–$$$ ✕ **Town House.** Most of the rich and famous people who have visited Jamaica over the decades have eaten here. You find daily specials, delicious variations of standard dishes (red snapper papillote is a specialty), and many Jamaican favorites (like the curried chicken with breadfruit and ackee). The 18th-century Georgian house is adorned with original Jamaican and Haitian art. There's alfresco dining on the stone patio. ⊠ *16 Church St.* ☎ *876/952–2660* ☜ *Reservations essential* ⊟ *AE, D, DC, MC, V.*

CLOSE UP

The Leeward Maroons

Southeast of Montego Bay lies one of the island's most rugged regions, the Cockpit Country. Since the mid-1700s this area has been the home of the Leeward Maroons, much as the Portland area was home to the Windward Maroons. Both groups made up the island's Maroon population, a name derived from *Cimarron*, meaning "wild" in Spanish. The Maroons, descendants of the escaped slaves, were fierce fighters who took to the hills and stayed there, never to again be recaptured.

The Windward Maroons were led by an Ashanti priestess named Nanny; her brothers Cudjoe and Accompong each took a group west. Cudjoe settled in today's St. James parish, while Accompong took his group south to St. Elizabeth parish. Both were in Cockpit

Country, a land of steep hills, impenetrable vegetation, and terrain pocked with sinkholes and caves.

When the British took the island, they called Cockpit Country the "land of look behind." Soldiers rode two to a horse, one facing forward and one back, to guard against an ambush. After years of fighting, the British and the Leeward Maroons eventually signed a peace treaty, later joined by the Windward Maroons.

Today the Maroons are self-governing, with their own elected officials. The most visited community in Cockpit Country is Accompong. Tours often depart for this unique region. The Maroons, who for so long lived a completely self-sustained existence, are still known as the island's greatest herbalists.

$-$$ ✕**Margaritaville.** Along Montego Bay's "Hip Strip," this colorful restaurant is a favorite nightspot, but is also popular during the day thanks to its 110-foot waterslide into the sea, two water trampolines, and a rooftop whirlpool tub. When it's time to settle down for lunch, the menu offers some Caribbean-influenced items such as jerk burgers and conch fritters, but the offerings are pretty much all-American. ✉*Gloucester Ave.* ☎*876/952–4777* ▭*AE, D, MC, V.*

$-$$ ✕**Royal Stocks English Pub & Steakhouse.** In Half Moon Shopping Village, this pub brings a slice of jolly old England to Jamaica, from its wood-paneled decor to its menu featuring shepherd's pie, bangers and mash, and plenty of fish-and-chips. Umbrella-shaded tables in the courtyard are the most popular, except on the hottest of days, when visitors

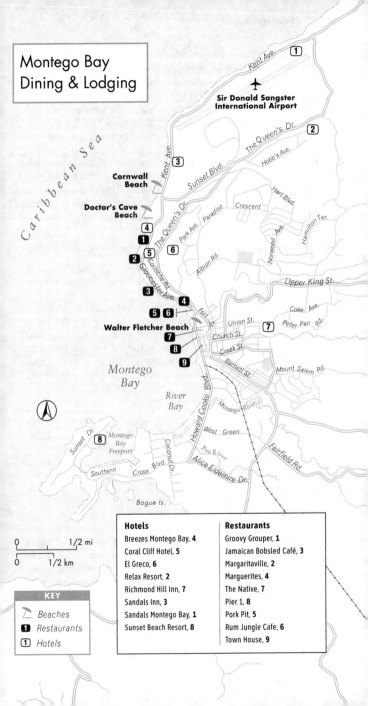

Montego Bay
Dining & Lodging

Caribbean Sea

Sir Donald Sangster International Airport

Cornwall Beach

Doctor's Cave Beach

Walter Fletcher Beach

Montego Bay

River Bay

Hotels
Breezes Montego Bay, **4**
Coral Cliff Hotel, **5**
El Greco, **6**
Relax Resort, **2**
Richmond Hill Inn, **7**
Sandals Inn, **3**
Sandals Montego Bay, **1**
Sunset Beach Resort, **8**

Restaurants
Groovy Grouper, **1**
Jamaican Bobsled Café, **3**
Margaritaville, **2**
Marguerites, **4**
The Native, **7**
Pier 1, **8**
Pork Pit, **5**
Rum Jungle Cafe, **6**
Town House, **9**

0   1/2 mi
0   1/2 km

KEY
~ *Beaches*
■ *Restaurants*
▢ *Hotels*

Jamaican Bobsled Team

Ice is a rare sight in Jamaica—except in the cocktails enjoyed at many beach bars. But in the 1980s, the idea of founding an Olympic bobsled team wasn't as crazy as it seemed. After all, a Jamaican pushcart derby uses many of the same moves as bobsledding. The team that debuted at the Calgary Olympics in 1988 drew worldwide attention; in the 1992 Winter Olympics in Albertville, France, the team finished in 14th place. The team inspired the 1993 movie *Cool Runnings*. What became of the team? It continues to train in Evanston, Wyoming. Proceeds come from the Jamaica Bobsled Café, on Montego Bay's Hip Strip and at the Sangster International Airport.

retreat to the dark pub. ⊠*Half Moon Shopping Village, N. Coast Rd., 7 mi (11 km) east of Montego Bay* ☎876/953–9770 ▭*AE, MC, V.*

¢–$$ ✕**Jamaican Bobsled Café.** The trials and triumphs of Jamaica's Olympic bobsled team, inspiration for the 1993 film *Cool Runnings*, are remembered at this Hip Strip eatery. Offerings like the barbecue burger and the barbecue chicken pizza make up the family-friendly menu. A percentage of the café's profits go toward supporting the team. ⊠*69 Gloucester Ave.* ☎876/940–7009 ▭*AE, D, MC, V.*

JAMAICAN

$$–$$$ ✕**Rum Jungle Café.** Decorated like an indoor rain forest, this expansive restaurant in the Coral Cliff is casual and fun. Large buffets feature Caribbean dishes ranging from escovitch fish to jerk chicken. Bartenders pour from a selection of rums from the Caribbean and beyond. Sunday brunch is popular. ⊠*Coral Cliff, 165 Gloucester Ave.* ☎876/952–4130 ▭*AE, D, MC, V.*

$$–$$$ ✕**Sugar Mill.** Seafood is served with flair at this terrace res-
★ taurant on the Half Moon golf course. Caribbean specialties, steak, and lobster are usually offered in a pungent sauce that blends Dijon mustard with Jamaica's own Pickapeppa sauce. Otherwise, choices at this dinner-only restaurant include the daily à la carte specials and anything flame-grilled. Live music and a well-stocked wine cellar round out the elegant experience. ⊠*Half Moon, 7 mi (11 km) east of Montego Bay* ☎876/953–2228 ⚷*Reservations essential* ▭*AE, MC, V.*

$-$$$ ✕**Groovy Grouper Beach Bar & Grill.** On Doctor's Cave Beach, this casual eatery may be a tourist favorite because of its location, but its menu is full of authentic dishes from Jamaica and other Caribbean islands. Sit outside beneath the thatched roof and start with conch fritters or fish tea (a local soup), then move on to a grouper burger, fish and bammy, or the signature dish, a half-pound grouper fillet dusted with jerk spices. Steaks and burgers round out the menu options. ✉*Beach Club, Gloucester Ave.* ☎876/952–8287 ═AE, D, MC, V.

¢–$$ ✕**The Native.** Shaded by a large poinciana tree and overlook-
★ ing Gloucester Avenue, this open-air stone terrace is the place for Jamaican dishes. To go native, start with smoked marlin, then move on to the *boonoonoonoos* platter (a sampler of local dishes). Round out your meal with coconut pie or *duckanoo* (a sweet dumpling of cornmeal, coconut, and banana wrapped in a banana leaf and steamed). Live entertainment and dimly lighted tables make this a romantic choice for dinner. ✉*29 Gloucester Ave.* ☎876/979–2769 ⚓*Reservations essential* ═AE, MC, V.

¢–$ ✕**The Pork Pit.** A favorite with many MoBay locals, this no-frills eatery serves Jamaican specialties including some fiery jerk—note that it's spiced to local tastes, not watered down for foreign palates. Many order their food to go, but you can also find picnic tables just outside. ✉*27 Gloucester Ave.* ☎876/940–3008. *No credit cards.*.

¢–$ ✕**Scotchies.** Many call this jerk eatery the best in Jamaica, but the new Scotchies Too in Ocho Rios certainly makes it a tough decision. Like its sister restaurant, Scotchies serves up genuine jerk—chicken, pork, fish, sausage, and more—with fiery sauce and delectable side dishes including festival (similar to a Southern hush puppy) and rice and peas. This restaurant is a favorite with Montego Bay residents; on a typical day, you're likely to see a slap-the-table game of dominoes. ✉*N. Coast Hwy., across from Holiday Inn SunSpree* ☎876/9953–3340. *No credit cards.*.

SEAFOOD

$$–$$$ ✕**Marguerites Seafood By the Sea.** At this romantic dining room, flambé is the operative word. Lobster, shrimp, fish, and several desserts are prepared in dancing flames as you sip exotic cocktails. The Caesar salad, prepared tableside, is also a treat. You wouldn't know this restaurant is part of the same operation as the rowdy and rollicking Margaritaville next door. ✉*Gloucester Ave.* ☎876/952–4777 ⚓*Reservations essential* ═AE, D, MC, V ⊗*No lunch.*

Jamaican Cuisine

CLOSE UP

Jamaican cuisine, like its people, is a product of a mix of cultures from around the world. Spanish, English, Chinese, East Indian, and other groups each brought their own tastes to the island.

Ackee: A red fruit that's poisonous until ripe

Alligator pear: A local name for an avocado

Bammy: Fried bread made from cassava flour

Bun: Spicy bread eaten with cheese

Callaloo: A leafy vegetable that resembles spinach

Cho-Cho: A member of the squash family

Cut cake: A sweet cake made with diced coconut and ginger toffee

Dasheen: A root vegetable used like a potato; some Jamaicans call it coco yam

Duckanoo: A dessert of African origin made with cornmeal, coconut, spices and brown sugar, tied up in a banana leaf and slowly cooked in boiling water

Escovitch: A style of cooking using vinegar, onions, and spices brought to Jamaica by the Spanish Jews

Festival: A bread similar to hush puppies served with jerk

Fish tea: A spicy fish bouillon

Garden egg: The local name for an eggplant

Gizzada: A coconut tart

Grater cake: A grated coconut and sugar confection

Janga: Crayfish cooked and sold as hot peppered shrimp by the woman of Middle Quarters on the South Coast

Jerk: Jamaican barbecue

Mannish water: A spicy soup—a reported aphrodisiac—made from goat's head

Matrimony: A dessert using the star apple; usually served during the holidays

Otaheiti Apple: An apple that looks like a small, red pear

Pawpaw: Local name for papaya

Pepperpot soup: A peppery callaloo soup

Pimento: Called allspice in other parts of the world; the wood from these trees give jerk its distinctive taste

Red pea soup: Made with kidney beans

Rice and peas: Rice and red kidney beans, an omnipresent lunch and dinner dish

Rundown: Pickled fish cooked in a seasoned coconut milk

Solomon gundy: An appetizer made of pickled fish

Spinners: Twisted dumplings used in soup

Stamp and go: Small fish fritters

1

$$–$$$ ✕**Pier 1.** After tropical drinks at the deck bar, you'll be ready to dig into the international variations on fresh seafood; the best are the grilled lobster and any preparation of island snapper. Several party cruises leave from the marina here, and on Friday night the restaurant is mobbed by locals who come to dance. ⊠*Off Howard Cooke Blvd.* ☎*876/952–2452* ⊟*AE, MC, V.*

WHERE TO STAY

Montego Bay has miles of hotels and resorts ranging from inexpensive properties in town and in the hills overlooking town to larger hotels and all-inclusive resorts west and east of town. Montego Bay has the added advantage of being the closest resort area to the island's main airport.

$$$$ ▥**Half Moon.** With its shopping village, hospital, school, ○ ★ golf course, and equestrian center, Half Moon almost seems more like a town than a mere resort. What started out in 1954 as a group of private beach cottages offered for rent during off-season months has blossomed into one of Jamaica's most extensive resorts. Those beach cottages are still available and—just steps away from the sand as well as public areas—remain a great choice. Now, however, you also can choose villas with three to seven bedrooms. Some accommodations are a long walk from public areas, although you can arrange for a golf cart to pick you up. The villas come with a private golf cart for your use. **Pros:** expansive beach, many types of rooms, numerous on-site activities. **Cons:** long walk to some public areas, some rooms need renovation. ⊠*N. Coast Hwy., 7 mi (11 km) east of Montego Bay, Box 80* ☎*876/953–2211* ⊟*876/953– 2731* ⊕*www.halfmoon.com* ⇆*34 rooms, 164 suites, 33 villas* ��*In-room: safe, kitchen (some), refrigerator, dial-up, Wi-Fi (some). In-hotel: 6 restaurants, room service, bars, golf course, tennis courts, pools, gym, spa, beachfront, diving, water sports, bicycles, no elevator, children's programs (infant–17), laundry service, concierge, public Internet, public Wi-Fi, airport shuttle, parking (no fee), no-smoking rooms* ⊟*AE, D, DC, MC, V* ⫚*EP.*

$$$$ ▥**Ritz-Carlton Golf & Spa Resort, Rose Hall.** With the high- ○ brow service for which this chain is renowned, this expansive resort lies across the road from historic Rose Hall. Although the luxury hotel is elegant and has solid service, little here calls to mind the Caribbean except the ocean-front location. If you like high tea, it's offered daily. Along with a full-service spa, there's a fully supervised children's club, making it a popular choice for families. **Pros:** excellent business facilities, great golf course, varied children's program. **Cons:** generic atmosphere, small beach, overly formal atmosphere. ⊠ *1 Ritz-Carlton Dr., Montego Bay* ☎ *876/953–2800* 🖷 *876/518–0110* ⊕ *www.ritzcarlton.com* ↪ *427 rooms* ☐ *In-room: safe, refrigerator, Ethernet. In-hotel: 6 restaurants, room service, bars, golf course, tennis courts, pool, gym, spa, beachfront, diving, concierge, executive floor, children's programs (ages 5–12), public Internet, public Wi-Fi, airport shuttle* 🖃 *AE, D, DC, MC, V* |◉| *EP.*

$$$$ 🖼 **Round Hill Hotel & Villas.** A favorite of celebrities thanks to
★ its secluded feel, this peaceful resort sits 8 mi (13 km) west of MoBay. The 36 traditional hotel rooms in the Pineapple House are decorated in a refined Ralph Lauren style—done by the designer himself, who owns one of the 27 villas that dot the resort's 98 acres. Each villa includes a maid and a cook to make your breakfast, and most have its own pool. It's a fairly quiet place, with a small beach and limited dining options, but most guests return again and again because of the personal service and excellent management. **Pros:** personal service, stylish accommodations, quiet atmosphere. **Cons:** pricey, rather remote location, some villas lack pools. ⊠ *N. Coast Hwy., Box 64* ☎ *876/956–7050* 🖷 *876/956–7505* ⊕ *www.roundhilljamaica.com* ↪ *36 rooms, 27 villas* ☐ *In-room: refrigerator, dial-up. In-hotel: restaurant, room service, bar, tennis courts, pool, gym, spa, beachfront, diving, water sports, concierge, no elevator* 🖃 *AE, D, DC, MC, V* |◉| *EP.*

$$$$ 🖼 **Sandals Inn.** If you can forego a private beach at your doorstep (there's a public one across the street, and an hourly shuttle that takes you to other Sandals properties), you can stay here for much less than at the other Sandals. Managed more as a small hotel than a large resort, this property is intimate and relatively quiet. The charming rooms are compact; most have balconies that face the small pool area. Although the hotel has fewer on-site facilities than its sister properties, it does have the added benefit of 24-hour room service. The in-town location puts you close to shops and sights, a bonus if you like to get out and explore. Like others in the Sandals chain, this property is for couples only (but no longer restricted to male–female duos). **Pros:** less expensive than other Sandals resorts, complimentary shuttle to sister properties, convenient location. **Cons:** no private beach, small pool, limited on-site dining

options. ⊠*Kent Ave.* ☎*876/952–4140* 🖷*876/952–6913* ⊕*www.sandals.com* ⚲*52 rooms* ⚘*In-room: safe, Ethernet. In-hotel: 2 restaurants, room service, bars, tennis court, pool, no elevator, laundry service, concierge, public Internet, airport shuttle, no kids under 18* ▭*AE, D, DC, MC, V* ⦿*AI.*

$$$$ 🏨**Sandals Montego Bay.** The largest private beach in Montego Bay is the highlight of this Sandals—one of the most popular upscale resorts in the Caribbean. It's one big party, despite the planes that zoom overhead (the airport is minutes away, making it a good option for quick departures). Rooms are done in tropical colors and have four-poster beds; for top-notch luxury the rooms and suites in the Bay Roc Villa Suites are the resort's nicest. The pricier rooms offer butler service and 24-hour room service. **Pros:** good beach, convenient to transportation, butler service in some rooms. **Cons:**airport noise, not walking distance to other restaurants, some rooms need upgrading. ⊠*N. Kent Ave.* ☎*876/952–5510* 🖷*876/952–0816* ⊕*www.sandals.com* ⚲*251 rooms* ⚘*In-room: safe, refrigerator (some), Ethernet. In-hotel: 5 restaurants, room service (some), bars, tennis courts, pools, gym, spa, beachfront, diving, water sports, no elevator, laundry service, concierge, executive floor, public Internet, airport shuttle, no kids under 18* ▭*AE, D, DC, MC, V* ⦿*AI.*

$$$$ 🏨**Sandals Royal Caribbean Resort & Private Island.** This ele-
★ gant resort—the most upscale of the three Sandals properties in MoBay—consists of Jamaican-style buildings arranged in a semicircle around attractive gardens. Less boisterous than Sandals Montego Bay, it offers a few more civilized touches, including afternoon tea. The latest additions to the resort are the St. James River Suites, rooms that open out onto the resort's lazy river. In the evenings, a colorful "dragon boat" transports you to Sandals's private island for meals at a Thai restaurant. **Pros:** delightful dining, lovely landscaping, complimentary shuttle to sister resorts. **Cons:** too quiet for some, small beach ⊠*N. Coast Hwy., Box 167* ☎*876/953–2231* 🖷*876/953–2788* ⊕*www.sandals.com* ⚲*176 rooms, 14 suites* ⚘*In-room: safe, refrigerator (some), Ethernet. In-hotel: 4 restaurants, room service (some), bars, tennis courts, pools, gym, spa, beachfront, diving, water sports, no elevator, laundry service, concierge, public Internet, airport shuttle, parking (no fee), no kids under 18, no-smoking rooms* ⚲*2-night minimum* ▭*AE, D, DC, MC, V* ⦿*AI.*

$$$$ ⬚ **The Tryall Club.** Well known among golf aficionados, Try-
★   all lies 15 mi (24 km) west of MoBay. The sumptuous villas—each of which has a private pool—and pampering staff
lend a home-away-from-home atmosphere. The beautiful
seaside golf course is considered one of the meanest in the
world and hosts big-money tournaments. Golfers are more
than willing to accept the relative isolation for easy access
to the great course, but this resort is even farther out than
Round Hill. **Pros:** challenging golf course, good amenities,
popular family program. **Cons:** remote location, shared
public facilities, too formal for some. ✉ *N. Coast Hwy.,
Box 1206, Sandy Bay* ☎*876/956–5660* 📠*876/956–5673*
⊕*www.tryallclub.com* 🛏*56 villas* ⌂*In-room: kitchen. In-
hotel: restaurant, bars, golf course, tennis courts, pool,
gym, spa, beachfront, water sports, children's programs
(ages 5–12), no elevator* ☰*AE, D, DC, MC, V* 🍴*EP.*

$$$–$$$$ ⬚ **Coyaba Beach Resort & Club.** Owners Joanne and Kevin
Robertson live on the grounds of this small resort, chatting
with guests and giving the intimate property a relaxing,
welcoming ambience. From the plantation-style greathouse
to the elegant guest rooms, which are decorated with colo-
nial prints and hand-carved mahogany furniture, you feel
the graciousness and comforting atmosphere reminiscent of
a country inn. Although families are welcome at this resort,
in late December and early January no children under age
12 are permitted. **Pros:** quiet atmosphere, excellent restau-
rants, beautiful beach. **Cons:** on busy highway, small pool,
stairs to upper-floor rooms. ✉*Montego Bay, Little River*
☎*876/953–9150* 📠*876/953–2244* ⊕*www.coyabaresort-
jamaica.com* 🛏*50 rooms* ⌂*In-room: safe, refrigerator
(some), VCR. In-hotel: 3 restaurants, room service, bars,
tennis court, pool, gym, spa, beachfront, water sports, no
elevator, laundry service, concierge, public Internet, park-
ing (no fee), no-smoking rooms* ☰*AE, D, MC, V* 🍴*EP.*

$$$–$$$$ ⬚ **FDR Pebbles.** This resort bills itself as a soft-adventure
☻   experience for families. Although you're still assigned a
nanny if you have young kids, the family experience is
taken a step further here with many more supervised pro-
grams for teens, including campouts. Located 30 minutes
east of Montego Bay, the resort has the feel of a camp-
ground, with rooms in wooden buildings. Each junior
suite is paneled with cedar and pine, highlighted with trim
in tropical colors. Up to three children under age 16 can
share a room with two parents; kids under 6 stay and eat
free when sharing a room with parents. **Pros:** nannies for
families, supervised children's program, good selection of

activities for older kids. **Cons:** common areas can be noisy, set apart from local attractions. ⊠*Main St., Falmouth* ☎*876/954–4821* 📠*876/617–2512* ⊕*www.fdrholidays. com* ⌑*96 junior suites* ↻*In-room: refrigerator, Wi-Fi. In-hotel: 3 restaurants, bar, tennis, pool, gym, spa, beachfront, water sports, bicycles, no elevator, children's programs (ages newborn–16), laundry service, public Internet, public Wi-Fi, airport shuttle, no-smoking rooms* ⊟*AE, D, MC, V* ⊙*AI.*

$$$–$$$$ 🛏**Holiday Inn SunSpree Resort.** Family fun is tops here, ↻ although many couples and singles are also drawn to the moderate prices and good location, 6 mi (9½ km) east of the airport. You can find seven-room blocks spread along the long beach and large public areas that can, at times, feel a bit overrun with kids. Adults can find some peace in the quiet pool, which has its own swim-up bar. On the other side of the grounds, a lighted 9-hole miniature golf course offers night play. Shoppers will be happy with the moderately priced shopping mall directly across the street. Children 12 and under stay and eat free. **Pros:** good family atmosphere, easy access to shopping, complimentary laundry room. **Cons:** common areas can be noisy, no motorized water sports, on busy highway. ⊠*N. Coast Hwy., Box 480* ☎*876/953–2485* 📠*876/953–3274* ⊕*www.montegobay-jam.sunspreeresorts.com* ⌑*524 rooms, 27 suites* ↻*In-room: safe, dial-up, Wi-Fi. In-hotel: 4 restaurants, room service, bars, tennis courts, pools, gym, spa, beachfront, diving, water sports, concierge, children's programs (ages 6 months–12), laundry facilities, laundry service, concierge, public Internet, public Wi-Fi, airport shuttle, parking (no fee), no-smoking rooms* ⊟*AE, D, DC, MC, V* ⊙*AI.*

$$$–$$$$ 🛏**Iberostar Rose Hall Beach.** Twenty minutes east of the ↻ Montego Bay airport, this all-inclusive resort has opened the first of several planned phases. An extensive array of dining options (including three à la carte restaurants that require reservations) and activities are offered (although motorized water sports and scuba diving incur an additional fee). Operated by a European company, the resort has some of the same feel as the brand's popular Mexico properties, with thatch-roofed poolside palapas, Spanish lessons, tropical dance lessons, and around-the-clock action. **Pros:** numerous on-site activities, easy access to transportation, complimentary minibars. **Cons:** construction noise, long waits for elevators, limited all-inclusive program. ⊠*N. Coast Hwy.* ☎*876/680–0000* 📠*876/680–0007* ⊕*www.iberostar.com* ⌑*334 rooms, 32 suites* ↻*In-*

room: safe, refrigerator, dial-up. In-hotel: 4 restaurants, room service, bars, pools, gym, spa, beachfront, diving, water sports, children's programs (ages 4–12), laundry service, concierge, public Internet, airport shuttle, parking (no fee) ▤*AE, D, MC, V* ©*AI.*

$$$ ▦**Rose Hall Resort & Country Club.** Popular with conference
☼ groups, this self-contained resort lies 4 mi (6½ km) east of the airport on the grounds of the 400-acre Rose Hall Plantation. Kids love the huge water park, complete with lagoons and lazy rafting river, while golfers head across the street to the challenging course. The lack of a good beach is the biggest drawback; the waters are sometimes better for sailing. However, the expansive pool and water-park complex is a good alternative. **Pros:** extensive renovations in 2007, family-friendly dining and pool area, easy access to golf course. **Cons:** beach is lackluster, pool can be crowded with kids, some activities across highway. ▨*N. Coast Hwy., Box 999* ☎*876/953–2650* ▧*876/518–0203* ⊕*www.rosehallresort.com* ⬐*488 rooms, 14 suites* ⬩*In-room: safe, Wi-Fi. In-hotel: 5 restaurants, room service, bars, golf course, tennis courts, pools, gym, beachfront, diving, water sports, children's programs (ages 4–12)* ▤*AE, D, DC, MC, V* ©*AI.*

$$–$$$ ▦**Sunset Beach Resort & Spa.** Often packed with charter
☼ groups, this expansive resort is a good value if you don't mind mass tourism. With one of Jamaica's best (and most used) lobbies, a water park, teen center, and excellent beaches on a peninsula jutting out into the bay, the facilities here help to redeem the motel-style rooms. You can choose among three beaches (one nude) or, when it's time to take a break from the sun, hit the spa or the slots-only casino. **Pros:** excellent beaches, good restaurants, numerous on-site activities. **Cons:** can be crowded, waits for the elevator, somewhat remote location.   ▨*Freeport, Box 1168* ☎*876/979–8800* ▧*876/979–8039* ⊕*www.sunsetbeachresort.com* ⬐*430 rooms, 15 suites* ⬩*In-room: safe, dial-up. In-hotel: 4 restaurants, bars, tennis courts, pools, gym, spa, beachfront, water sports, children's programs (ages 2–12), laundry service, concierge, public Internet, airport shuttle, parking (no fee)* ▤*AE, MC, V* ©*AI.*

$–$$$ ▦**Relax Resort.** This family-owned hotel is a budget-friendly option for travelers who don't mind not being on the beach (although a complimentary shuttle is available). Simple rooms have tile floors and balconies, but the best bargain is the studios and apartments; these have kitchens that can be stocked with the groceries you've requested in advance.

Only the bedrooms of the apartments are air-conditioned. **Pros:** good value, access to transportation, family-friendly atmosphere. **Cons:** not on the beach, drab room decor, limited on-site activities. ⊠*26 Hobbs Ave.* ☎*876/979–0656* 📠*876/952–7218* ⊕*www.relax-resort.com* ⇘*36 rooms* ♿*In-room: no a/c (some), safe, kitchen (some), refrigerator. In-hotel: restaurant, room service, bar, pool, gym, no elevator, laundry service, public Internet, airport shuttle, parking (no fee)* ⊟*AE, MC, V* ⑩*EP.*

$-$$ ▦**Breezes Montego Bay.** A good choice for those on a budget, this active resort near the airport is favored by young travelers. Right on Montego Bay's "Hip Strip," the resort places you steps away from nightclubs and shops. Rather than a private beach like most all-inclusives, this property takes advantage of the beach-club atmosphere of Doctor's Cave Beach (whether that's a plus or a minus is up to you). Rooms have white-tile floors, cozy love seats (leather sofas in the oceanfront suites), carved wooden headboards, and big marble bathrooms. A popular circus workshop and free weddings are also part of the package. **Pros:** close to restaurants and bars, easy access to transportation, good value. **Cons:** can be noisy, no private beach, lacks resort feel. ⊠*Gloucester Ave.* ☎*876/940–1150* 📠*876/940–1160* ⊕*www.superclubs.com* ⇘*124 rooms* ♿*In-room: safe, VCR (some). In-hotel: 3 restaurants, bars, tennis court, pool, beachfront, diving, water sports, public Internet, airport shuttle, no kids under 14* ⇗*2-night minimum* ⊟*AE, D, DC, MC, V* ⑩*AI.*

$-$$ ▦**El Greco.** For visitors who don't have to be on the beach, El Greco is a budget-friendly option. Thanks to an elevator, there's direct service from the hilltop hotel to Doctor's Cave Beach. Somewhat bare bedrooms are air-conditioned, although they also have glass doors and usually an ample breeze. An on-site restaurant serves lunch and dinner (a full breakfast is included), and full kitchens make it easy to prepare your own meals. **Pros:** good value, near many dining options, kitchens in rooms. **Cons:** no private beach, bland room décor. ⊠*11 Queens Dr.* ☎*876/940–6116* 📠*876/940–6115* ⊕*www.elgrecojamaica.com* ⇘*96 suites* ♿*In-room: safe, kitchen, refrigerator, dial-up. In-hotel: restaurant, room service, bar, tennis courts, pool, laundry service, public Internet* ⊟*AE, MC, V* ⑩*BP.*

$-$$ ▦**Starfish Trelawny.** This all-inclusive resort operated by ♻ SuperClubs is a real bargain, so you might not mind that it has fewer extras than at the company's other resorts. For beach lovers, the best option is the garden-level cottages (especially popular with larger groups). Most guest rooms, however, are in high-rise towers. The resort is perfect for families, with kid-friendly restaurants and entertainment. The resort has a rock-climbing wall, a circus workshop, "ice-skating" on a special plastic surface, and, for an additional cost, unlimited trapeze sessions. **Pros:** good value, excellent children's program, numerous activities. **Cons:** limited all-inclusive program, some water sports not included, many kids. ⊠ *N. Coast Hwy., Falmouth* ☎ *876/954–2450* ⊟ *876/954–9923* ⊕ *www.starfishresorts. com* ⇌ *349 rooms* ⸜ *In-room: safe, Wi-Fi (some). In-hotel: 6 restaurants, room service, bars, tennis courts, pools, gym, spa, beachfront, diving, water sports, children's programs (ages 6 months–12), public Internet, airport shuttle* ⇋ *2-night minimum* ⊟ *AE, D, DC, MC, V* ⦿ *AI.*

$ ▣ **Coral Cliff Hotel and Entertainment Centre.** This hotel has two main assets: a good location on the Hip Strip and on-site gambling at Montego Bay's largest casino. Non-gamers will find themselves occupied by a jungle-theme restaurant, small pool, and—best of all—the fun of nearby Doctor's Cave Beach. Most guests spend their time at the casino or on the Hip Strip rather than in the motel-style rooms. **Pros:** good value, walking distance to restaurants and clubs, interesting decor. **Cons:** no private beach, can get noisy, little privacy. ⊠ *165 Gloucester Ave.* ☎ *876/952–4130* ⊟ *876/952–6532* ⊕ *www.coralcliffjamaica.com* ⇌ *30 rooms* ⸜ *In-room: dial-up. In-hotel: 2 restaurants, room service, bars, pool, gym, no elevator, laundry service, parking (no fee)* ⊟ *MC, V* ⦿ *EP.*

$ ▣ **Richmond Hill Inn.** This hilltop inn—a 200-year-old great-house originally owned by the Dewars clan—has spectacular views of the Caribbean and a great deal of peace. The decor tends toward the dainty, frilly lace curtains and doilies, lots of lavenders and mauves, and crushed-velvet furniture here and there. A free shuttle takes you to shops and beaches about 10 minutes away. **Pros:** good value, eye-popping view, delicious dining. **Cons:** somewhat dated decor, not on beach, not within walking distance of attractions. ⊠ *Union St.* ☎ *876/952–3859* ⊟ *876/952–6106* ⊕ *www. richmond-hill-inn.com* ⇌ *20 suites* ⸜ *In-room: refrigerator (some), dial-up. In-hotel: restaurant, room service, bar, pool, no elevator, laundry service* ⊟ *MC, V* ⦿ *EP.*

PRIVATE VILLAS

⬚ **The Wharf House.** A short drive from Round Hill, this stylish 18th-century home is comprised of five buildings connected by walkways. The main house includes the living and dining rooms as well as two bedrooms sharing a bath; two other bedrooms are in private cottages. A play cottage welcomes young visitors with a wealth of toys and games while a fifth building offers Ping-Pong and a bar. The house (which can also be rented as just a two-bedroom) includes membership at nearby Round Hill with complimentary access to that resort's beach and fitness center. **Pros:** excellent facilities for families, beautiful decor, good location. **Cons:** need car to get around, layout not good for families with small children. ✉*Rte. A1, west of Montego Bay* ☎ ⊕ ⤴*4 bedrooms, 2 baths* ⌂*In-villa: no a/c (some), safe, kitchen, refrigerator, dial-up, daily maid service, cook, on-site security, fully staffed, pool, beachfront, water toys, laundry facilities* ❢*EP.*

BEACHES

★ **Doctor's Cave Beach.** Montego Bay's tourist scene has its roots right on the Hip Strip, the bustling entertainment district along Gloucester Avenue. Here a sea cave whose waters were said to have healing powers drew travelers from around the world. Although the cave was destroyed by a hurricane generations ago, the beach is always busy and has a perpetual spring-break feel. It has the best facilities in Jamaica, thanks to the plantation-style clubhouse with changing rooms, showers, gift shop, restaurant, and Internet café. There's a fee for admission; beach chairs and umbrellas are also for rent. Its location within the Montego Bay Marine Park—where there are protected coral reefs and plenty of marine life—makes it a good spot for snorkeling. More active travelers can opt for parasailing, glass-bottom boat rides, or jet skiing. ✉*Gloucester Ave., Montego Bay.*

Walter Fletcher Beach. Although it's not as pretty (or as tidy) as Doctor's Cave Beach, Walter Fletcher Beach is home to Aquasol Theme Park, which offers a large beach (with lifeguards and security personnel), glass-bottom boats, snorkeling, tennis, go-kart racing, a disco at night, a bar, and a restaurant. Several times a week Aquasol throws a beach bash with live reggae performances. Near the center of town, the beach has unusually fine swimming; the calm

waters make it a good bet for children. ⊠*Gloucester Ave.,
Montego Bay.*

SPORTS & THE OUTDOORS

BIRD-WATCHING

Jamaica is a major bird-watching destination, thanks to
its various natural habitats. The island is home to more
than 200 species, some seen only seasonally or in particular
parts of the island. Many bird-watchers flock here for the
chance to see the vervain hummingbird (the world's sec-
ond-smallest bird, larger only than Cuba's bee hummingbird) or the Jamaican tody (which nests underground). The
early-morning and late-afternoon hours are usually the best
time for spotting birds.

★ A great place to spot birds is the **Rocklands Bird Sanctuary
& Feeding Station** (⊠*Anchovy* ☎876/952–2009), south of
Montego Bay. The station was the home of the late Lisa
Salmon, one of Jamaica's first amateur ornithologists. Here
you can sit quietly and feed birds—including the doctor
bird, recognizable by its long tail—from your hand. A visit
costs $10. Not recommended for families with young chil-
dren (they'll scare the birds), this memorable attraction
offers Jamaica's easiest bird-watching.

CANOPY TOURS

There are many ways to see Jamaica's thick tropical forests,
but perhaps none quite as exciting as canopy tours, also
known as zip-line tours. Following a short introductory
lesson, you climb platforms, hook up to steel cables strung
between trees and, with the help of local operators, literally
zip throughout the canopy of trees.

From its operation west of Montego Bay, **Chukka Caribbean Adventures** (⊠*Sandy Bay, Hanover* ☎876/972–2506
⊕*www.chukkacaribbean.com*) offers a canopy tour over
the Great River. Nine lines traverse the trees, at times buzzing you through the canopy at 35-mi (56-km) per hour. On
the tour you can catch a glimpse of a 150-year-old dam.
The three-hour tour is $80 per person and is open to those
ages 10 and up.

DIVING & SNORKELING

Jamaica isn't a major dive destination, but you can find a few rich underwater regions, especially off the north coast. Montego Bay, known for its wall dives, has **Airport Reef** at its southwestern edge. The site is known for its coral caves, tunnels, and canyons. The first marine park in Jamaica, the **Montego Bay Marine Park** was established to protect the natural resources of the bay; a quick look at the area and it's easy to see the treasures that lie beneath the surface. The north coast is on the edge of the Cayman Trench, so it boasts a wide array of marine life.

Prices on the island range from $45 to $80 for a one-tank dive. All the large resorts have dive shops, and the all-inclusive places sometimes include scuba diving in their rates. To dive, you need to show a certification card, though it's possible to get a small taste of scuba diving and do a shallow dive—usually from shore—after taking a one-day resort diving course, which almost every resort with a dive shop offers.

Scuba Jamaica (⌧*Half Moon, N. Coast Hwy., Montego Bay* ☎*876/381–1113* ⊕*www.scuba-jamaica.com*) offers serious scuba facilities for dedicated divers. This operator is a PADI and NAUI operation and also offers Nitrox diving as well as instruction in underwater photography, night diving, and open-water diving. There's a pickup service for the Montego Bay, Runaway Bay, Discovery Bay, and Ocho Rios areas.

Nondivers—even nonswimmers—can get into the undersea action during the **Sea Trek Adventure** (⌧*Doctor's Cave Beach, Montego Bay* ☎*876/972–2506* ⊕*www.chukkacaribbean.com*). Participants take a short introductory lesson before donning a high-tech dive helmet (beneath which you can even leave on prescription glasses) and taking a walk on the sea floor. For half an hour, visitors age 12 and up explore the undersea world while attached to a breathing tube. The experience costs $60 per person.

A good way to peek beneath the waves is a cruise with **MoBay Undersea Tours** (⌧*Pier One, Howard Cooke Blvd.* ☎*876/940–4465* ⊕*www.mobayunderseatours.com*). Twice-daily tours ($40) are offered every day except Wednesday aboard this specially built semisubmersible vehicle. You sit in the hull and view the sea through panoramic windows. At any point you can return to the top deck (a good option for families with small children).

DOLPHIN SWIMS

Under the same management as the public Dolphin Cove in Ocho Rios, Montego Bay is home to a private dolphin experience, **Dolphin Lagoon Half Moon** (⊠*N. Coast Hwy., Montego Bay* ☎*876/953–2211* ⊕*www.dolphinswimjamaica.com*). The Beach Encounter ($89) allows you to interact with dolphins in shallow water. The 35-minute Deep Water Encounter ($155) and the 40-minute Swim Encounter ($199) are better for stronger swimmers. Private swims ($400) and trainer for a day programs ($890) are also available.

FISHING

Deep-sea fishing is excellent in Montego Bay; anglers have the opportunity to go out and try to land yellowfin tuna, kingfish, wahoo, marlin, sailfish, and more. Many of the larger resorts offer deep-sea fishing; several operators in town also provide half- and full-day excursions. East of Montego Bay near Falmouth, **Glistening Waters Marina** (⊠*N. Coast Hwy., Falmouth* ☎*876/954–3229* ⊕*www.glisteningwaters.com*) offers charter trips. The 30 boats moored at the Glistening Waters Marina offer deep-sea fishing charters. There are also nighttime pontoon boat trips across the shimmering the lagoon, which glows because of microscopic dinoflagellates in the water.

Charter fishing excursions are available aboard the *No Problem* **and** *Reel E'zee* (☎*876/381–3229*). Half- and full-day excursions take anglers in search of big catch. Plan on about $400 for a half-day charter and $780 for a full-day on the seas; fees includes drinks and equipment.

Located at Half Moon, **North Coast Marine Sports** (⊠*Half Moon, N. Coast Hwy.* ☎*876/ 953–9266*) offers deep-sea fishing as well as other water sports.

Half-day charters ($380) are the specialty of **Salty Angler Fishing Charters** (☎*876/863–1599* ⊕*www.flyfishingjamaica.com*). Fly-fishing and light tackle are offered on open-water fishing excursions as well as casting sessions in the area's lagoons, flats, estuaries, and reefs.

GOLF

Golfers appreciate both the beauty and the challenges offered by Jamaica's courses, the most prestigious on the island. Caddies are almost always mandatory, and rates are $15 to $45 per round of golf. Cart rentals costs $20 to $40.

At Rose Hall Resort & County Club, **Cinnamon Hill Ocean Course** (⊠*N. Coast Hwy., Montego Bay* ☎*876/953–2650* ⊕*www.rosehallresort.com*) has hosted several invitational tournaments. The course was designed by Robert von Hagge and Rick Baril (the designers of the White Witch course at the Ritz-Carlton) and is adjacent to historic Cinnamon Hill. Greens fees run $115 for guests, $150 for nonguests.

East of Montego Bay, **Grand Lido Braco Golf Club** (⊠*Trelawny* ☎*876/954–0010* ⊕*www.superclubs.com*), between Duncans and Rio Bueno, is home to a 9-hole course. Nonguests should call for greens fees. Caddies are not mandatory on this course.

★ **Half Moon** (⊠*N. Coast Hwy.* ☎*876/953–2560* ⊕*www.half moongolf.com*), a Robert Trent Jones–designed 18-hole course 7 mi (11 km) east of town, is the home of the Red Stripe Pro Am (greens fees are $105 for guests, $150 for nonguests). In 2005 the course received an upgrade from Jones protégé Roger Rulewich, and once again draws international attention. The course is also home of the Caribbean headquarters of the David Leadbetter Golf Academy, which offers one-day sessions, multiday retreats, and hour-long private sessions.

SuperClubs Golf Club (⊠*Off N. Coast Hwy., Montego Bay* ☎*876/953–7319* ⊕*www.superclubs.com*), 3 mi (5 km) east of the airport at Ironshore, is an 18-hole links-style course (greens fees are $50). Designed by Robert Moote, the course also includes a restaurant, pro shop, and bar.

★ **Fodor's**Choice Probably the best-known golf course in Jamaica is the **Tryall Club** (⊠*N. Coast Hwy., Sandy Bay* ☎*876/956–5681* ⊕*www.tryallclub.com*) is 15 mi (24 km) west of Montego Bay. The 18-hole championship course is on the site of a 19th-century sugar plantation. The famous 7th hole tees off between the stone pillars of an historic aqueduct; the adjacent waterwheel has been the subject of many photos. The course was designed by Ralph Plummer and is an official PGA tour–approved course, having hosted events such as the Johnnie Walker World Championship. Greens fees are $85 for guests, $125 for nonguests. The newest course in Jamaica is at the Ritz-Carlton Golf & Spa Resort. The **White Witch Course** (⊠*1 Ritz-Carlton Dr., Rose Hall, St. James* ☎*876/518–0174*), designed by Robert von Hagge and Rick Baril, is literally on the grounds of historic Rose Hall. The greens fees at this 18-hole championship course are $179 for resort guests, $199 for nonguests, and $99 for a twilight round.

HELICOPTER TOURS

Departing from the domestic terminal of Montego Bay's Sangster International Airport, **Island Hoppers** (☎*876/974–1285* ⊕*www.jamaicahelicoptertours.com*) offers three helicopter tours of the Montego Bay area. The longest is the hour-long Western Showcase ($1,000 for up to four persons), which flies as far away as Negril. The 30-minute Memories of Jamaica tour ($520 for up to four persons) travels west over the cruise pier and over Round Hill. On the 20-minute Montego Bay Ecstasy Tour ($360 for up to four persons) you fly east over Rose Hall.

HORSEBACK RIDING

Although it doesn't have quite the long history of horseback rides as Ocho Rios (which began offering horseback swims at Chukka Cove after visitors saw the polo ponies being exercised in the sea), Montego Bay has a growing number of horseback options for both beginning and experienced riders.

In the Braco area between Montego Bay and Ocho Rios, **Braco Stables** (✉*Rte. A1, Duncans* ☎*876/954–0185* ⊕*www.bracostables.com*) offers a bareback romp in the sea for $70. For more experienced riders, a two-hour advanced ride costing $84 takes you into the mountains. The trips include complimentary refreshments served poolside at the Braco Great House as well as transportation to and from Montego Bay hotels.

From its location west of Montego Bay, **Chukka Caribbean Adventures** (✉*Sandy Bay, Hanover* ☎*876/972–2506* ⊕*www.chukkacaribbean.com*) offers tours for beginning riders. You travel through rain forest and open countryside before heading to the sea for an exhilarating ride through the surf. The three-hour excursion ($69) is available for riders 6 and older. **Half Moon Equestrian Centre** (✉*N. Coast Hwy.* ☎*876/953–2286* ⊕*www.horsebackridingjamaica.com*) offers horseback rides for all ages and abilities. Twice a day, 10-minute pony rides thrill children under 6. Those 6 and older can join in the 45-minute beginner's ride ($50) that starts with an introductory lesson before progressing to the trails. The 90-minute beach ride ($60), available for ages 8 and up, includes a romp in the sea.

DID YOU KNOW? **The thermometer may say the temperatures are in the 80s, but combined with the high humidity days in Jamaica are hot, hot, hot. You'll need to take extra precautions. It's a good idea to plan strenuous activities in the cooler morning hours.**

JEEP & ATV TOURS

Open-air jeeps and all-terrain vehicles are an exciting way for travelers to combine the experience of a guided tour with the thrills of an amusement-park ride. The fairly rugged landscape around Montego Bay adds to the fun.

West of Montego Bay, **Chukka Caribbean Adventures** (⊠*Sandy Bay, Hanover* ☎*876/972–2506* ⊕*www.chukkacaribbean. com*) offers ATV tours for adventurous travelers 16 and older. The noisy vehicles jostle and splash their way along trails on a 10-mi (16-km) ride through the hills before returning so you can take a dip in the sea. It also offers four-hour jeep trips across the countryside. The bouncy ride can be enjoyed by those 6 and over. Either ride costs $73 per person.

MOUNTAIN BIKING

Jamaica's hilly terrain makes the island a challenge for experienced mountain bikers, although beginners can also find easier rides, especially near the beaches and on the western end of the island. Heavy, unpredictable traffic on the North Coast Highway makes it off-limits for bikers, but country roads and hilly trails weave a network through the countryside.

Half Moon Equestrian Centre (⊠*N. Coast Hwy.* ☎*876/953–2286* ⊕*www.horsebackridingjamaica.com*) offers mountain-bike rides ($40) on the Mount Zion trail. The one-hour rides across the Rose Hall plantation grounds are for ages 12 and over.

SAILING

Ahoy, it's "shiver me timbers" time aboard **Calico Pirate Cruises** (⊠*Pier One, Howard Cooke Blvd., Montego Bay* ☎*876/940–4465* ⊕*www.calicopiratecruises.com*). The three-hour cruise ($60), aimed at a family audience, includes pirate stories, snorkeling in Montego Bay Marine Park, and unlimited punch, soda, and beer. Cruises depart daily except Wednesday at 10 AM. Geared more to an adult audience, the daily Calico Sunset Cruise features a four-course meal served onboard.

Dreamer Catamaran Cruises (✉*10 Queens Dr.* ☎*876/979–0102* ⊕*www.dreamercatamarans.com*) offers sails on three catamarans ranging from 53 to 65 feet. The cruise ($60) includes a snorkel stop and a visit to Margaritaville before the final leg of the cruise. There are foot massages for women, followed by dance instruction for all. Children are allowed on only the morning cruise.

TENNIS

Many hotels have tennis facilities that are free to their guests, but a few will allow nonguests to play for a fee. Court fees generally run $5 to $8 per hour for nonguests; lessons generally run $30 to $65 per hour.

The most extensive tennis center in the area, **Half Moon** (✉*N. Coast Hwy.* ☎*876/953–2211*) offers tennis buffs the use of 13 courts lighted for night play. There's also a resident pro and a pro shop. You need to buy a membership card if you're not a guest; a day pass is $40.

WHITE-WATER RAFTING

Cruising down the rivers of Jamaica aboard bamboo rafts had its start in Port Antonio—first with loads of bananas and later with tourists—but it has definitely caught on in Montego Bay. Today's travelers have their choice of lazy floats or energetic white-water excursions.

If you're looking for a more rugged adventure, then consider a white-water rafting trip with **Caliche Rainforest Park and Adventure Tours** (✉*Montego Bay* ☎*876/957–5569* ⊕*www.whitewaterraftingmontegobay.com*). Two tours, both offered in inflatable rafts, traverse the waters of the Great River. The Grade II Rainforest Rafting Tour glides along with stops for a swim; ages 4 and up can participate. The Canyon White Water Rafting tour traverses rapids up to Grade IV; travelers must be at least 14.

For more active water lovers, several operators offer guided tours of varying levels, ranging from tubing to kayaking. **Chukka Caribbean Adventures** (✉*Sandy Bay, Hanover* ☎*876/972–2506* ⊕*www.chukkacaribbean.com*) offers white-water tubing on the White River, a mild trip that doesn't require any previous rafting experience. Rafters travel in a convoy along the river and through some gentle rapids.

Jamaica Tours Limited (✉*Providence Dr., Montego Bay* ☎*876/953–3700* ⊕*www.jamaicatoursltd.com*) conducts trips through Mountain Valley, approximately 12 mi (19

1

km) southwest of MoBay. The four-hour excursion costs about $54 per person, including lunch, and takes you through unspoiled hill country. Bookings can be made through hotel tour desks.

River Raft Ltd. (✉*66 Claude Clarke Ave., Montego Bay* ☎*876/952–0889* ⊕*www.jamaicarafting.com*) leads trips down the Martha Brae River, about 25 mi (40 km) from MoBay. The cost is $45 per person for the 1½-hour river run.

SHOPPING

Shopping is not one of Jamaica's high points, though you will certainly be able to find things to buy. Good choices include Jamaican handicrafts, which range from batik fabrics to woven baskets. Wood carvings are one of the top purchases; the finest carvings are made from Jamaica's national tree, the lignum vitae, or tree of life, a dense wood that requires a talented carver to transform the hard, blond wood into dolphins, iguanas, or fish. Bargaining is expected with crafts vendors.

Naturally, Jamaican rum is another top souvenir—there's no shortage of opportunities to buy it at gift shops and liquor stores—as is Tia Maria, the Jamaican-made coffee liqueur. Coffee (both Blue Mountain and the less expensive High Mountain) is sold at every gift shop on the island. The cheapest prices are found at the local grocery stores, where you can buy beans or ground coffee. As one of two major cruise ports on the island, Montego Bay has some good duty-free shops as well. Fine jewelry and watches are top buys in the duty-free shops.

AREAS & MALLS

★ The most serious shopping in town is presently at **Half Moon Village**, east of Half Moon resort. The bright yellow buildings are filled with the finest and most expensive wares money can buy, but the park benches and outdoor pub here make the mall a fun stop for window-shoppers as well.

At this writing, final work was underway on **The Shoppes at Rose Hall**, an upscale shopping center designed to resemble an old-fashioned main street. The center, across the highway from Rose Hall, includes jewelry, cosmetics, and designer-apparel shops as well as a handful of restaurants.

CLOSE UP

The Man in Black

Jamaica has been home to many famous foreigners—Ian Fleming and Noël Coward in Ocho Rios, Errol Flynn in Port Antonio. Montego Bay had Johnny Cash, the "man in black" himself.

Cash found a home away from home in Jamaica, coming to the island for nearly 30 years to his winter residence at the Cinnamon Hill greathouse near Rose Hall. "Jamaica has saved and renewed me more times than I can count," wrote the famous musician in his autobiography. The country singer enjoyed fishing in local streams, visiting the markets for fresh fruits and vegetables, and being surrounded by the country atmosphere that reminded him of his boyhood home.

Cash and his wife June were very active in the establishment of an S.O.S. Children's Village for orphaned and abandoned children in Barrett Town, just east of Montego Bay. The duo worked to finance the first family home, performing concerts at nearby Rose Hall to raise funds for the project. Cash later wrote "The Ballad of Annie Palmer," a song about the legendary occupant of Rose Hall. All the profits, of course, fund the children's home.

Less serious shopping takes place at the **Holiday Inn Shopping Centre,** directly across the street from the Holiday Inn Sunspress. The casual shopping area has jewelry, clothing, and crafts stores.

Unless you have an extremely early flight, you'll find plenty of shopping in the new terminal of the Sangster International Airport, considered the largest shopping mall in Jamaica.

SPECIALTY ITEMS

ART

The **Gallery of West Indian Art** (⊠11 Fairfield Rd., Montego Bay ☎876/952–4547) is the place to find Jamaican and Haitian paintings. A corner of the gallery is devoted to hand-turned pottery (some painted) and beautifully carved and painted birds and animals.

HANDICRAFTS

In Montego Bay, the largest crafts market is on **Market Street,** a compendium of stalls, each selling pretty much the same thing. Come prepared to haggle over prices and to be given the hard sell; if you're in the right mood, though, the whole experience can be a lot of fun and a peek into Jamaican commerce away from the resorts.

Things Jamaican (⊠*Devon House, 26 Hope Rd., Kingston* ☎*876/926–1961* ⊠*Sangster International Airport, Montego Bay* ☎*876/952–4212*) sells some of the best Jamaican crafts—from carved wooden bowls and trays to reproductions of silver and brass period pieces.

LIQUOR & TOBACCO

As a rule, only rum distilleries, such as Appleton's and Sangster's, have better deals than the airport stores. Best of all, if you buy your rum at the airport, you don't have to tote all those heavy, breakable bottles around. Remember that if you purchase rum (or other liquids, such as perfumes) outside the airport, you'll need to place them in your checked luggage when returning home. If you purchase liquids inside the secured area of the airport, you may board with your liquids. The most extensive liquor stores in the airport are Jamaica Farewell and Sunshine Liquor.

Fine handmade cigars are available at the Montego Bay airport or at one of the area's cigar stores. You can also buy Cuban cigars almost everywhere, but remember that they can't legally be brought back to the United States. The Cigar Hut, the Tobacco Shop, and Jamaica Farewell sell a wide selection of cigars.

MUSIC

The **Bob Marley Experience & Theatre** (⊠*Half Moon Shopping Village, Montego Bay* ☎*876/953–3449*) has shops filled with Marley memorabilia, including CDs.

NIGHTLIFE & THE ARTS

This island is all about music. For starters there's reggae, popularized by the late Bob Marley and performed today by his son, Ziggy Marley, as well as Jimmy Tosh (the late Peter Tosh's son), Gregory Isaacs, Jimmy Cliff, and many others. If your experience with Caribbean music has been limited to steel drums and Harry Belafonte, then the political, racial, and religious messages of reggae may set you on your ear; listen closely and you just might hear the heartbeat of the people. Dancehall is another island favorite type of music, as is soca.

A Splash of Reggae

Since its birth in the 1960s, reggae has been the cultural heartbeat of Jamaica. Each summer, the pulsating rhythm reverberates as the genre's top performers take the microphone at the Red Stripe Reggae Sumfest. Not to be confused with the now-defunct Reggae Sunfest in Kingston, Sumfest is held in Montego Bay and includes a week of performances.

This bash, billed as the world's premier reggae event, draws more than 30,000 fans. The festival's message of "promot-ing music, the universal force" is spread at the main concert, as well as through a series of minitours held throughout the Caribbean.

Reggae Sumfest has broadened its musical horizons since its launch in 1992, embracing a wider spectrum of music. Reggae stars like Ziggy Marley and the Melody Makers, Burning Spear, and Beenie Man now share the same bill with performers like Kanye West, 50 Cent, G-Unit, Jay-Z, Ja Rule, and Sean Paul.

ANNUAL EVENTS

★ Fodor's Choice Those who know and love reggae should visit Montego Bay between mid-July and August for the **Red Stripe Reggae Sumfest** (⊕*www.reggaesumfest.com*). This weeklong concert—at the Bob Marley Performing Arts Center in the Freeport area—attracts such big-name performers as Third World and Ziggy Marley and the Melody Makers. Tickets are sold for each night's performances or by multievent passes.

BARS & CLUBS

The liveliest late-night happenings throughout Jamaica are in the major resort hotels, with the widest variety of spots probably in Montego Bay. Some of the all-inclusive resorts offer a dinner and disco pass from $50 to $100. Call ahead to check availability and bring photo identification. Pick up a copy of the *Daily Gleaner*, the *Jamaica Observer*, or the *Star* for listings on who's playing when and where.

The **Brewery** (⊠*Miranda Ridge, Gloucester Ave., Montego Bay* ☎876/940–2433) is a popular sports bar. **Hurricanes Disco** (⊠*Breezes Montego Bay Resort, Gloucester Ave., Montego Bay* ☎876/940–1150) is packed with locals and visitors from surrounding small hotels thanks to a $50 night pass (which includes dinner and drinks). **Walter's**

(⊠*39 Gloucester Ave., Montego Bay* ☎*876/952–9391*) is a downtown favorite.

CASINOS

You won't find massive casinos in Jamaica, although a growing number of resorts have slots-only gaming rooms. In Montego Bay, the largest of these is the **Coral Cliff** (⊠*165 Gloucester Ave., Montego Bay* ☎*876/952–4130*). Right on the Hip Strip, it has more than 120 slot machines. Weekly slot tournaments and complimentary drinks keep you in the mood. The gaming room is open 24 hours daily.

MONTEGO BAY ESSENTIALS

To research prices, get advice from other travelers, and book travel arrangements, visit www.fodors.com.

TRANSPORTATION

BY AIR

Jamaica is well served by major airlines. From the United States, Air Jamaica, American, Continental, Delta, Northwest, Spirit, United, and US Airways offer nonstop and connecting service. Air Canada offers service from several major airports in Canada. Air Jamaica, Virgin Atlantic, and British Airways offer service from the United Kingdom. Cayman Airways connects Jamaica to Grand Cayman and Cayman Brac.

Airlines **Air Canada** (☎*876/952–5160*). **Air Jamaica** (☎*876/952–4300*). **AmericanAirlines** (☎*800/744–0006*). **British Airways** (☎*876/929–9020*). **Cayman Airways** (☎*876/924–8092*). **Continental** (☎*800/231–0856*). **Delta** (☎*800/221–1212*). **Northwest Airlines** (☎*800/225–2525*). **Spirit Airlines** (☎*586/791–7300 or 800/772–7117*). **United Airlines** (☎*800/538–2929*). **US Airways** (☎*800/622–1015*). **Virgin Atlantic** (☎*800/744–7477*).

AIR TRAVEL AROUND JAMAICA

TimAir and International Airlink offer charter service from Montego Bay's Sangster International Airport to airports in Port Antonio, Ocho Rios, Runaway Bay, Kingston, and Negril. Scheduled service is available on International Airlink between Montego Bay and Kingston. Charter helicopter service is provided by Island Hoppers to Ocho Rios.

Information **International Airlink** (☎*888/247–5465* ⊕*www.intlairlink.com*). **Island Hoppers** (☎*876/974–1285* ⊕*www.jamaicahelicoptertours.com*). **TimAir** (☎*876/952–2516* ⊕*www.timair.com*).

AIRPORTS & TRANSFERS

Jamaica's busiest airport is the Sangster International Airport (MBJ) in Montego Bay. Many hotels offer shuttles to pick you up at the airport. The airport's new arrivals hall is home to hotel lounges for Sandals, Beaches, SuperClubs, Ritz-Carlton, Couples, Sunset, and Half Moon resorts; check in at the desk and relax until the bus leaves.

If your hotel does not offer a shuttle, the best way into the city is by taxi. The authorized airport taxi desk is just beyond the exit past Customs.

Information **Sangster International Airport** (✉ *Rte. A1, Montego Bay* ☎ *876/952–3124* ⊕ *www.mbjairport.com*).

BY CAR

Driving in Jamaica can be extremely frustrating. You must constantly be on guard—for enormous potholes, people and animals darting out into the street, and aggressive drivers. With a narrow road encircling the island, local drivers are quick to pass other cars. Sometimes two cars will pass simultaneously, inspiring the UNDERTAKERS LOVE OVERTAKERS signs seen throughout the island. Driving in Jamaica is on the left, British-style.

Because many car renters are returning Jamaicans, the breakdown between high season and low season for car rentals is different than the high and low hotel seasons. Car-rental prices are highest over the winter holidays, Easter, and July and August. To rent a car you must be between the ages of 23 (with at least one year possessing a valid driver's license) and 70.

Information **Alex's Car Rentals and Tours** (☎ *876/971–2615*). **Avis Rent a Car** (☎ *876/952–0762* ⊕ *www.avis.com.jm*). **Budget** (☎ *876/979–0438* ⊕ *www.budget.com*). **Fiesta Car Rentals** (☎ *876/953–9444* ⊕ *www.fiestacarrentals.com*). **Hertz** (☎ *876/952–4250* ⊕ *www.hertz.com*). **Island Car Rentals** (☎ *876/952–7225* ⊕ *www.islandcarrentals.com*). **Jamaica Car Rental** (☎ *876/952–5586*).

BY CRUISE SHIP

Montego Bay is one of three Jamaican cruise ports (along with the very busy Ocho Rios and the very quiet Port Antonio). Ships dock at the Montego Cruise Terminal. Located west of Montego Bay, the cruise terminal has five berths and accommodates both cruise and cargo shipping. The terminal includes specialty shops, a communications center, a visitor information booth, and a taxi stand supervised by the Jamaica Tourist Board.

1

The Montego Cruise Terminal is a short ride from town. The Freeport Shopping Centre is within walking distance of the docks. If you just want to visit a beach, then Doctor's Cave Beach is a very good nearby option, and it's right in town.

From the terminal, both taxis and buses shuttle passengers to downtown. Taxi service is about US$10 each way to downtown. Expect to pay $2 per person each way by shuttle bus to the City Centre Shopping Mall or $3 each way to Doctor's Cave Beach.

Information **Carnival Cruise Line** (☎*888/227–6482*). **P&O Cruises** (☎*0845/678–0014*). **Royal Caribbean Cruises** (☎*866/562–7625*).

BY TAXI

Some, but not all, of Montego Bay's taxis are metered. If you accept a driver's offer of his services as a tour guide, be sure to agree on a price before the vehicle is put into gear. A one-day tour should run about $150 to $180, in U.S. dollars, depending on distance traveled. All licensed taxis display red Public Passenger Vehicle (PP) plates. Cabs can be summoned by phone or flagged down on the street. Rates are per car, not per passenger, and 25% is added to the metered rate between midnight and 5 AM. Licensed minivans are also available and bear the red PP plates. JUTA is the largest taxi franchise and has offices in all resort areas.

Information **JCAL Taxi** (☎*876/952–7574* ⊕*www.jcaltours.com*). **JUTA Montego Bay** (☎*876/952–0813* ⊕*www.jutatours.com*).

CONTACTS & RESOURCES

BANKS & EXCHANGE SERVICES

Currency exchange is available at Sangster International Airport (just past immigration) as well as in hotels, banks, and exchange offices. But few Americans bother—especially if they'll be in Montego Bay for their entire trip—since U.S. dollars are widely accepted.

Not all ATMs in Jamaica accept American ATM cards, so you may have to try more than one. Some ATMs dispense either Jamaican or U.S. dollars. NCB ATMs offer U.S. dollars using debit or credit cards; these machines are at the Montego Bay Cruise Ship Terminal and Half Moon Resort. Cool Cash ATMs provide U.S. currency; in the Montego

Bay area, you can find these machines at Rose Hall Resort, Holiday Inn, Iberostar, Coral Cliff, Sunset Beach Resort, City Centre Shopping Plaza, and four locations at Sangster International Airport.

The official currency is the Jamaican dollar. At this writing the exchange rate was about J$66.27 to US$1. Prices quoted throughout this chapter are in U.S. dollars, unless otherwise noted.

Banks are generally open Monday through Thursday from 9 to 2, Friday 9 to 4. Exchange offices have more extended hours.

Information **Cambio King** (⌧ *Casa Montego Arcade, Montego Bay* ☏ *876/952-2570*). **DB&G's Cambio** (⌧ *8 Market St., Montego Bay* ☏ *876/940-0691*). **First Caribbean International Bank** (⌧ *59 St. James St., Montego Bay* ☏ *876/952-4045*). **First Global Bank** (⌧ *53 Gloucester Ave., Montego Bay* ☏ *876/971-5260*). **Scotiabank** (⌧ *6-7 Sam Sharpe Sq., Montego Bay* ☏ *876/952-4440*).

ELECTRICITY

The current in Jamaica is 110 volts but only 50 cycles, with outlets that take two flat prongs. Some hotels provide 220-volt plugs as well as special shaver outlets. If you plan to bring electrical appliances with you, it's best to ask when making your reservation.

EMERGENCIES

Outside of Kingston, Montego Bay is home to the island's most extensive medical facilities. For travelers, the major hospital is the MoBay Hope Medical Center on the grounds of the Half Moon Resort.

Emergency Services **Ambulance & Fire Emergencies** (☏ *110*). **Police Emergencies & Air Rescue** (☏ *119*). **Hurricane Update** (☏ *116*). **Scuba-Diving Emergencies** (⌧ *St. Ann's Bay Hospital, St. Ann's Bay* ☏ *876/972-2272*).

Hospitals **Cornwall Regional Hospital** (⌧ *Mount Salem, Montego Bay* ☏ *876/952-5100*). **MoBay Hope Medical Center** (⌧ *Half Moon, Montego Bay* ☏ *876/953-3981*).

Pharmacies **Corn-Med Pharmacy** (⌧ *38 Barnett St., Shop 21, Oneness Plaza, Montego Bay* ☏ *876/971-9108*). **Greysville Pharmacy** (⌧ *3 Barnett St., Trinity Mall, Montego Bay* ☏ *876/971-1075*). **Zack's Pharmacy** (⌧ *30 Union St., Montego Bay* ☏ *876/979-2870*).

HOLIDAYS

Public holidays include New Year's Day, Ash Wednesday (beginning of Lent, 6 weeks before Easter), Good Friday, Easter Monday, Labor Day (May 23), Independence Day (1st Monday in August), National Heroes Day (October 15), Christmas, and Boxing Day (December 26). Along with the closure of many attractions, numerous tours do not operate on these days.

INTERNET, MAIL & SHIPPING

Internet service is becoming far more common, and most hotels offer at least limited service, either at public terminals (sometimes free at the all-inclusive resorts) or wireless service.

Post office hours are weekdays from 9 to 5. Postcards may be mailed anywhere in the world for J$50. Letters cost J$60 to the United States and Canada, J$70 to Europe, and J$90 to Australia and New Zealand. Due to costly and slow air-shipping service, most travelers carry home packages, even large wooden carvings.

Internet Cafés **Cyber Cafe** (⊠*Doctor's Cave Beach, Montego Bay* ☎*876/971–8907*).

Post Offices **Main Post Office** (⊠*122 Barnett St., Montego Bay* ☎*876/952–7389*).

Shipping Companies **Airpak Express** (⊠*Sangster International Airport, Montego Bay* ☎*876/952–5299*). **DHL** (⊠*34 Queens Dr., Montego Bay* ☎*888/225–5345*). **FedEx Express** (⊠*Chatwick Plaza, 10 Queens Dr., Montego Bay* ☎*888/463–3339*).

TAXES

The departure tax of $27 must be paid in cash if it's not added to the cost of your airline tickets; this policy varies by carrier, although most ticket prices now include the departure tax. Jamaica has replaced the room occupancy tax with a V.A.T. of 15% on most goods and services, which is already incorporated into the prices of taxable goods. Since May 2005, incoming air passengers were charged a US$10 tourism-enhancement fee; incoming cruise passengers pay a $2 fee. Both these fees are almost always included in the price of your airline ticket or cruise passage.

TOUR OPTIONS

Montego Bay offers a wide array of guided tours. JUTA, the island's largest tour operator, offers a greathouse tour and a rafting tour, as well as tours to other parts of the island like Black River, Negril, and Ocho Rios. Glamour Tours is another large tour operator with a wide selection of guided visits to Rose Hall and Greenwood Great House.

Guided plantation and countryside visits are also popular. The 8-hour Hilton High Day Tour takes visitors 45 minutes into the hills for a country-style breakfast followed by a visit to the German-immigrant-founded Seaford Town, and a Jamaican buffet lunch. The Croydon Plantation Tour visits the birthplace of Jamaican hero Sam Sharpe, who led the rebellion that helped put an end to slavery on the island. John's Hall Adventure Tour visits a plantation near the town of John's Hall in Cockpit Country to taste fresh fruit and enjoy a barbecue lunch. The John's Hall Adventure Tours company also leads visits to Negril and Ocho Rios and organizes "Jamaica Rhythm," an evening of folk dancing and dinner.

Information **Croydon Plantation Tour** (⊠ Box 1348, Montego Bay 🖀 876/979–8267 ⊕ www.croydonplantation.com). **Glamour Tours** (⊠ 2 Gloucester and Kent Aves., Montego Bay 🖀 876/940–3277 ⊕ www.glamourtoursdmc.com). **Hilton High Day Tour** (⊠ Box 162, Reading 🖀 876/952–3343 ⊕ www.jamaicahiltontour.com). **John's Hall Adventure Tour** (⊠ 26 Hobbs Ave., Montego Bay 🖀 876/971–6958 ⊕ www.johnshalladventuretour.com). **JUTA** (⊠ Box 1155, Montego Bay 🖀 876/952–0813 ⊕ www.jutatours.com).

VISITOR INFORMATION

The Jamaica Tourist Board has a full office downtown filled with visitor information, maps, and brochures; the office is open weekdays 8:30 to 4:30 and Saturday 9 to 1. At the city's Sangster International Airport, arriving passengers will find a JTB booth in the customs hall. The airport information desk is open 6 am to 10 pm daily.

Information **Jamaica Tourist Board** (⊠ Cornwall Beach, Montego Bay 🖀 876/952–4425 ⊕ www.visitjamaica.com).

Ocho Rios & Runaway Bay

WORD OF MOUTH

"We took a day [in Ocho Rios] to explore the stores (those that the locals shop in) and the locals market. It was one of the most memorable days of our trip."

—travelincane

"Climbing the Dunn's River Falls is a complete blast. It is something that you've never done in your life. It is really super fun."

—kellibellie

By Paris
Permenter
and John
Bigley

PICTURE THE JAMAICA OF TRAVEL brochures—the towering waterfalls, the colorful flowers, the ferns so thick they form a canopy—and you'll be envisioning Ocho Rios. Located 67 mi (111 km) east of Montego Bay, Ocho Rios (often just Ochi) is favored by honeymooners and other romantic types for its natural beauty. Often called the garden center of Jamaica, this community is perfumed by flowering hibiscus, bird of paradise, bougainvillea, and other beautiful blooms throughout the year. (All that tropical growth, of course, means more rain than most other locations in Jamaica, but more on that later.)

Ocho Rios is where you can find one of the island's most famous attractions: Dunn's River Falls, where travelers climb up in daisy-chain fashion behind a sure-footed guide. This spectacular sight is actually a series of waterfalls cascading from the mountains to the sea. Dunn's River Falls is just one of several eye-popping natural wonders in the region. Several botanical gardens invite you to enjoy a few hours surrounded by tropical beauty.

Ocho Rios is a popular destination, so you won't be wandering through those gardens on your own. But it's easy to escape the crowds. Many people take advantage of the many rivers and go kayaking or white-water rafting. Ocho Rios is also home to a growing number of land-based adventure companies, so you can also go mountain biking, take a trip in an all-terrain vehicle, or whiz through the rain forest on a zip line.

In quiet contrast to Ocho Rios is Runaway Bay, the smallest of Jamaica's resort areas. About 12 mi (19½ km) west of Ocho Rios and 50 mi (80 km) east of Montego Bay, Runaway Bay is home to a few all-inclusive resorts and an 18-hole golf course. It has little of the tropical lushness for which Ocho Rios is known.

EXPLORING OCHO RIOS & RUNAWAY BAY

Exploring the Ocho Rios area can be explored on a guided excursion, on a tour with a licensed taxi driver, or even by rental car (although the latter is not recommended due to poor road conditions). When planning an itinerary, the distance can be misleading; plan for almost twice as long as you think it should take to get from one place to another. For example, although Ocho Rios is 67 mi (111 km) from Montego Bay, the drive takes about two hours. The North

OCHO RIOS TOP 5

Falling for the falls: Form a human daisy chain and climb up Dunn's River Falls, one of Jamaica's most popular attractions.

Being a secret agent: Create your own top-secret hideaway in a villa at Goldeneye, author Ian Fleming's former estate, where he wrote many James Bond novels.

Remembering a legend: Pay tribute to reggae great Bob Marley at his final resting place at Nine Mile.

Horsing Around: Splash through the waves—on horseback—at Chukka Cove, just west of Ocho Rios.

Getting close to nature: Swim with the dolphins, stingrays, and sharks at Dolphin Cove, just west of Ocho Rios.

Coast Highway, in the midst of a massive improvement project, is a faster route than it was years ago, but construction delays are something to keep in mind when visiting the surrounding area.

East of Ocho Rios, the North Coast Highway slows to a crawl, especially beyond Oracabessa to Port Antonio. The road is so slow, in fact, that many taxi drivers prefer to drive overland to Kingston and around the coast to Port Antonio rather than taking the direct route. Improvements are underway, but you should still budget about 3½ hours to get from Ocho Rios to Port Antonio.

South of Ocho Rios, the roads wind into the hills, with some of the prettiest (and, in some places, some of the slowest) drives you can take in Jamaica.

ABOUT THE RESTAURANTS

Although it's the setting for many all-inclusive resorts where guests take advantage of on-site restaurants, Ocho Rios is also home to many excellent stand-alone eateries. The city boasts a wide array of restaurants ranging from take-out jerk stands to sit-down dining rooms perched in the hills overlooking the city. During peak season, reservations are required at the most elegant establishments; otherwise, dining is a casual affair.

ABOUT THE HOTELS

With so much tropical beauty, Ocho Rios is the capital of Jamaica's couples-only and adults-only resorts. All-inclusive resorts claim the lion's share of hotel rooms—not surprising, as Ocho Rios was the birthplace of the Caribbean's all-inclusive movement. Although these sprawling resorts are the most visible (and often the most expensive) option in Ocho Rios, there are also standard hotels and a growing number of villas, complete with maid and chef service. The smaller Runaway Bay area is home to primarily all-inclusive resorts. Just beyond Runaway Bay, Discovery Bay is increasingly popular for its villas.

WHAT IT COSTS IN DOLLARS				
$$$$	$$$	$$	$	¢
RESTAURANTS				
Over $30	$20–$30	$12–$20	$8–$12	under $8
HOTELS*				
Over $350	$250–$350	$150–$250	$80–$150	under $80
HOTELS**				
Over $450	$350–$450	$250–$350	$125–$250	under $125

*EP, BP, CP; **AI, FAP, MAP; Restaurant prices are per person for a main course at dinner and do not include the 15% V.A.T. and 10% service charge. Hotel prices are per night for a double room in high season, excluding 15% V.A.T. and 10% service charge.

TIMING

Like the rest of Jamaica, Ocho Rios has a peak season that runs from mid-December through mid-April, although it also sees a surge in business during the increasingly popular Ocho Rios Jazz Festival in June. Another timing consideration: all that lush, tropical growth hints at the precipitation the area receives. The rainiest months are May and October, when the usual afternoon showers can stretch longer.

Travelers visiting Nine Mile, the hometown of Bob Marley, should note that on February 6, the anniversary of his birth, fans from around the world congregate here for concerts.

OCHO RIOS ATTRACTIONS

Ocho Rios isn't the prettiest town, but the surrounding area has several worthwhile attractions, including the very popular (and very touristy) Dunn's River Falls, located west of the city. When cruise ships are docked, the town can be incredibly crowded during the day. Evening, however, restores a calm feeling to the town of about 36,000 people.

In contrast, Runaway Bay is almost always a quiet getaway, a place where many travelers remain at their all-inclusive resort until they head back to the airport.

Numbers in the margin correspond to points of interest on the Jamaica map.

WHAT TO SEE

★ **❽ Bob Marley Centre & Mausoleum.** Those with an interest in Bob Marley won't want to miss Nine Mile, the community where reggae legend Bob Marley was born. Tucked behind a tall fence, the site is marked with green and gold flags. Tours are led by Rastafarians, who take visitors through the house and point out the single bed that Marley wrote about in "Is This Love." Visitors also step inside the mausoleum where the singer is buried with his guitar. The site also includes a restaurant and gift shop. Visitors from Ocho Rios can arrange transport by taxi, but the round-trip fare is about $175; a less expensive option is a guided tour. ⊠*Rhoden Hall, Nine Mile* ☎*876/995–1763* ⊠*$15* ⊙*Daily 9–4.*

❹ Coyaba River Garden & Museum and Mahoe Waterfalls. Jamaica's national motto is "Out of Many, One People," and at these gardens you can see the many cultural influences that have contributed this island's culture. The museum covers the island's history from the time of the Arawak Indians up to the present day. A 45-minute guided tour through the lush garden, which is 1½ mi (2½ km) south of Ocho Rios, introduces you to the island's flora and fauna. The complex includes a gift shop and a snack bar. ⊠*Shaw Park Estate, Shaw Park Ridge Rd.* ☎*876/974–6235* ⊕*www.coyabagardens.com* ⊠*$5* ⊙*Daily 8–5.*

❻ Cranbrook Flower Forest and River Head Adventure Trail. You can enjoy the region's natural wonders without the crowds at this garden filled with blooming orchids, ginger, and

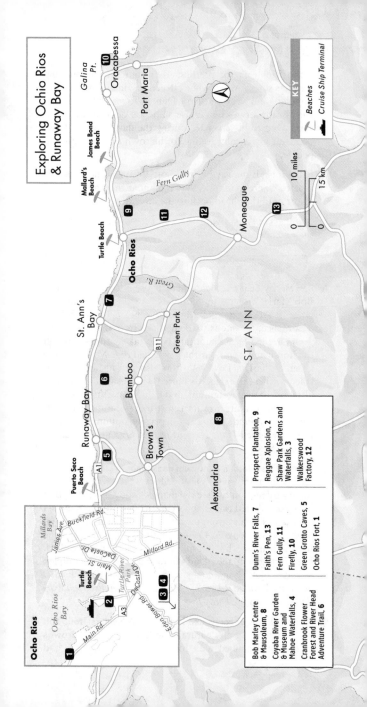

Exploring Ochio Rios & Runaway Bay

Ocho Rios

KEY

Beaches

Cruise Ship Terminal

Bob Marley Centre & Mausoleum, **8**	Prospect Plantation, **9**
Coyaba River Garden & Museum and Mahoe Waterfalls, **4**	Reggae Xplosion, **2**
Cranbrook Flower Forest and River Head Adventure Trail, **6**	Shaw Park Gardens and Waterfalls, **3**
	Walkerswood Factory, **12**
Dunn's River Falls, **7**	
Faith's Pen, **13**	
Fern Gully, **11**	
Firefly, **10**	
Green Grotto Caves, **5**	
Ocho Rios Fort, **1**	

0   10 miles
0   15 km

ST. ANN

ferns. This park is the brainchild of Ivan Linton, who has pampered the plants at this former plantation since the early 1980s. Linton proudly points out unusual specimens of plants such as birds of paradise, wild ginger, heliconia, and begonias. The grounds are perfect for a picnic and a hike along the shady banks of Laughlin's Great River. The path climbs high into the hills to a waterfall. Donkey rides, croquet, and volleyball are also available here. The complex includes a snack shop. ⊠ *5 mi (8 km) east of Runaway Bay, 1 mi (1½ km) off N. Coast Hwy.* ☎ *876/770–8071* ⊕ *www.cranbrookff.com* ⊠ *$10* ⊙ *Daily 9–5.*

7 ★ Fodor's Choice **Dunn's River Falls.** This series of waterfalls is an eye-catching sight: crystal-clear water splashing over a series of stone steps until it reaches the Caribbean. The best way to enjoy the falls is to climb the slippery steps: don a swimsuit, grasp the hand of the person ahead of you, and follow an experienced guide. The guides are personable fellows who reel off bits of local lore while telling you where to step; you can hire one for just a few dollars. After the climb, you exit through a crowded market—another reminder that this is one of Jamaica's top tourist attractions. If you can, schedule a visit on a day when no cruise ships are in port. ⚠ **Always climb with a licensed guide at Dunn's River Falls. Freelance guides might be a little cheaper, but the experienced guides can tell you just where to plant each footstep—helping you prevent a fall.** ⊠ *Off A1, between St. Ann's Bay and Ocho Rios* ☎ *876/974–2857* ⊕ *www. dunnsriverfallsja.com* ⊠ *$15* ⊙ *Daily 8:30–5.*

13 **Faith's Pen.** If you want to combine a cultural experience with lunch, stop by Faith's Pen. Rows of stalls with names like Johnny Cool No. 1 and Shut's Night and Day offer local specialties with home-cooked taste. For just a few dollars, buy a lunch of jerk chicken, curried goat, or roasted fish and enjoy it at one of the nearby picnic table. An unusual treat is the mannish water (a soup—and reported aphrodisiac—made from a goat's head). Faith's Pen is on Route A1, 12 mi (19½ km) south of Ocho Rios. ⊠ *Rte. A1, about 4 mi (6½ km) south of Rte. A3.*

11 **Fern Gully.** Don't miss a drive through Fern Gully, a natural canopy of vegetation that sunlight barely penetrates. (Jamaica has the world's largest number of fern species, with more than 570 types.) The 3-mi (5-km) stretch of fern-shaded forest includes many walking paths as well as numerous crafts vendors. Most tours through the area include a drive through Fern Gully, but to experience the damp, shady forest, stop and take a walk. ⊠*Rte. A3, south of Ocho Rios.*

NEED A BREAK? The drive from Montego Bay to Ocho Rios takes close to two hours, so take a break at a seaside jerk stand called **Yow's Restaurant and Beach Bar** (⊠*N. Coast Hwy., Rio Bueno* ☎*876/954–0366*). The restaurant has a couple of tables where you can enjoy favorites like jerk pork, chicken, and shrimp for about $6 per person.

★ ⑩ **Firefly.** Looking exactly as it did when it was visited by the late Queen Mother, Firefly was the home of playwright Noël Coward. Through the years this home received a who's who of celebrities like Sir Laurence Olivier, Alec Guiness, Peter O'Toole, Sophia Loren, Elizabeth Taylor, and Richard Burton. A guided tour includes a look at the surprisingly modest home and the simple grave where Coward is buried. The view from the house's hilltop perch is one of the best on the north coast, making Firefly well worth the price of admission. ⊠*Rte. A1, west of Port Maria* ☎*876/725–0920* ☎*$10* ⊗*Mon.–Thurs. and Sat. 9–5.*

❺ **Green Grotto Caves.** A good choice for rainy days, these caves offer 45-minute guided tours that include a look at a subterranean lake. The cave has a long history as a hiding place for everyone from fearsome pirates to runaway slaves to the Spanish governor (he was on the run from the British at the time). It's a good destination if you want to see one of Jamaica's caves without going too far off the beaten path. You'll feel like a spelunker, since you must wear a hard hat throughout the tour. ⊠*N. Coast Hwy., 2 mi (3 km) east of Discovery Bay* ☎*876/973–2841* ⊕*www.greengrottocavesja.com* ☎*$20* ⊗*Daily 9–4.*

DID YOU KNOW? Green Grotto Caves are the most popular in Jamaica— but they are by no means the only spelunking options. With porous limestone making up much of island, more than 1,100 caves have been discovered. Some are open for guided tours; others are explored primarily by adventure travelers that hire local guides. One of the top resources on the subject is *Jamaica Underground*, published by the University of the West Indies Press.

① Ocho Rios Fort. There's not much left of the 17th-century Ocho Rios Fort besides a wall and four cannons that still look out to the sea. Two of the cannons were brought here to protect the bay from the French, and the other two once protected nearby Mammee Bay (where the French did attack). ✉*Main St. next to Reynolds Pier* ☏*No phone* ⊕*www.jnht.com* 💵*Free* ☉*Open 24 hrs.*

⑨ Prospect Plantation. To learn about Jamaica's agricultural heritage, a trip to this working plantation, just west of town, is a must. It's not just a place for history lovers, however. Everyone enjoys the views over the White River Gorge and the tour in a tractor-pulled cart. The grounds are full of exotic flowers and tropical trees, some planted over the years by such celebrities as Winston Churchill and Charlie Chaplin. The estate includes a small aviary with free-flying butterflies. You can also saddle up for horseback rides and camel safaris on the plantation's 900 acres. ✉*Rte. A1, east of Ocho Rios* ☏*876/994–1058* 💵*$32* ☉*Daily 8–5; tours Mon.–Sat. 10:30, 2, and 3:30.*

② Reggae Xplosion. In the open-air Island Village shopping center, which is owned by Island Records tycoon Chris Blackwell, Reggae Xplosion traces the fascinating history of Jamaican music. Reggae, ska, mento, dancehall, and other genres are featured in a series of exhibits spanning two stories. Special sections highlight the careers of some of Jamaica's best-known talents, including Bob Marley, Peter Tosh, and Bunny Wailer. The museum has an extensive gift shop filled with recordings and collectibles. ✉*Turtle Beach Rd.* ☏*876/675–8895* ⊕*www.islandjamaica.com* 💵*$15* ☉*Mon.–Sat. 9–5.*

③ Shaw Park Gardens and Waterfalls. Originally used for growing sugarcane and later oranges, this estate became the original site of the exclusive Shaw Park Hotel (today relocated to the beach). The owner's daughter, appropriately named Flora, worked to create the lush gardens, which now fill the 25-acre site with flame flowers, birds of paradise, and orchids. ✉*Shaw Park Rd.* ☏*876/974–2723* ⊕*www.shaw-parkgardens.com* 💵*$10* ☉*Daily 8–4.*

★ **⑫ Walkerswood Factory.** To learn more about Jamaican cuisine (as well as the island's bountiful supply of herbs and spices), visit Walkerswood Factory. This company produces everything from jerk seasonings to pepper sauces. A one-hour guided tour provides a look at the herb gardens, a jerk marinade demonstration, and a sampling of

Getting Hitched

With its lush tropical backdrop and wide selection of romantic resorts, Ocho Rios is one of the island's top wedding spots. Weddings are big business, so your hotel will be happy to offer all the assistance you'll need for a happy honeymoon.

Several all-inclusive resorts, including Couples and Sandals, offer free wedding packages. These typically include a ceremony and small reception, although you'll pay for other expenses like the marriage license. All the major resorts have wedding coordinators that handle all the paperwork needed to be filled out before your arrival.

Getting married in Jamaica is easy and inexpensive, with just a 24-hour waiting period after you arrive on the island. No blood tests are required. You'll need to bring along a proof of citizenship, including a certified copy of your birth certificate. If applicable, you'll also need a proof of divorce, a copy of a deceased partner's death certificate, or a parent's written consent if you're under 21.

local products. The site includes a gift shop and snack bar featuring local dishes (well spiced, of course). The facility is about 6 mi (10 km) south of Ocho Rios. ⊠*Rte. A3, Walkerswood* ☎*876/917–2318* ⊕*www.walkerswood.com* ⊯*$15* ⊙*Mon.–Sat. 9–4.*

WHERE TO EAT

Although Ocho Rios is a hub of all-inclusive activity, travelers find a wide variety of independent dining options in the area as well, from jerk stands to fine-dining restaurants to familiar burgers-and-fries eateries. The area within walking distance of the cruise terminal is home to many casual restaurants that are especially popular for lunch; dinner options can range from seaside restaurants to open-air establishments high in the hills overlooking the city lights.

ASIAN

$–$$$ ✕ **The Ruins at the Falls.** Just as the name suggests, this restaurant is perched beside a waterfall. Tables sit at the base of the 40-foot cascade, making this a romantic spot for lunch or dinner. The menu here is diverse, with Asian specialties such as lotus lily lobster joining Jamaican favorites like curried goat. There are even a few vegetarian dishes.

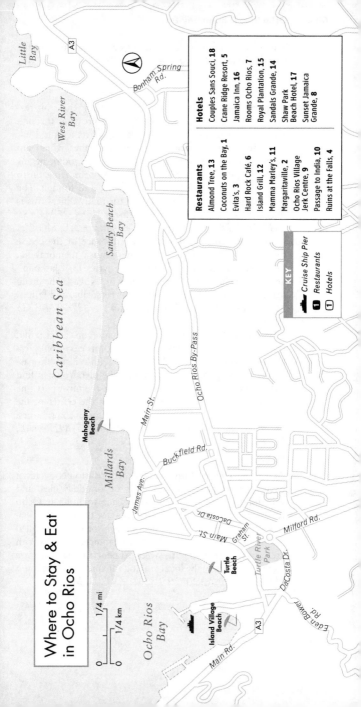

Where to Stay & Eat in Ocho Rios

Restaurants

Almond Tree, **13**
Coconuts on the Bay, **1**
Evita's, **3**
Hard Rock Café, **6**
Island Grill, **12**
Mamma Marley's, **11**
Margaritaville, **2**
Ocho Rios Village Jerk Centre, **9**
Passage to India, **10**
Ruins at the Falls, **4**

Hotels

Couples Sans Souci, **18**
Crane Ridge Resort, **5**
Jamaica Inn, **16**
Rooms Ocho Rios, **7**
Royal Plantation, **15**
Sandals Grande, **14**
Shaw Park Beach Hotel, **17**
Sunset Jamaica Grande, **8**

KEY

Cruise Ship Pier

1 Restaurants

① Hotels

Caribbean Sea

Little Bay

West River Bay

Sandy Beach Bay

Millards Bay

Mahogany Beach

Ocho Rios Bay

Island Village Beach

Turtle Beach

Bonham Spring Rd.

A3

Main St.

Ocho Rios By-Pass

Buckfield Rd.

James Ave.

DaCosta Dr.

Main St.

Graham St.

Turtle River Park

Milford Rd.

DaCosta Dr.

Eden Bower Rd.

Main Rd.

A3

0   1/4 mi
0   1/4 km

This place is popular for weddings and other big events, so call ahead. ✉ *17 Da Costa Dr.* ☎ *876/974–8888* ☐ *AE, MC, V.*

ECLECTIC

$$–$$$$ ✕ **Almond Tree.** A longtime favorite in Ocho Rios, this restaurant is named for the massive tree growing through the roof. For many diners, the evening starts with a drink at the terrace bar overlooking the sea. Dinner, which can be enjoyed on the terrace or in the dining room, begins with pumpkin and pepperpot soup before moving on to such entrées as fresh fish, veal piccata, and fondue. The service can be somewhat slow, so for many diners this is the evening's activity. ✉ *Hibiscus Lodge Hotel, 87 Main St.* ☎ *876/974–2813* ♦ *Reservations essential* ☐ *AE, MC, V.*

$$–$$ ✕ **Hard Rock Café.** Within walking distance of the cruise pier, this popular eatery is filled with music memorabilia, including Bob Marley's handwritten lyrics for "Jammin" and a guitar he used in the recording of "Kaya." The menu features the usual fare, including burgers, ribs, and fajitas. ✉ *Taj Mahal Shopping Centre, 4 Main St.* ☎ *876/974–3333* ☐ *AE, D, MC, V.*

$$–$$ ✕ **Margaritaville.** Part of the popular chain (you can also find branches in Montego Bay and Negril), this easy-going restaurant and bar is especially popular with cruise-ship passengers because of its location near the pier. You can find jerk burgers and conch fritters but, for the most part, the menu is all-American. The large bar in the center of the restaurant is packed, especially during the evening hours. ✉ *Island Village, Turtle Beach Rd.* ☎ *876/675–8977* ☐ *AE, D, MC, V.*

INDIAN

$$ ✕ **Passage to India.** With a downtown location convenient both to cruise passengers looking for a midday meal and vacationers headed to dinner, Passage to India is Ocho Rios's most popular Indian eatery. Start with savory chicken tikka (a rich stew) or samosas (mutton- or vegetable-filled dumplings), then work your way to minced mutton with green peas or shrimp with sweet peppers. All the dishes are flavored to satisfy the local craving for spicy food. ✉ *Soni's Plaza, Main St.* ☎ *876/795–3182* ☐ *AE, D, MC, V.*

ITALIAN

★ Fodor'sChoice ✕**Evita's.** Just about every celebrity who has vis-
$$–$$$ ited Ocho Rios has dined at this hilltop restaurant. (Evita
has the pictures to prove it.) You'll feel like a star yourself
as an attentive staff guiding you through a list of about 30
kinds of pasta, including *rotelle colombo* (crabmeat with
white sauce and noodles). Not all the dishes are traditional,
including the fiery jerk spaghetti. Light eaters will appreciate half portions. The restaurant offers free transportation from area hotels. ⊠*Mantalent Inn, Eden Bower Rd.*
☎*876/974–2333* ☐*AE, D, MC, V.*

$–$$$ ✕**Toscani's.** At Harmony Hall, this longtime favorite offers
seating in the dining room and on the garden verandah. The
menu features classic Italian dishes prepared with Jamaican
flair. Start with the savory minestrone soup, but save room
for the main courses: grilled snapper filet, chicken breast
simmered in tomatoes, and veal cutlets with fontina cheese
and proscuitto sautéed in butter and wine. Save room for
delicious desserts like tiramisu and chocolate and amaretto
cheesecake. If you're staying in an Ocho Rios hotel, call for
complimentary shuttle. ⊠*Harmony Hall, N. Coast Hwy.*
☎*876/795–3182* ⊘*Reservations recommended* ☐*AE,*
MC, V.

JAMAICAN

$$–$$$ ✕**Coconuts on the Bay.** This casual eatery, opposite the cruise
pier, features slightly upscale local specialties. Start with
jerk chicken wings or conch and shrimp fritters before mov-
ing on to specialties like tamarind shrimp or lobster served
grilled, curried, or creole style. Complimentary transpor-
tation from local hotels is available. ⊠*Turtle Beach Rd.*
☎*876/795–0064* ☐*AE, MC, V.*

¢–$$ ✕**Mamma Marley's Jammin' Bar and Grill.** Cedella Booker,
Bob Marley's mother, is the force behind this popular eat-
ery across from the largest crafts market in Ocho Rios.
Cedella's recipes include some of her son's favorite dishes.
You'll find jerk on the menu, but look for other local dishes
like ackee and saltfish, coconut curried vegetables, and
grilled lobster tails. Bob Marley memorabilia is for sale, of
course. ⊠*50 Main St.* ☎*876/795–4803* ☐*MC, V.*

¢ ✕**Bumperee Jerk Centre and Rest Stop.** This open-air eatery,
a popular stop for travelers headed out to Bob Marley's
house, is also a favorite with locals who come by for tasty
jerk and spicy patties. Pork and chicken take center stage
here, accompanied by rice and peas and tasty festival. A
separate bar, housed in a colorful rondoval, serves drinks

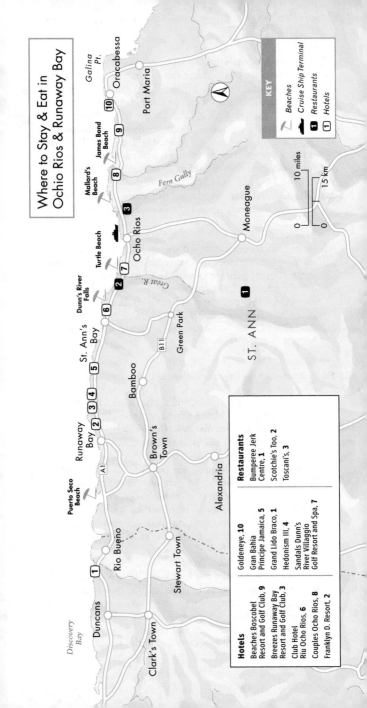

Where to Stay & Eat in Ocho Rios & Runaway Bay

Hotels

Beaches Boscobel Resort and Golf Club, **9**
Breezes Runaway Bay Resort and Golf Club, **3**
Club Hotel Riu Ocho Rios, **6**
Couples Ocho Rios, **8**
Franklyn D. Resort, **2**
Goldeneye, **10**
Gran Bahia Principe Jamaica, **5**
Grand Lido Braco, **1**
Hedonism III, **4**
Sandals Dunn's River Villaggio Golf Resort and Spa, **7**

Restaurants

Bumperee Jerk Centre, **1**
Scotchie's Too, **2**
Toscani's, **3**

KEY

↗ Beaches
⚓ Cruise Ship Terminal
⬛ Restaurants
① Hotels

and expensive sodas. Jerk is available Monday to Saturday; on Sunday you can only order the patties. ⊠*Claremont* ☎*No phone* ▭*No credit cards.*

¢   ⨉**Island Grill.** With several locations across the island, Island Grill is Jamaica's version of fast food. Jerk, patties, rice and peas—all spiced for the local palate—fill the menu of this eat-in or take-out restaurant about a block from the main tourist area. ⊠*12 Main St.* ☎*876/974–4061* ▭*MC, V.*

¢   ⨉**Ocho Rios Village Jerk Centre.** This blue-canopied eatery is a good place to park yourself for frosty Red Stripe beer and fiery jerk pork, chicken, or seafood. Milder barbecued meats sold by weight (a quarter- or half-pound serving is usually enough) turn up on the chalkboard menu posted on the wall. It's liveliest at lunch, especially when passengers from cruise ships swamp the place. ⊠*Da Costa Dr.* ☎*876/974–2549* ▭*D, MC, V.*

★ **Fodor'sChoice** ⨉**Scotchie's Too.** The Ocho Rios branch of the
¢   longtime Montego Bay favorite has already been lauded for its excellent jerk. The open-air eatery offers plates of chicken, sausage, fish, pork, and ribs, all accompanied by festival, bammy, and some fire-breathing hot sauce. Be sure to step over to the kitchen to watch them make jerk over the pits. The restaurant is in Drax Hall, a small community west of Ocho Rios. ⊠*N. Coast Hwy., Drax Hall* ☎*876/794–9457* ▭*AE, D, MC, V.*

WHERE TO STAY

OCHO RIOS

$$$$ ⊞**Beaches Boscobel Resort & Golf Club.** Although this all-
☾   inclusive resort is for anyone—including singles and couples—it's best suited for families. Children enjoy supervised activities in one of five kids' clubs divided by age, from infants to teens. Some rooms have pullout sofas, and there are also connecting rooms for large families. Special rates apply for kids under age 16 sharing a room with a parent. One drawback for families with a short vacation: the resort is farther from the airport than almost anywhere else in Ocho Rios, meaning a long drive with restless kids. **Pros:** excellent children's program, numerous dining options, relaxing. **Cons:** long drive from the airport, beach is far from the rooms, far from local attractions. ⊠*N. Coast Hwy., Box 2, St. Ann's Bay* ☎*876/975–7777* ⊟*876/975–7622* ⊕*www.beaches.com* ⇆*120 rooms, 110 suites* ⌂*In-room: safe, refrigerator. In-hotel: 5 restaurants, bars, tennis*

courts, pools, gym, spa, beachfront, diving, water sports, children's programs (ages infant–17), laundry service, concierge, public Internet, airport shuttle, parking (no fee), no-smoking rooms ⚲2-night minimum ▤AE, MC, V ⦿AI.

$$$$ 🏨**Couples Ocho Rios.** Renovations have spiffed the guest rooms at Jamaica's first all-inclusive resort. Although its romantic atmosphere is similar to Sandals, this resort tends to draw a somewhat older clientele thanks to its longtime popularity. Connected by long hallways, rooms are a short walk from the beach. The handful of villa suites tucked back in the gardens have private plunge pools or hot tubs. The resort is on a nice stretch of beach, and there's also a private island where you can sunbathe in the buff if you want. Weddings are included in the package, as are off-site excursions. **Pros:** numerous dining options, free weddings, private island for clothing-optional sunbathing. **Cons:** long hallways, drab public areas, villas a long walk from the beach. ✉*Tower Isle* ☎*876/975–4271* 🖷*876/975–4433* ⊕*www.couples.com* ⚲*189 rooms, 17 suites* &*In-room: safe, refrigerator (some). In-hotel: 5 restaurants, bars, tennis courts, pools, gym, spa, beachfront, diving, water sports, concierge, public Internet, airport shuttle, parking (no fee), no kids under 18 ⚲3-night minimum* ▤*AE, D, MC, V* ⦿*AI.*

$$$$ 🏨**Couples Sans Souci Resort & Spa.** This all-inclusive resort emphasizes relaxation. The accommodations—all suites—are soothing, with tile floors, large balconies, and a style more Mediterranean than Caribbean. Bathrooms are particularly large and luxurious. Romantic oceanfront suites have generous whirlpool tubs. You have your choice of beaches (one is clothing-optional), but both have pebbly sand, and neither is as appealing as the pools. Though the resort is open to couples only, they do not have to be male–female couples. **Pros:** excellent spa, gorgeous rooms, spacious grounds. **Cons:** public areas a long walk from some rooms, beaches are not as good as others in area ✉*N. Coast Hwy., Box 103, Mammee Bay ⊹2 mi (3 km) east of Ocho Rios* ☎*876/994–1206* 🖷*876/994–1544* ⊕*www.couples.com* ⚲*148 suites* &*In-room: safe, refrigerator (some). In-hotel: 4 restaurants, room service, bars, tennis courts, pools, gym, spa, beachfront, concierge, laundry service, airport shuttle, no kids under 18, no elevator ⚲3-night minimum* ▤*AE, D, DC, MC, V* ⦿*AI.*

$$$$ 🏨**Goldeneye.** Whether you're a James Bond buff or just a
★   fan of luxurious getaways, this exclusive resort 20 minutes east of Ocho Rios holds special appeal. Once the home of

2

Bond, James Bond

CLOSE UP

Jamaica was a seductive muse for author Ian Fleming, who penned every line of his 13 James Bond novels at his Oracabessa residence, Goldeneye. The beauty of the island played a starring role in more than one of Agent 007's on-screen adventures, so it's easy to retrace the footsteps of Sean Connery and Roger Moore.

Bikini-clad Ursula Andress sang "Under the Mango Tree" as she emerged from the cobalt-blue ocean at **Laughing Waters Beach** in *Dr. No*, 007's first foray in film. Known today as the original James Bond Beach, this Ocho Rios oasis is known for its golden sand. Link hands with fellow travelers as you climb nearby **Dunn's River Falls**, where the secret agent and Honey Ryder enjoyed a seductive swim.

The sound of Paul McCartney singing "Live and Let Die" in the opening credits will ring in your head much like the echo of footsteps that reverberate inside **Green Grotto Caves**, which served as a stalagmite-filled sanctuary for Bond's adversary Dr. Kananga in the 1973 film of the same name.

The spy showed his softer side in the eighth installment of the movie franchise with a picnic scene filmed on the grounds of **The Ruins at the Falls** restaurant.

author Ian Fleming, the estate is now one of the unique Island Outpost properties. The 15-acre property consists of the main house, complete with its own private pool and beach, and three villas tucked into the lush gardens, each with outdoor showers and lots of privacy. Plans call for the addition of more villas as well as a private residential section. **Pros:** unique and spacious accommodations, excellent food, plenty of privacy. **Cons:** remote location, limited dining options, may be too quiet for some travelers. ⊠*N. Coast Hwy., Oracabessa* ☎*876/975–3354* 🖷*876/975–3620* ⊕*www.goldeneyehotel.com* ↩*1 house, 3 villas* ⌖*In-room: no a/c (some), safe, kitchen, refrigerator, DVD, VCR, Wi-Fi. In-hotel: restaurant, bar, pool (some), beachfront, water sports, no elevator, concierge, parking (no fee)* ▤*AE, D, MC, V* ⏣*AI.*

$$$$ ⊡**Gran Bahia Principe Jamaica.** Somewhat bare grounds surround this massive property, one of the island's newest resorts. Guest rooms, decorated in muted tropical tones, are a good value for travelers who don't mind some dining restrictions (and plenty of fellow travelers at the buffet

line). All in all, this is one of the island's most economical all-inclusives. A special Club Golden Principe offers separate check-in, concierge service, room service, and some exclusive facilities. **Pros:** on-site numerous activities, expansive pool areas, good value. **Cons:** limited dining options, lack of landscaping, long walks to public areas. ⊠*N. Coast Hwy., Runaway Bay* ☎*876/973–7000* ☎*876/670–8503* ⊕*www.bahia-principe.com* ⌑*589 suites* ☖*In-room: safe, refrigerator, Ethernet, dial-up, Wi-Fi. In-hotel: 5 restaurants, room service (some), bars, tennis courts, pools, gym, spa, beachfront, diving, water sports, children's programs (ages 4–12), laundry service, concierge, executive floor, public Internet* ⊟*AE, MC, V* ⊙*AI.*

$$$$ ⌂**Jamaica Inn.** Start a conversation about elegant resorts and this quietly sophisticated hotel will surely be mentioned. A favorite with the rich and famous (one suite is named for guest Winston Churchill), this genteel resort is known for its attentive staff. Each suite has its own verandah (larger than most hotel rooms) on the private cove's powdery, champagne-color beach. The cliff-top spa is known for its exotic treatments. No children under 12 are allowed in high season, and none under 10 the rest of the year. **Pros:** elegant rooms, exceptional service, good spa. **Cons:** somewhat stodgy atmosphere, no children's facilities, no in-room TVs. ⊠*N. Coast Hwy., Box 1* ☎*876/974–2514* ☎*876/974–2449* ⊕*www.jamaicainn.com* ⌑*47 suites* ☖*In-room: no TV. In-hotel: restaurant, room service, bars, pool, gym, spa, beachfront, water sports, laundry service, no elevator, laundry service, concierge, no elevator, parking (no fee)* ⊟*AE, D, MC, V* ⊙*EP.*

$$$$ ⌂**Royal Plantation.** More exclusive than any of the island's
★ chain hotels, Royal Plantation puts an emphasis on personal service, fine dining, and a refined atmosphere. Built high atop a bluff, it has stunning ocean views. The suites have luxurious linens, fully stocked in-room bars, mahogany furniture, and marble baths, many with whirlpool tubs. The most expensive suites have special check-in and luggage services; optional butler service is also available. Steps lead to the beach, where the luxury continues with the services of a beach butler. **Pros:** stylish rooms, good dining options, beach butler service. **Cons:** small pool, steps down to the beach. ⊠*N. Coast Hwy., Box 2* ☎*876/974–5601* ☎*876/974–5912* ⊕*www.royalplantation.com* ⌑*74 suites* ☖*In-room: safe, VCR (some), dial-up. In-hotel: 4 restaurants, room service, tennis courts, pool, gym, spa,*

beachfront, diving, water sports, concierge, no kids under 18 ☞*2-night minimum* ☰*AE, MC, V* ⬛*EP.*

$$$$ ⬛**Sandals Dunn's River Villaggio Golf Resort & Spa.** This couples-only retreat is built around a large pool complex with its own miniature version of the falls for which the resort is named. Eight room categories offer a variety of budget options—some basic, some with butler service. Most rooms are contained in fairly generic high-rise hotel towers, but the honeymoon rooms are best for those who want a low-rise building and easy beach access. You can hop a shuttle to the other Sandals properties. **Pros:** nice pool areas, newly renovated rooms, numerous dining options. **Cons:** some rooms overlook a rooftop, golf course a long distance from hotel. ⊠*N. Coast Hwy., Mammee Bay* ☎*876/972–1610* 🖷*876/972–1611* ⬀*www.sandals.com* ⬅*250 rooms* ⬤*In-room: safe, refrigerator, Ethernet. In-hotel: 6 restaurants, room service, bar, tennis courts, pools, gym, spa, beachfront, diving, water sports, laundry service, concierge, public Internet, airport shuttle, parking (no fee), no-smoking rooms* ☞*2-night minimum* ☰*AE, D, DC, MC, V* ⬛*AI.*

$$$$ ⬛**Sandals Grande Ocho Rios Beach & Villa Resort.** This sprawling resort began years ago as two separate properties, and today it continues to have a split personality. The "Riviera" section sits right on the ocean; its lush grounds are a shady alternative to the sunny beach. Across the road (accessible by shuttle or tunnel), the "Manor" side is home to both traditional hotel rooms in the faux greathouse and suites in primarily four-unit villas that share a common pool. Some villas are a quite distance from the public areas and the beach. **Pros:** lots of privacy, numerous swimming options, romantic dining options. **Cons:** villas a long way from the beach, some rooms removed from public areas, long wait for the shuttle. ⊠*Main St.* ☎*876/974–2691* 🖷*876/974–5700* ⬀*www.sandals.com* ⬅*529 rooms* ⬤*In-room: safe, kitchen (some), refrigerator (some), Ethernet. In-hotel: 11 restaurants, room service, bars, tennis courts, pools, gym, spa, beachfront, diving, water sports, no elevator, laundry service, concierge, public Internet, airport shuttle, parking (no fee), no kids under 18, no-smoking rooms* ☞*2-night minimum* ☰*AE, D, DC, MC, V* ⬛*AI.*

$$$–$$$$ ⬛**ClubHotel Riu Ocho Rios.** This sprawling resort, built in two U-shape wings each overlooking a pool, is presently the largest in Jamaica. Rooms are generously sized and well maintained, although there are long walks to public areas. All rooms come with an all-inclusive package, but suites include such extras as 24-hour concierge service. Some activities including billiards and scuba diving (except for an introductory lesson in the pool) are not part of the all-inclusive package. **Pros:** numerous dining options, large rooms, expansive beach. **Cons:** long walk to beach, some public areas feel cramped, all-inclusive package is limited. ⊠*N. Coast Hwy., Mammee Bay* ☎*876/972–2200* 🖷*876/972–2203* ⊕*www.riu.com* ⇌*475 rooms, 371 suites* ♿*In-room: safe, refrigerator, Ethernet. In-hotel: 7 restaurants, bars, tennis courts, pools, gym, spa, beachfront, diving, water sports, children's programs (ages 4–12), laundry service, concierge, executive floor, public Internet, airport shuttle* ▭*AE, DC, MC, V* ⎸⊙⎹*AI.*

$$$ 🖪 **Sunset Jamaica Grande Resort & Spa.** Jamaica's busiest conference hotel, in the heart of Ocho Rios, is always buzzing with activity. Following an extensive renovation, it now also attracts leisure travelers. The simple rooms in a pair of high-rise towers have been brightened with tropical colors; the best views are found in the north tower. Many guests spend their time at the pool, built to resemble Dunn's River Falls. It includes a meandering river and even a lighthouse with a slide. Kids are kept busy in the complimentary Club Mongoose program, and teens can head to the Jamrock Center. Parents can play in an 80-machine slot and video blackjack room. **Pros:** nice pool area, good location for exploring Ocho Rios, lovely sunset views from some rooms. **Cons:** frequent conventions, crowded restaurants, bland rooms. ⊠*Main St., Box 100* ☎*876/974–2200* 🖷*876/974–2289* ⊕*www.sunsetjamaicagrande.com* ⇌*730 rooms, 12 suites* ♿*In-room: safe, refrigerator (some), dial-up. In-hotel: 6 restaurants, bars, tennis courts, pools, gym, spa, beachfront, water sports, concierge, children's programs (ages 2–12), laundry service* ▭*AE, D, DC, MC, V* ⎸⊙⎹*AI.*

$$ 🖪 **Shaw Park Beach Hotel & Spa.** With its hospital-green corridors and motel-style rooms, the Shaw Park won't win any awards for its designer. But it just might be the friendliness place around. The staff at this smaller property makes up for any shortcomings. Guest rooms have either a patio or balcony overlooking a long stretch of beach that ends near the White River. Most guests opt for dining on the open-air terrace, where excellent local and international dishes are featured. Meals are served at specified hours (not around the clock, as at larger all-inclusives). For an additional fee, you can opt for meals at the gourmet restaurant. A nightclub and casino are quiet during the week but busy Friday and Saturday night. **Pros:** beachfront rooms, excellent

2

food, friendly staff. **Cons:** very basic rooms, limited on-site dining options, limited activities. ✉*Cutlass Bay, Ocho Rios* ☎*876/974–2552* ⊕*www.shawparkbeachhotel.com* ⤢*81 rooms, 13 suites* ⌂*In-room: safe, dial-up. In-hotel: 2 restaurants, room service, bars, pool, gym, spa, beachfront, water sports, no elevator, laundry service, concierge, parking (no fee)* ☐*AE, MC, V* ⦿*AI.*

$–$$ ▨**Crane Ridge Resort.** In the hills west of the city center, Crane Ridge Resort is a good option for travelers who don't demand a beachfront property or all the bells and whistles of an all-inclusive. A complimentary shuttle takes you to the beach, but you might prefer the on-site pool. The lemon-tinted building consists primarily of one- and two-bedroom suites with private balconies (standard guest rooms share balconies). **Pros:** good value, spacious rooms, convenient location. **Cons:** no beach, limited on-site dining, dated decor. ✉*17 Da Costa Dr.* ☎*876/974–8056* 🖷*876/974–8070* ⊕*www.craneridge.net* ⤢*30 rooms, 60 suites* ⌂*In-room: safe, kitchen (some), refrigerator, Ethernet. In-hotel: Restaurant, room service, bar, tennis courts, pool, gym, no elevator, parking (no fee), no-smoking rooms* ☐*AE, D, MC, V* ⦿*EP.*

$ ▨**Rooms Ocho Rios.** Adjacent to Sunset Jamaica Grande Resort, this hotel offers a rooms-only plan (though with ★ continental breakfast). This family-friendly facility is favored by those who plan to explore the region rather than settle down at a resort. Rooms, decorated in tropical tones, have ocean views. The long stretch of beach and excellent location within walking distance of downtown make this a good option for those on a budget. **Pros:** good value, lovely beach, good location for exploring Ocho Rios. **Cons:** small pool area, limited on-site dining options, limited activities. ✉*Main St.* ☎*876/974–6632* 🖷*876/516–1554* ⊕*www. roomsresorts.com* ⤢*73 rooms, 26 suites* ⌂*In-room: safe, kitchen (some), Ethernet, Wi-Fi. In-hotel: restaurant, room service, bar, pool, gym, beachfront, water sports, no elevator, laundry facilities, laundry service, public Internet, public Wi-Fi, parking (no fee), no-smoking rooms* ☐*AE, D, MC, V* ⦿*CP.*

RUNAWAY BAY

$$$$ ▨**Franklyn D. Resort.** A favorite for families with very young ☺ children, this relaxed resort goes a step beyond the usual supervised kids' programs, assigning you a professional caregiver who will assist you throughout your stay. Nannies help with in-room tasks, from washing out bathing suits to supervising naps. You'll enjoy spacious one-, two-, and three-bedroom suites in low-slung stucco buildings. Children under six stay and eat free when staying with their parents. **Pros:** good supervised kids' programs, convenient nanny service, spacious accommodations. **Cons:** small pool area, rooms need updating. ⌂*Main St., Runaway Bay* ☎*876/973–4591* ⌨*876/973–6987* ⊕*www.fdrholidays. com* ⤶*76 suites* ⌂*In-room: safe kitchen, refrigerator, Wi-Fi. In-hotel: 4 restaurants, bars, tennis court, pool, gym, spa, beachfront, diving, water sports, bicycles, no elevator, children's programs (ages newborn–16), laundry facilities, laundry service, public Wi-Fi, airport shuttle, no-smoking rooms* ⊟*AE, D, MC, V* ⊚*AI.*

$$$$ 🏨**Grand Lido Braco.** If you want an experience that's equal parts Jamaica and Disneyland, this resort's for you. Fifteen minutes west of Runaway Bay, the resort is built around a "village" complete with a town square with a fruit lady and peanut man. Here you can also find the island's largest clothing-optional facilities, including a pool, hot tub, and tennis courts. The beach—with both clothed and clothing-optional sections—is expansive, although not the island's best strip of sand. **Pros:** upscale property, 9-hole golf course within distance, separate clothing-optional facilities. **Cons:** pebbly beach, theme-park architecture, somewhat remote location. ⊠*N. Coast Hwy., Trelawny* ☎*876/954–0000* ⌨*876/954–0021* ⊕*www.superclubs.com* ⤶*226 rooms, 58 suites* ⌂*In-room: safe. In-hotel: 5 restaurants, room service, bars, golf course, tennis courts, pools, gym, spa, beachfront, diving, water sports, no elevator, concierge, laundry service, public Internet, public Wi-Fi, airport shuttle, no kids under 16* ⤳*2-night minimum* ⊟*AE, D, DC, MC, V* ⊚*AI.*

$$$–$$$$ 🏨**Hedonism III.** Like its more spartan cousin in Negril,
★   Hedonism III is an adults-only hotel that appeals to those looking for fun. Here that means nude body painting and volleyball and a waterslide (through the disco, no less). Unlike its sister property, Hedonism III offers luxurious rooms with mirrored ceilings, hot tubs, and music systems. The beach is divided into "nude" and "prude" sections, although a quick look shows that most people leave their suits at home. The resort even holds Jamaica's only nude weddings. **Pros:** swim-up accommodations, good in-room amenities, around-the-clock activities. **Cons:** beach not as good as others in area, noisy atmosphere. ⊠*Main Rd., Box 250* ☎*876/973–4100* ⌨*876/973–5402* ⊕*www.super-clubs.com* ⤶*210 rooms, 15 suites* ⌂*In-room: refrigerator*

(some), safe. In-hotel: 5 restaurants, bars, tennis courts, pools, gym, spa, beachfront, diving, water sports, airport shuttle, no kids under 18, no elevator ☞2-night minimum ⊟AE, D, DC, MC, V ⊚AI.

$$$ 🗻**Breezes Runaway Bay Resort & Golf Club.** This moderately priced resort underwent an extensive renovation and expansion, reopened with much fanfare in 2007. The all-inclusive property emphasizes an active, sports-oriented vacation—including golf, tennis, a circus workshop, and an array of water sports. Expert instruction and top-rate equipment are part of the package. Guests flock here to dive and snorkel around the reef right off the beach (which no longer includes a clothing-optional section). Like other SuperClubs resorts, Breezes Runaway Bay offers complimentary weddings and even has a beachfront chapel. **Pros:** extensive activities, good dining options, easy beach access. **Cons:** some public areas feel crowded, small spa, crowded restaurants. ⊠*N. Coast Hwy., Runaway Bay* ☎*876/973–6099* ⊟*876/516–4155* ⊛*www.superclubs.com* ⬎*220 rooms, 46 suites* ⬥*In-room: safe, refrigerator, dial-up, Wi-Fi. In-hotel: 5 restaurants, bars, golf course, tennis courts, pools, gym, spa, beachfront, diving, water sports, bicycles, no elevator, laundry service, public Internet, public Wi-Fi, airport shuttle, parking (no fee), no kids under 14, no-smoking rooms ☞2-night minimum ⊟AE, D, DC, MC, V ⊚AI.*

VILLAS RENTALS

Ocho Rios is filled with private villas, especially in the Discovery Bay area. In Jamaica, most luxury villas come with a full staff including a housekeeper, cook, butler, gardener, and often a security guard. Many can arrange for a driver, either for airport transfers, for daily touring, or for a prearranged number of days for sightseeing.

The island's villas were once mostly smaller homes, but recent years have seen an increased demand for larger, more luxurious properties. Numerous villas have five or more bedrooms spread around different parts of the building—or in different buildings altogether—for extra privacy.

Most villas come fully stocked with linens. You can often arrange for the kitchen to be stocked with groceries upon your arrival. Air-conditioning, even in the most luxurious villas, is typically limited to the bedrooms.

A four-night minimum stay is average for many villas although this can vary by season and property. Gratuities, usually split among the staff, typically range from 10% to 15%.

Since 1967, the **Jamaica Association of Villas and Apartments** (⊠ *2650 W. Montrose, Suite 309, Chicago, IL 60618* ☎ *800/ 845–5276* ⊕ *www.villasinjamaica.com*) has handled villas, cottages, apartments, and condos across the island.

Several private companies specialize in villa rentals, matching up vacationers with accommodations of the right size and price range. **Jamaica Villas by Linda Smith** (⊠ *8029 Riverside Dr., Cabin John, MD 20818* ☎ *301/229–4300* ⊕ *www. jamaicavillas.com*) offers more than 60 fully-staffed villas on the island. **Luxury Retreats International** (⊠ *740 Notre Dame W, Suite 1305, Montréal, Quebec, Canada H3C3X6* ☎ *877/993–0100* ⊕ *www.luxuryretreats.com*) offers numerous luxury villa rentals in Negril, Montego Bay, Ocho Rios (including the Discovery Bay area), and Port Antonio.

PRIVATE VILLAS

☒ **Blue Harbour.** This complex of three beachfront villas includes Noël Coward's original Jamaica home, the two-bedroom Villa Grande. The complex also includes the playwright's former art studio, the three-bedroom Villa Rose, and the former guest quarters, now the one-bedroom Villa Chica. Villa Grande, where Coward entertained stars like Marlene Dietrich, Katherine Hepburn, and Patricia Neal, includes some original furnishings, including a sleigh bed in the main bedroom. Downstairs, the kitchen and verandah are shared by other guests at Blue Harbour, just as they were in Coward's day. You'll also share a small saltwater pool and the beach on the half-moon cove. You can opt for an all-inclusive meal plan for $100 per person daily; it does not include alcoholic beverage. The entire complex can be rented as a single unit or separately. **Pros:** private beach, interesting history, good value. **Cons:** dated accommodations, shared public facilities, need car to get around. ⊠ *N. Coast Hwy. between Oracabessa and Port Maria* ☎ *505/586–1244* ⊕ *www.blueharb.com* ⤙ *3 villas* ⚐ *In-room: no a/c, safe, VCR, daily maid service, cook, on-site security, pool* ⊟ *No credit cards* �ﻪ⊙*AI.*

☒ **Goldenfoot.** This stylish Oracabessa getaway is perfect for travelers seeking luxury accommodations without a budget-busting price tag. You're welcomed at the bamboo bar for a taste of the Goldenfoot Jamosa, a blend of white wine and the island's Ting soda. Each day you're served two meals—breakfast and either lunch or dinner, depending on your schedule. Bedrooms, like the rest of the property, are painted in subtle tropical shades and have an island ambience; the main bath includes its own bamboo-screened outdoor bath. Unlike most Jamaican villas, this property is wheelchair accessible (although stairs leads down to the pool). **Pros:** good value, stylish decor, wheelchair accessible. **Cons:** too quiet for some travelers, need car to get around, long distance from airport ✉*Off Rte. A3, Oracabessa* ☎*876/842–1237* ⊕*www.agoldenfootvilla.com* ⇄*2 bedrooms, 3 baths* ⌂*In-villa: no a/c (some), DVD, VCR, daily maid service, cook, on-site security, fully staffed, pool* ⊟*AE, MC, V* ⍩*MAP.*

★ ⚏**Ian Fleming Villa.** Jamaica has larger and more luxurious private homes, but none with the panache of Ian Fleming Villa. This one-story home was the winter escape of author Ian Fleming. Here he wrote the 17 James Bond novels at the desks in the living room and main bedroom. Other than the desks, the villa is furnished in a Balinese style with bamboo furniture, hand-carved sculptures, and plenty of elegant touches like private outdoor showers for each bedroom. A koi pond, sunken garden (where Fleming liked to dine), and exquisite pool round out the offerings of this very private getaway. The villa includes a private beach, accessible by steps down the sea cliff; follow the path to a quiet sea cave and you'll feel a little like Agent 007. **Pros:** elegant accommodations, private beach and cove, beautiful pool. **Cons:** remote location, fairly long drive from airport, too quiet for some. ✉*N. Coast Hwy., Oracabessa* ☎*876/975–3354* ⊕*www.islandoutpost.com* ⇄*3 bedrooms, 4 baths* ⌂*In-villa: no a/c (some), safe, kitchen, refrigerator, DVD, VCR, Wi-Fi, daily maid service, cook, on-site security, tennis court, pool, beachfront, water toys* ⊟*AE, D, MC, V* ⍩*AI.*

⚏**Makana.** Teak floors add an exotic touch to this elegant villa. Downstairs you'll find two bedrooms with lots of privacy. Upstairs, four bedrooms share a family room with a flat-screen television and a home office complete with a computer and phone service. Wireless Internet access throughout the house makes it easy to get a little work done. Outdoor amenities including an infinity pool, hot tub, gazebo with a view of the sea and nearby mountains, and a private beach with a calm lagoon. **Pros:** beautiful decor, great facilities, perfect location for families with chil-

CLOSE UP

Mad Dogs and Englishmen

A two-week vacation led to a lifelong love affair for Noël Coward. After visiting Jamaica in 1944, the playwright and songwriter would return 4 years later to claim an 8-acre tract of land upon which his home, Blue Harbour, was constructed.

A haven for members of high society, such luminaries as Marlene Dietrich, Katharine Hepburn, Vivien Leigh, and Laurence Olivier would flit about the two-story main house, christened Villa Grande, and its two guesthouses, Villa Rose and Villa Chica. Perhaps they inspired the name of the British bon vivant's next abode, Firefly. Coward moved up the hill to a perch with a grand view of Port Maria, constructing Firefly as an escape from the continuous commotion caused by his celebrity houseguests at Blue Harbour.

Perched on a hillside that was once the domain of Sir Henry Morgan, one of the original pirates of the Caribbean, Firefly became a peaceful retreat where the sophisticated wordsmith could pursue his passion for painting, a hobby encouraged by another famous figure who dabbled in oils, Sir Winston Churchill. Tubes of cobalt blue and vermilion lie to this day next to a set of paintbrushes in his studio, waiting to be picked up by an artist who was stilled by a heart attack in 1973.

A slab of stone, etched solely with the playwright's name and the dates of his birth and passing, marks Coward's final resting place in the garden on Firefly Hill. Perhaps, in the end, no written epitaph could sum up the life of the man dubbed "The Master." A more fitting tribute can be found in Firefly's living room, where rows of photographs grace the grand piano, each an image of a smiling celebrity face that once reveled in his company.

dren. **Cons:** expensive, need a car to get around, may be too quiet for some. ✉*Fortlands Rd., Discovery Bay* 🌐*www.luxuryretreats.com* *6 bedrooms, 6½ baths* *In-villa: no a/c (some), safe, kitchen, refrigerator, DVD, VCR, Ethernet, Wi-Fi, tennis court, pool, daily maid service, cook, on-site security, fully staffed, tennis court, pool, beachfront, water toys, laundry facilities, no-smoking rooms* ▭*AE, MC, V* *EP.*

Roaring Pavilion Villa & Spa. A favorite with celebrities (Celine Dion, Tom Cruise, and Jack Nicholson have each stayed here), this villa is convenient to Ocho Rios, yet extremely private. The one-story house is especially noted for its on-site spa with two full-time masseuses. There's no extra charge for spa treatments if you opt for an all-inclusive package. Most bedrooms are in the main villa, but a separate bedroom in the Balinese Wing includes a luxurious private bath. Beyond the pool and well-manicured lawn is a private beach that just might look familiar: this is where Ursula Andress emerged from the surf in *Dr. No*. **Pros:** on-site spa, beautiful decor, separate wing ideal for those looking for more privacy. **Cons:** expensive, no beach view, need car to get around. ⊠*N. Coast Hwy., 3 mi (4 km) west of Ocho Rios* ⊕*www.roaringpavilion.com* ⚲*4 bedrooms, 6 bathrooms* ⚐*In-room: no a/c (some), safe, dishwasher, DVD, Ethernet, Wi-Fi, daily maid service, cook, on-site security, fully staffed, hot tub, pool, gym, beachfront, water toys, laundry facilities* ⊟*AE, D, MC, V* ⏃❙*EP*.

▩**A Summer Place.** More economical than many of the villas in the Fortlands Road neighborhood, this slightly older home can sleep more than a dozen people in its seven bedrooms. (One more private bedroom is housed in a garage conversion.) Just outside the living area awaits a pool and a yard that leads to a 100-foot private beach. **Pros:** good value, nice beach, private bedroom good for those looking for more privacy. **Cons:** dated decor, few water toys, need car to get around. ⊠*Fortlands Rd., Discovery Bay* ⊕*www. luxuryretreats.com* ⚲*7 bedrooms, 7 baths* ⚐*In-room: no a/c (some), safe (some), dishwasher, DVD, VCR, dial-up, daily maid service, cook, on-site security, pool, beachfront, water toys, laundry facilities* ⊟*AE, MC, V* ⏃❙*EP*.

▩**Whispering Waters.** This stylish villa can accommodate 14 guests, making it perfect for large families. (For even bigger groups, there's a six-bedroom property next door.) A staff of seven keeps things immaculate with attentive butler, housekeeping, and chef service. Constructed with many local materials including breadnut floors and blackheart ceiling beams, the elegant home has individual climate control in all the bedrooms as well as a sound system throughout the grounds. A private pool and hot tub overlook a private white-sand beach. **Pros:** beautiful grounds, attentive staff, great beach, and swimming cove. **Cons:** expensive, too large for some groups, need car to get around. ⊠*Fortlands Rd., Discovery Bay* ☎*876/670–0549* ⊕*www.luxuryretreats.com* ⚲*7 bedrooms, 7 baths* ⚐*In-villa: no a/c (some), safe, kitchen, refrigerator, DVD, VCR,*

*Ethernet, Wi-Fi, daily maid service, cook, on-site security,
fully staffed, hot tub, tennis court, pool, gym, beachfront,
water toys, laundry facilities, no-smoking rooms* ⊟AE,
MC, V ⦵EP.

BEACHES

Although it boasts no stretches as spectacular as those in
Negril, Ocho Rios has many good beaches ranging from
quiet to bustling, depending on the location and whether
there's a cruise ship in town.

OCHO RIOS

Beach World. Especially popular with cruise passengers
thanks to its proximity to the pier, Beach World offers a
small beach and a full array of water toys at Island Village. Admission to the beach is $3; for an extra fee, you
can rent umbrellas, towels, and beach chairs. Activities
include kayaking, snorkeling, scuba diving, and glass-
bottom-boat rides. Changing rooms and lockers are also
available. ⊠*Island Village Shopping Complex, Main St.*
☎*876/842–9406.*

★ **Dunn's River Falls Beach.** You'll also find a crowd (especially
if there's a cruise ship in town) at the small beach at the
foot of the falls. Although tiny—especially considering the
masses of people—its got a great view, as well as a beach
bar and grill. Look up from the sands for a spectacular
view of the cascading water, whose roar drowns out the
sea as you approach. ⊠*Rte. A1, between St. Ann's Bay
and Ocho Rios.*

James Bond Beach. Another alternative near Ocho Rios—if
you don't mind the drive—is in the community of Oracabessa. This beach is on the former estate of James Bond's
creator, the late Ian Fleming. Today record producer Chris
Blackwell runs the show, so it's no surprise that the beach
often rocks with live music on the bandstand. Admission
is $5 per person. The beach is open daily except Monday
from 9:30 to 6. ⊠*Orcabessa.*

Turtle Beach. One of the busiest beaches in Ocho Rios is not
the prettiest, but it's usually lively and has a mix of residents and visitors. It's next to the Sunset Jamaica Grande
and looks out over the cruise port. ⊠*Main St..*

RUNAWAY BAY

Puerto Seco Beach. This public beach looks out on Discovery Bay, the place where, according to tradition, Christopher Columbus first came ashore. The explorer searched for freshwater but found none, so he named this stretch of sand Puerto Seco, or "dry port." Today the beach is anything but dry; concession stands sell bottles of Red Stripe to a primarily local crowd. Admission is $5. ⊠*Discovery Bay, 5 mi (8 km) west of Runaway Bay.*

SPORTS & THE OUTDOORS

CANOPY TOURS

With so much lush vegetation, it's no surprise that canopy tours are a popular way to enjoy the forests surrounding Ocho Rios. West of town at Cranbrook Flower Forest, canopy tours are operated by **Chukka Caribbean Adventures** (⊠*St. Ann's Bay* ☎*876/972–2506* ⊕*www.chukkacaribbean.com*). A short walk takes you to the first of nine zip lines traversing the Laughlands River gorge. Participants must be 10 or older.

DIVING & SNORKELING

These waters have been protected since 1966, which is why the Ocho Rios region is a popular diving destination. The **Ocho Rios Marine Park** stretches from Mammee Bay to Frankfort Point. Some of the top dive sites in the area include **Jack's Hall,** a 40-foot dive dotted with many types of coral, **Top of the Mountain,** a 60-foot dive near Dunn's River Falls filled with many coral heads, and the *Katryn,* a 50-foot dive to the wreck of a 140-foot minesweeper.

Five Star Watersports (⊠*121 Main St.* ☎*876/974–2446* ⊕*www.fivestarwatersports.com*) operates the "Cool Runnings" catamaran cruise to Dunn's River Falls. Along with a guided climb up the falls, the trip includes a reef snorkeling excursion. Tours includes admission to Dunn's River Falls. **Jamaqua Dive Centre** (⊠*Club Ambiance, Runaway Bay* ☎*876/973–4845* ⊕*www.jamaqua.com*) is a five-star PADI facility specializing in small dive groups. Along with dives, Jamaqua Dive Centre has a variety of courses ranging from snorkeling to rescue diving. You can also find underwater cameras for rent here.

FISHING

Although not as popular as in Montego Bay or Port Antonio, deep-sea fishing is another option for dedicated anglers who don't mind the high cost. Plan on about $400 to $450 for a half-day tour or $800 for a full day of fishing. Local hotels will make arrangements with area captains. For a less-expensive option, local fishermen will also take out travelers for a few hours of reef fishing; this generally runs $50 to $70. Ask at your hotel about local anglers.

Although open-water adventures are usually associated with Jamaica, the **Wilderness Resort** (⊠*Goshen* ☎*876/974–5189*) offers freshwater fishing at an altitude of 1,000 feet. The park, which also offers paddleboats and kayaks, has large ponds filled with tilapia; visitors can have the chef prepare their catch and enjoy a picnic on the grounds. To get here, take the road to Frankfort, which leads off Route A3.

GOLF

Ocho Rios courses don't have the prestige of those around Montego Bay, but duffers will find challenges at a few lesser-known courses.

The 18-hole course at **Breezes Runaway Bay Resort & Golf Club** (⊠*N. Coast Hwy., Runaway Bay* ☎*876/973–7319* ⊕*www.superclubs.com*) has hosted many championship events. The course is also home to an extensive golf academy. Greens fees are $80 for nonguests; guests at Breezes Runaway Bay and Grand Lido Braco play for free.

The course at **Sandals Dunn's River Villaggio Golf Resort & Spa** (⊠*N. Coast Hwy., Mammee Bay* ☎*876/972–1610* ⊕*www. sandals.com*) sits at 700 feet above sea level, so there are eye-popping views. Greens fees for nonguests are $100.

HELICOPTER TOURS

Just west of the small fort in Ocho Rios, **Island Hoppers** (⊠*Reynolds Pier* ☎*876/974–1285* ⊕*www.jamaicahelicoptertours.com*) offers three helicopter tours of the region. The longest tour is the hour-long Jamaican Showcase ($1,000 for up to four persons), circling over Spanish Town, Kingston, and the Blue Mountains. The 30-minute Memories of Jamaica tour ($520 for up to four persons) travels east to Port Maria for an aerial view of Noël Coward's and Ian Fleming's former homes. For diehard 007 fans, James Bond's Jamaica Tour ($360 for up to four persons) provides a half-hour look at the sites made famous by the movies and novels.

HORSEBACK RIDING

With its combination of hills and beaches, Ocho Rios is a natural for horseback excursions. Most are guided tours taken at a slow pace and perfect for those with no previous equestrian experience. Many travelers opt to pack long pants for horseback rides, especially those away from the beach.

★ Fodor's Choice Ocho Rios has excellent horseback riding, and the best company is **Chukka Caribbean Adventures** (⊠*St. Ann's Bay* ☎*876/972–2506* ⊕*www.chukkacaribbean. com*). Trainers here once exercised polo ponies by taking them for rides in the sea; soon there were requests from visitors to ride the horses through the surf. The company now offers a three-hour beach ride that ends with a bareback ride in the sea. This experience—a highlight of many people's trip to the island—costs $73 per person. There's also a ride through the White River Valley. The ride, priced at $62 per person, takes you through the rain forest and through the mountains. All riders must be 6 or older.

Between Falmouth and Runaway Bay, **Braco Stables** (⊠*Rte. A1, Duncans* ☎*876/954–0185* ⊕*www.bracostables.com*) takes you across an 18th-century plantation before heading to the sea for a swim. Rides costing $70 per person begin daily at 10:30 and 2:30. More experienced rides can join a two-hour mountain ride that costs $84 per person. All riders must be age 5 or older. The company arranges transportation from local hotels.

Hooves (⊠*61 Windsor Rd., St. Ann's Bay* ☎*876/972–0905* ⊕*www.hoovesjamaica.com*) has several guided tours along beach, mountain, and river trails. One of the most interesting is the Bush Doctor Mountain Ride, which takes you back on a two-hour trek through the countryside, where locals still depend on bush doctors who utilize plants for treatments. The tour, which costs $55, include round-trip transportation from hotels in Ocho Rios, Runaway Bay, and Discovery Bay.

Riders with an interest in history should take a horseback tour at the 600-acre **Annandale Plantation** (⊠*Ocho Rios* ☎*876/974–2323*). It's still a working farm, and in its glory days it hosted dignitaries such as England's late Queen Mother. Rides cost $59 per person.

At **Prospect Plantation** (⊠*Ocho Rios* ☎*876/994–1058* ⊕*www.dolphincovejamaica.com*), 90-minute rides take

CLOSE UP

Goodbye, Columbus

During his second voyage to the New World, rumors of a "land of blessed gold" lured Christopher Columbus to what would later be called Jamaica. Although the promise of riches turned out to be unfounded, the explorer could lay claim to discovering a tropical treasure for Spain's rulers.

Although St. Anne's Bay was to be his first glimpse of the island, Columbus first set foot on the swath of sand then known as Xaymaca, today referred to as Discovery Bay. His arrival, on May 5, 1494,

marked the beginning of the end for the native Arawak people, who would be killed off by strange new diseases and the cruelties of slavery brought by those who followed in the explorer's path.

Columbus fared little better here, as a shipwreck necessitated his return to the island on his fourth voyage in 1503. Enduring an unsuccessful mutiny attempt by some of his crew, Columbus was rescued a year later, never returning to the "land of blessed gold."

you across the 18th-century estate and along the White River. Tours are $58 per person, and riders must be 8 or older. If you're feeling adventurous, you can even book 90-minute camel ride ($89).

JEEP & ATV TOURS

Since most visitors to the island don't rent cars, it's not surprising that guided jeep and all-terrain vehicle tours are a popular options for travelers who want to combine some sightseeing with a little adventure travel.

Three guided jeep tours are offered in the Ocho Rios area by **Chukka Caribbean Adventures** (⊠*St. Ann's Bay* ☎*876/972–2506* ⊕*www.chukkacaribbean.com*), each in a zebra-striped safari vehicle. The five-hour Dunn's River Safari Jeep Tour ($70) takes you to Murphy Hill for a view of the city before continuing to a cattle farm, a small coffee plantation, and the famous falls. The 3½-hour Coyaba Gardens Safari Tour ($66) includes stops at the gardens as well as Murphy's Hill and the White River Valley. The five-hour Bob Marley Jeep Tour ($70) visits the reggae star's birthplace in the community of Nine Mile.

The company also has guided ATV tours for those 16 and older. The two-hour trip ($74) takes you through the farm, past a historic sugar factory, and to a local school before heading to the beach for a dip.

Wilderness ATV Tours (✉*Reynolds Pier* ☎*876/969–6653* ⊕*www.wildernessatvtours.com*) offers two different tours. One takes you to Murphy Hill, the highest point in Ocho Rios, and the other heads to Dunn's River Falls. Tours range from $50 to $80 per person. All tours, offered daily, start at Reynolds Pier, so they're popular with cruise passengers. Transportation is included if you're staying in nearby hotels.

KAYAKING

Many beachside resorts have sea kayaks available for their guests. For something more challenging, paddle up the White River on a tour with **Chukka Caribbean Adventures** (✉*St. Ann's Bay* ☎*876/972–2506* ⊕*www.chukkacaribbean.com*). The three-hour trip is $66 per person.

MARINE-LIFE PROGRAMS

☼ Dolphin lovers will find a well-run operation near Dunn's River Falls. **Dolphin Cove at Treasure Reef** (✉*N. Coast Hwy., Ocho Rios* ☎*876/974–5335* ⊕*www.dolphincovejamaica.com*) offers dolphin swims as well as lower-price dolphin encounters for ages 8 and up and dolphin touch programs for ages 6 and up. Programs cost as much as $195, depending on your level of involvement with the dolphins. Advance reservations are required. The facility also has stingray and shark swims available.

Stingray City Jamaica (✉*James Bond Beach, Oracabessa* ☎*876/726–1630* ⊕*www.stingraycityjamaica.com*) offers a 45-minute interaction with these interesting ocean dwellers. The adventure begins with instructions on how to hold the slippery creatures, then moves on to snorkeling among them. The cost is $55 for adults and $25 for children, and includes use of snorkel gear.

MOUNTAIN BIKING

Blue Mountain Bicycle Tours (✉*121 Main St., Ocho Rios* ☎*876/974–7075* ⊕*www.bmtoursja.com*) takes you on guided rides in the spectacular Blue Mountains. The all-day excursion starts high and heads downhill, so you don't have to be in peak condition. The trip ends with a refreshing dip in a waterfall. The price includes transportation from Ocho Rios, meals, and all equipment.

Chukka Caribbean Adventures (✉*St. Ann's Bay* ☎*876/972–2506* ⊕*www.chukkacaribbean.com*) offers a three-hour bike tour of St. Ann's Bay and the village of Mount Zion, ending with a snorkeling adventure. The tour, costing $60 per person, is for those 12 and older.

TENNIS

Many hotels have tennis facilities that are free for their guests, but a few will allow nonguests to play for a fee. Fees generally run $5 to $8 per hour for nonguests; lessons generally run $30 to $65 per hour.

Breezes Runaway Bay Resort & Golf Club (⊠*N. Coast Hwy., Runaway Bay* ☎*876/973–2436* ⊕*www.superclubs.com*) has four tennis courts. **Sandals Dunn's River Villaggio Golf Resort & Spa** (⊠*N. Coast Hwy., Ocho Rios* ☎*876/972–1610*) has two courts lighted for night play as well as the services of a pro.

WHITE-WATER RAFTING

White-water rafting is increasingly popular in the Ocho Rios area. For the most options, however, check out the operators in Montego Bay. **Chukka Caribbean Adventures** (⊠*St. Ann's Bay* ☎*876/972–2506* ⊕*www.chukkacaribbean.com*) offers white-water fun on the White River—an easy trip that doesn't require any previous experience. Rafters travel in a convoy along the river and through some gentle rapids. The 3½-hour tour costs $60 for adults.

SHOPPING

Thanks to the large number of cruise-ship passengers, duty-free shopping is big business in Ocho Rios. Fine jewelry and watches, rum and other liquors, and cigars are popular purchases. Most of the duty-free shops are found in the malls.

AREAS & MALLS

Ocho Rios has several malls that draw day-trippers from the cruise ships. The best are **Soni's Plaza** and the **Taj Mahal,** two malls on the main street with stores selling jewelry, cigars, and clothing. Another popular mall on the main street is **Ocean Village.** On the North Coast Highway east of Ochos Rios are **Pineapple Place** and **Coconut Grove.**

★ A fun mall that also serves as an entertainment center is **Island Village** (⊠*Turtle River Rd., near cruise port*). The open-air mall includes Reggae Xplosion, a Margaritaville restaurant, shops selling local handicrafts, duty-free goods, and designer clothing, and a small beach area with a variety of water sports.

MARKETS

Ocho Rios is home to several interesting crafts markets, including those at Dunn's River Falls and Fern Gully. The largest craft market is the **Ocho Rios Crafts Market** (⊠*Main St.* ☎*876/795–2286*), with stalls selling everything from straw hats to wooden figurines to T-shirts. Vendors can be aggressive, and haggling is expected for all purchases. Your best chance of getting a good price is to come on a day when there's no cruise ship in port. The **Pineapple Craft Market** (⊠*N. Coast Hwy.* ☎*No phone*) is a small, casual market east of Ocho Rios that's operated at the site for two decades. Look for everything from carved figurines to coffee-bean necklaces.

SPECIALTY ITEMS

HANDICRAFTS

★ **Harmony Hall** (⊠*Rte. A1, Ocho Rios* ☎*876/975–4222*), an eight-minute drive east of town, is a restored greathouse where Annabella Proudlock sells her unique wooden boxes with covers decorated with reproductions of local art. Also on sale—and magnificently displayed—are larger reproductions of paintings, lithographs, and signed prints of Jamaican scenes. In addition, Harmony Hall is well-known for its exhibits by local artists.

Hemp Heaven (⊠*Island Village, Turtle River Rd., Ocho Rios* ☎*876/675–8969*) sells apparel and accessories made of hemp.

Starfish Essentials (⊠*Island Village, Turtle River Rd., Ocho Rios* ☎*876/901–7113*) sells Jamaican-made candles. Don't miss the Blue Mountain candle, with whole coffee beans in the wax.

Wassi Art Pottery Works (⊠*Bougainvillea Dr., Great Pond* ☎*876/974–5044*) produces one-of-a-kind works of art in terra-cotta. Visitors at this gallery just east of Ocho Rios can stroll through the studio, watching local artists produce colorful pots in an array of shapes and sizes. The pottery is made of clay from Castleton, a small town in the mountains of northeast Jamaica.

LIQUOR & TOBACCO

Rum Roast & Royals (⊠*Island Village, Turtle River Rd., Ocho Rios* ☎*876/675–8796* ⊕*www.rumroastroyals.com*)

sells premium local cigars, all stored in a humidor in the back of the store. For nonsmokers, the store also sells Blue Mountain Coffee, Jamaican rums and other spirits, and local spices and jerk products.

MUSIC

Reggae Yard & Island Life (✉ *Island Village, Turtle River Rd., Ocho Rios* ☎ *876/675–8795*), the largest music store in Ocho Rios, is adjacent to Reggae Xplosion. The offerings include an extensive selection of reggae recordings as well as other types of Caribbean music.

NIGHTLIFE & THE ARTS

Since many of its visitors set sail at the end of the day, Ocho Rios has a quieter after-dark scene than Negril or Montego Bay. Nonetheless, evening events range from discos to romantic cruises.

ANNUAL EVENTS

In Ocho Rios, the biggest event of the year is the **Ocho Rios Jazz Festival** (☎ *876/927–3544* ⊕ *www.ochoriosjazz.com*) held each June. The event, which started in 1991 as a one-day concert, now spans eight days and draws many top names.

BARS & CLUBS

For the most part, the liveliest late-night happenings in Ocho Rios are at the larger resort hotels. Some of the all-inclusive resorts offer a dinner and disco pass for $50 to $100; to buy a pass, call ahead to check for availability. Pick up a copy of the *Daily Gleaner*, the *Jamaica Observer*, or the *Star* (available at newsstands throughout the island) for listings on what musicians are playing and where.

Carnival only occurs once a year, but thanks to **Five Star Watersports** (✉ *121 Main St.* ☎ *876/974–2446* ⊕ *www.five starwatersports.com*), you can experience it every Thursday aboard a special evening cruise.

The colorful **Margaritaville Caribbean Bar & Grill** (✉ *Island Village, Turtle River Rd., Ocho Rios* ☎ *876/675–8800*) boasts a fun-loving atmosphere any night of the year. It's very popular with younger travelers, reflected in a calendar of weekly nightlife activities, which includes plenty of all-night parties.

At Shaw Park Beach Hotel, **Silks** (✉ *Cutlass Bay, Ocho Rios* ☎ *876/974–2552*) is a disco with a DJ that keeps the crowd on its toes.

OCHO RIOS ESSENTIALS

To research prices, get advice from other travelers, and book travel arrangements, visit www.fodors.com.

TRANSPORTATION

BY AIR

Mostly charter flights use Boscobel Aerodrome, 10 mi (14 km) east of Ocho Rios. Helicopter service from Island Hoppers is also available from Montego Bay.

Information **International Airlink** (☎ *888/247–5465* ⊕ *www.intlairlink.com*). **Island Hoppers** (☎ *876/974–1285* ⊕ *www.jamaicahelicoptertours.com*). **TimAir** (☎ *876/952–2516* ⊕ *www.timair.com*).

AIRPORTS & TRANSFERS

Ocho Rios has a small domestic airport east of the city. The Boscobel Aerodrome has limited charter service from Montego Bay and Kingston. Most visitors to Ocho Rios arrive via Montego Bay's Sangster International Airport. Many of the area's larger hotels arrange for shuttle service, so you don't have to worry about transportation. JCAL Tours, Jamaica Tours, and Clive's Transport Service provide round-trip transportation for about $60 to $80 per person.

Some people choose to fly into Kingston's Norman Manley International Airport, but Ocho Rios hotels do not operate shuttles service there. Clive's Transport Service will provide charges about $280 per person round-trip.

Information **Clive's Transport Service** (✉ *Lucea* ☎ *876/956–2615 or 876/869–7571* ⊕ *www.clivestransportservicejamaica.com*). **Jamaica Tours** (✉ *Providence Dr., Ironshore, Montego Bay* ☎ *876/953–2107* ⊕ *www.jamaicatoursltd.com*). **JCAL Tours** (✉ *Claude Clarke Ave., Montego Bay* ☎ *876/952–7574* ⊕ *www.jcaltours.com*).

BY CAR

Ocho Rios, like most of the island, is plagued by poor roads and daredevil drivers. Renting a car is not recommended, especially when you consider the island's extremely high auto fatality rate—the third highest in the world. If you do opt to rent a car, consider taking a taxi the first day or two to get accustomed to being on the left side of the road.

Car travel in downtown Ocho Rios can be very slow, especially on cruise-ship days. Traveling west from Ocho Rios is now speedier, thanks to the newly improved North Coast Highway. Travel east of Ocho Rios remains extremely slow due to ongoing road construction.

Note that some car-rental agencies, such as Avis, do not have a local office but will deliver cars to hotels in Ochos Rios.

Information **Avis** (☎876/974–8047 ⊕www.avis.com.jm).**Budget** (✉Couples Ocho Rios, Tower Isle ☎876/975–4986 ⊕www.budget. com). **Caribbean Car Rentals Limited** (✉Main St., Ocho Rios ☎876/974–2513). **Caribbean Car Rentals Limited** (✉Salem Crescent, Runaway Bay ☎876/973–5188).

BY CRUISE SHIP
Ocho Rios has quickly become the island's busiest cruise port. On many days the number of ships exceeds the capacity of the two-berth Turtle Bay Pier, so ships dock at Reynolds Pier.

Information **Carnival Cruise Line** (☎888/227–6482). **P&O Cruises** (☎0845/678–0014). **Royal Caribbean Cruises** (☎866/562–7625).

BY TAXI
Taxi service is readily available in Ocho Rios, but take care to hire a licensed taxi, indicated by the red PP license plate. The largest taxi operator is JUTA. Agree on a price before departure, as most taxis are not metered.

Information **JUTA** (☎876/974–2292).

CONTACTS & RESOURCES

BANKS & EXCHANGE SERVICES
Ocho Rios travelers can exchange money at hotels (usually with a less favorable exchange rate) or local banks. Many travelers, however, opt to use U.S. dollars throughout their trip.

Some local ATMs give you the option of obtaining U.S. or Jamaican dollars. Cool Cash ATM machines offer U.S. cash.

Information **National Commercial Bank** (✉Ocho Rios Cruise Ship Pier, Ocho Rios). **Scotiabank** (✉Main St., Ocho Rios).

EMERGENCIES

The area's largest medical facility is St. Ann's Bay Hospital, west of Ocho Rios.

Emergency Services **Ambulance & Fire Emergencies** (☎110). **Police Emergencies & Air Rescue** (☎119). **Hurricane Update** (☎116). **Scuba-Diving Emergencies** (✉St. Ann's Bay Hospital, St. Ann's Bay ☎876/972–2272).

Hospitals **St. Ann's Bay Hospital** (✉Main St., St. Ann's Bay ☎876/972–2272).

Pharmacies **Ocho Rios Pharmacy** (✉Ocean Village Shopping Centre, Main St., Ocho Rios ☎876/974–2398).

INTERNET, MAIL & SHIPPING

Outside the major resort hotels, Internet service is somewhat limited in Ocho Rios. You can find a few Internet cafés, however. Expect to pay about $2 for 20 minutes of high-speed access.

If you find yourself purchasing that 5-foot-tall wooden giraffe at the crafts market, Ocho Rios has international shipping service. Hotels with concierge service will also assist with wrapping and shipping purchases.

Internet Cafés **Jerkin** (✉Taj Mahal Centre, Main St. and DaCosta Dr., Ocho Rios ☎876/974–7438) offers numerous terminals for staying in touch while traveling.

Post Offices **Ocho Rios Post Office** (✉Main St., Ocho Rios ☎876/974–2526).

Shipping Companies **AirPak Express** (✉Ocean Village Shopping Centre, Ocho Rios ☎876/974–0910).

TOUR OPTIONS

Half-day and full-day tours can be arranged with many taxi drivers. Be sure to agree on a price before heading out on the tour.

Scheduled tours are also available, including the Chukka Caribbean Adventures journey in a colorfully painted bus to Bob Marley's birthplace. Jamaica Tours Ltd. offers several Ocho Rios tours with stops ranging from gardens to Dunn's River Falls.

Information **Chukka Caribbean Adventures** (✉Llandovery, St. Ann's Bay ☎876/972–2506 ⊕www.chukkacaribbean.com). **Jamaica Tours Ltd.** (✉Ocho Rios ☎876/974–6447 ⊕www.jamaicatoursltd.com).

VISITOR INFORMATION

The main Jamaica Tourist Board offices on the island are in Montego Bay, Port Antonio, and Kingston. There's a Tourism Product Development Company office in Ocho Rios, however. The hours for this office are Monday through Thursday 8:30 to 5 and Friday 8:30 to 4.

Information **Ocho Rios Information Office** (✉ *Ocean Villa Plaza, Main St., Ocho Rios* ☎ *876/974–2582*).

Port Antonio

WORD OF MOUTH

"Porty is rainforest Jamaica, so timing is everything. But even in the rain—for diehard and non-Jamaica fans—Porty is hard to beat. Like Treasure Beach, it's largely ignored by package tourists and those unwilling to rough it a bit, which is much rewarded."

—tivertonhouse

by Paris
Permenter
and John
Bigley

ONCE THE DARLING OF THE Hollywood set, this eastern getaway is Jamaica's most remote resort destination. In terms of sheer distance, the town isn't that far removed— 60 mi (97 km) east of Ocho Rios and 133 mi (220 km) from Montego Bay—but Port Antonio is worlds apart.

The North Coast Highway–construction project that has finally improved the road from Negril all the way to Ocho Rios is still underway between Ocho Rios and Port Antonio. The result is a 3½-hour obstacle course marked by gaping potholes and unexpected detours. Some taxi drivers taking travelers from Ocho Rios to Port Antonio actually prefer to get there by way of Kingston. Flying would be a better option, except that Port Antonio's aerodrome is served only by expensive charter flights.

The best way to reach Port Antonio is by yacht—just as swashbuckling actor Errol Flynn did in the 1940s. Even if you're not among the lucky few who arrive via the high seas, you're likely to spend a good deal of time on the water. After all, Port Antonio is home to Jamaica's best marina. Anglers are attracted by the region's excellent deep-sea fishing. Dolphin (the delectable fish, not the lovable mammal) is the likely catch here, along with tuna, kingfish, and wahoo. Each October, the weeklong Blue Marlin Tournament draws crowds from around the world.

Instead of fish, you'll find that pork, chicken, and goat take center stage at Boston Beach, east of Port Antonio. This small area was the birthplace of modern jerk, dating back to the 1930s when the first roadside (locally known as wayside) stands first began offering fiery jerk. Today about half a dozen jerk stands tempt diners with modestly priced meals. Jerk may have spread throughout the island, but many aficionados still return to Boston Beach for a taste of the "real thing."

EXPLORING PORT ANTONIO

Since it's so difficult to get to Port Antonio, most visitors come for a stay of a week or more. This gives them plenty of time to explore the town, its twin harbors, and the surrounding countryside. To the east of the city, the road winds beyond many beaches and bays that are waiting to be discovered. To the south, the terrain quickly turns rugged, approaching the John Crow Mountains and the Blue Mountains. This area is the home of the Windward

Maroons, descendants of the former slaves who sought freedom in these mountains centuries ago.

ABOUT THE RESTAURANTS

Dining options in Port Antonio range from rickety jerk stands to gourmet restaurants, with plenty of options in between. Seafood usually takes center stage, especially at upscale dining rooms where locally caught snapper and tuna are often on the menus. With Port Antonio experiencing a tourism lull, reservations usually aren't required except during peak winter months. The mood is casual at most lunch spots, but slacks or sundresses fit the bill for evening dress.

ABOUT THE HOTELS

If you've had your fill of the all-inclusive resorts in Montego Bay and Ocho Rios, then head to Port Antonio. Don't look for mixology classes or limbo dances, as the hotels here are extremely quiet. Popular with repeat customers, Port Antonio's little lodgings (many of them older and some looking a bit haggard) are also joined by some villas and even some camping options.

WHAT IT COSTS IN DOLLARS				
$$$$	$$$	$$	$	¢
RESTAURANTS				
Over $30	$20–$30	$12–$20	$8–$12	under $8
HOTELS*				
Over $350	$250–$350	$150–$250	$80–$150	under $80
HOTELS**				
Over $450	$350–$450	$250–$350	$125–$250	under $125

*EP, BP, CP; **AI, FAP, MAP; Restaurant prices are per person for a main course at dinner and do not include the 15% V.A.T. and 10% service charge. Hotel prices are per night for a double room in high season, excluding 15% V.A.T. and 10% service charge.

TIMING

Like the rest of Jamaica, Port Antonio has a high season ranging from mid-December through mid-April. The lowest prices coincide with the peak of hurricane season, September and October. As Jamaica's rainiest resort area, Port Antonio can experience daily deluges between May

PORT ANTONIO TOP 5

Jerking Around: Enjoy a lunch of jerk chicken, pork, or fish made by one of the vendors at Boston Beach, said to be among the best jerk in Jamaica.

Telling Fish Tales: Talk about the one that got away as you cast a line for marlin on a fishing charter.

Rolling Down the River: Glide along on the gentle Rio Grande River atop a tradi-tional bamboo raft.

Seeing the Back Side of Water: Take a boat beneath the cascade of Somerset Falls.

Taking a Hike: Follow in the footsteps of the Maroons as you visit Nanny Falls to get your blood pumping.

and October; if your plans revolve around many outdoor activities (and most do in this area), plan accordingly. Also, access into some of the more remote regions surrounding Port Antonio can be restricted if heavy rains lead to road closures.

PORT ANTONIO ATTRACTIONS

For most travelers, Port Antonio means an active vacation, one that involves hiking (from easy walks to multiday treks), swimming, surfing, and beachcombing. The town's few attractions are all outdoors: waterfalls, rivers, and swimming holes. With that in mind, planning a day's activities can revolve around the weather, which can often be rainy. Usually morning hours are the sunniest, with afternoon heat bringing in tropical showers. During the rainy season that runs from May through October, expect longer and more frequent rainfalls.

Exploring the region also means taking into account the distances between attractions. Although on the map many attractions may look easily accessible, it takes time and patience to navigate these roads. Try to group attractions and activities by region to minimize drive time.

Numbers in the margin correspond to points of interest on the Port Antonio Region and Port Antonio maps.

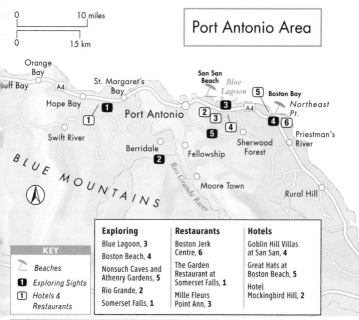

Port Antonio Area

0 — 10 miles
0 — 15 km

Orange Bay · uff Bay · Hope Bay · St. Margaret's Bay · San San Beach · Blue Lagoon · Boston Bay · Northeast Pt. · Port Antonio · Swift River · Berridale · Fellowship · Sherwood Forest · Priestman's River · Rio Grande River · Moore Town · Rural Hill · BLUE MOUNTAINS

KEY

Beaches

1 Exploring Sights

1 Hotels & Restaurants

Exploring	Restaurants	Hotels
Blue Lagoon, **3**	Boston Jerk Centre, **6**	Goblin Hill Villas at San San, **4**
Boston Beach, **4**	The Garden Restaurant at Somerset Falls, **1**	Great Hats at Boston Beach, **5**
Nonsuch Caves and Athenry Gardens, **5**	Mille Fleurs Point Ann, **3**	Hotel Mockingbird Hill, **2**
Rio Grande, **2**		
Somerset Falls, **1**		

WHAT TO SEE

❸ Blue Lagoon. One of Port Antonio's best-known attractions is the Blue Lagoon, whose azure waters have to be seen to be believed. The colors of the spring-fed lagoon are a real contrast to the warmer waters of the ocean. Catch some rays on the floating docks, or relax on the small beach. Just how deep is the Blue Lagoon? You might hear it's bottomless, but the lagoon has been measured at a depth of 180 feet. At this writing the lagoon was closed, but was expected to reopen soon. Check with tourism officials for an update. ⊠9 mi (13 km) east of Port Antonio, 1 mi (1½ km) east of San San Beach.

❹ Boston Beach. A short drive east of Port Antonio is Boston Beach, a don't-miss destination for lovers of jerk pork. The recipe originated with the Arawaks, the island's original inhabitants, but was perfected by the Maroons. Eating almost nothing but wild hog preserved over smoking coals enabled these former slaves to survive years of fierce guerrilla warfare with the English. Jerk resurfaced in the 1930s, and the spicy barbecue drew diners from around the island. Today a handful of small jerk stands, collectively known as the Boston Jerk Centre, offers fiery flavors cooled by some festival bread and a cold Red Stripe. ⊠*Rte. A4, east of Port Antonio.*

❻ DeMontevin Lodge. On Titchfield Hill, the DeMontevin Lodge is owned by the Mullings family. The late Gladys Mullings was Errol Flynn's cook, and you can still sample her recipes here. The lodge, and a number of structures on nearby Musgrave Street, is built in a traditional seaside style that's reminiscent of New England. ⊠*21 Fort George St.* ☎*876/993–2604.*

NEED A BREAK? **Coronation Bakery** (⊠*18 West St.* ☎*876/993–2710*)has served up freshly made baked goods for more than seven decades. Grab some hard-dough bread (originally brought to Jamaica by the Chinese), an unleavened bun called bulla, or even spicy patties.

❼ Folly. A favorite photo stop in Port Antonio, Folly is little more than ruins these days. This structure, spanning 60 rooms in its heyday, was the home of a Tiffany heiress. The house didn't last long because seawater, rather than freshwater, was used in the cement. In July the grounds serve as the setting for the annual Portland Jerk Festival. ⊠*Folly Point.*

❽ Folly Lighthouse. Since 1888, this red-and-white-stripe masonry lighthouse has stood watch at the tip of Folly Point. Administered by the Jamaica National Heritage Trust, the lighthouse is an often-photographed site near Port Antonio's East Harbour. ⊠*Folly Point.*

❺ Nonsuch Caves and Athenry Gardens. About 6 mi (9½ km) northeast of Port Antonio, these tropical gardens include the Nonsuch Caves, whose underground beauty has been made accessible by concrete walkways, railed stairways, and discrete lighting. Call ahead before heading out to these caves, as the road has become difficult to navigate. ⊠*Nonsuch Rd., Nonsuch* ☎*876/779–7144* ☎*$6* ⊙*Daily 10–4.*

❷ Rio Grande. Jamaica's river-rafting operations began here, on an 8-mi- (13-km-) long swift green waterway from Berrydale to Rafter's Rest. (Beyond that, the Rio Grande flows into the Caribbean at St. Margaret's Bay). The trip of about three hours is made on bamboo rafts pushed along by a guide who is likely to be quite a character. You can pack a picnic lunch to enjoy on the raft or on the riverbank; wherever you lunch, a Red Stripe vendor is likely to appear. A restaurant, a bar, and several souvenir shops can be found at Rafter's Rest. ✉*Rte. A4, 5 mi (8 km) west of Port Antonio.*

❶ Somerset Falls. On the Daniels River, these falls are in a veritable botanical garden. A concrete walk to the falls takes you past the ruins of a Spanish aqueduct and Genesis Falls before reaching Hidden Falls. At Hidden Falls, you board a boat and travel beneath the fumbling water; more daring travelers can swim in a whirlpool or jump off the falls into a pool of water. A bar and restaurant specializing in local seafood is a great place to catch your breath. ✉*Rte. A4, west of Port Antonio* ☎*876/913–0046* ⊕*www.somerset fallsjamaica.com* ☜*$7.50* ⊙*Daily 9–5.*

WHERE TO EAT

Attracting primarily European travelers, Port Antonio has slightly later dining hours than in the more Americanized resort areas of the North Coast. Dining is fairly casual, with long pants and sundresses fitting the bill for just about any establishment.

JAMAICAN

$–$$$ ✕**Mille Fleurs.** At this restaurant you can sit on a terrace surrounded by tropical vegetation and enjoy the sunset. The menu changes daily, but always features dishes prepared with local ingredients such as ackee-fruit soufflé or plantain fritters with black-bean dip. Chicken in June plum sauce is a favorite; for something more unique, try the jerk rabbit or the callaloo and goat cheese quiche. ✉*Hotel Mockingbird Hill, Point Ann, Box 254* ☎*876/993–7267* ⌂*Reservations essential* ⊟*AE, MC, V.*

$–$$ ✕**Norma's at the Marina.** A showcase for the culinary talents of Jamaican celebrity chef Norma Shirley (other locations include Kingston, Montego Bay, and Negril), this seaside restaurant serves gourmet dishes with a Jamaican twist. Start with an appetizer of smoked marlin or grilled deviled ocean crab, then move on to entrées such as grilled shrimp with mango salsa or pork riblets with local seasonings. ✉*Errol Flynn Marina, Ken Wright Dr.* ☎*876/ 993–9510* ⌂*Reservations essential* ⊟*AE, MC, V* ⊙*Closed Mon.*

¢–$ ★ Fodor'sChoice ✕**Boston Jerk Centre.** This casual collection of about half a dozen open-air stands is a culinary capital thanks to its fiery jerk pits. Stroll up to the open pits, fired by pimento logs and topped with a piece of corrugated

Port Antonio

Exploring
DeMontevin Lodge, **6**
Folly, **7**
Folly Lighthouse, **8**

Restaurants
Norma's at the Marina, **7**

Hotels
Frenchman's Cove
Resort, **8**
Jamaica Palace, **9**

◆ Trident Castle

KEY
1 Exploring Sights
1 Hotels & Restaurants

Caribbean Sea

Navy Island

West Harbour

East Harbour

Soldiers Bay

Salt Creek

Woods Island

Folly Point

Folly Estate

Turtle Crawle Bay

Queen St.
King St.
Fort George St.
Harbour St.
West St.
Summers Town Rd.
Red Hassell Rd.
Port Maria Rd.
Nuttall Rd.
W. Palm Ave.
E. Palm Ave.
Allan Ave.
A4

0   1/2 mi
0   1/2 km

CLOSE UP

Erroll Flynn in Jamaica

Foul weather caused Errol Flynn to veer off course during a voyage to the Galápagos Islands in 1942, docking in Port Antonio. Perhaps, though, fate brought "Captain Blood" to the Jamaican town he called "the most beautiful woman he had ever laid eyes upon"—high praise from a man as renowned for his amorous exploits as his silver screen adventures.

The charms of the seaside community lingered in his thoughts long after the visit, and eight years later he returned to live on the idyllic island with his third bride, Patrice Wymore. A Port Antonio resident for nearly a decade, he lived on Navy Island, just off the coast of Port Antonio, and entertained many celebrities in his verdant hideaway.

In the 1950s, Flynn started what has become one of Jamaica's top tourist activities, river rafting. Flynn, who had watched workers transporting bananas down the Rio Grande on bamboo rafts, began taking his female guests down the river, nicknaming one section winding between two boulders "Lovers Lane." Before long, tourists were floating down the river on rafts poled by expert raftsmen.

Flynn apparently had plans to make Port Antonio into a top tourist getaway. He purchased the Titchfield Hotel, at the time one of the region's best, but he died before his dreams could be realized. The Titchfield Hotel burned down in the 1960s and was never rebuilt.

roofing metal, and order meat by the quarter, half, or full pound. Chicken, pork, goat, and fish are most popular options. Side dishes are few, but generally include rice and peas or festival (rolled bread similar to a Southern hushpuppy). ⊠*Rte. A4, east of Port Antonio, Boston Beach* ☎*No phone* ☐*No credit cards.*

SEAFOOD

¢–$$ ✕**The Garden Restaurant at Somerset Falls.** Surrounded by tropical gardens and the flowing waters of the Daniel River, this restaurant offers lunch and dinner in a casual yet romantic setting. Seafood—including peppered shrimp, grilled lobster, and local catch such as snapper—are served daily. Some days bring Jamaican dishes such as jerk to the menu. ⊠*Rte. A4, west of Port Antonio* ☎*876/913–0046* ☐*MC, V.*

CLOSE UP

Barbecue, Jamaica-Style

Jamaica is well-known for its contributions to the world of music, but the island is also the birthplace of a cooking style known as jerk. Modern jerk originated in the 1930s along Boston Beach, east of Port Antonio. Here the first wayside stands sprang up on the side of the road, offering fiery jerk served in a casual atmosphere. Today jerk stands are everywhere on the island, but many aficionados still return to Boston Beach for the "real thing."

The historic origins of jerk are unknown (some say the Maroons brought the practice from Africa; others say the cooking style came to the island with the Caribs and the native Arawaks). The practice of cooking and preserving meat by smoking it was first recorded in 1698 by a French priest, who wrote of a jerk pit made with four forked sticks with crosspieces covered with a grill made of sticks. On the grill was placed a whole pig, stuffed with lime juice, salt, pimento, and spices that helped preserve the meat in the hot climate.

Today jerk is still cooked in a pit that contains a fire made from pimento wood. The meat, which is primarily pork but can also be chicken, goat, or fish, is marinated with jerk sauce. Every cook has his own favorite recipe, but most include allspice (pimento) berries, cloves, garlic, onion, ginger, cinnamon, thyme, and peppers. Commercial jerk sauces are also available. Once the jerk is cooked to perfection, it's served up with side dishes such as breadfruit, rice and peas, and a bread called festival.

WHERE TO STAY

$$–$$$ ⚁ **Hotel Mocking Bird Hill.** With 10 rooms, some overlooking the sea and others taking in the 7 acres of lush greenery, Mocking Bird Hill is much more like a bed-and-breakfast than a hotel. You'll be pleased at the way owners Barbara Walker and Shireen Aga run this environmentally-sensitive operation, which saves energy by using solar-heated showers. Meals made with local produce are served in the Mille Fleurs restaurant. There's a free shuttle to Frenchman's Cove Beach, about five minutes away. Wedding packages are available. **Pros:** environmentally conscious, excellent food, lovely views. **Cons:** not on beach, limited on-site dining options, rather remote location. ✉*Point Ann, Box 254, Port Antonio* ☎*876/993–7267* 🖷*876/993–7133* ⊕*www.*

hotelmockingbirdhill.com ↝*10 rooms* ⌂*In-room: no a/c, no phone, safe. In-hotel: restaurant, bar, pool, laundry service, no-smoking rooms, no elevator* ⊟*AE, MC, V* ⊚|*BP.*

$$ ⊺**Jamaica Palace.** This hotel is known for its Jamaica-shaped swimming pool and its black-and-white terrace, but that's just the beginning of its unusual attributes. The white building, distinguished by palatial columns indoors and out, is constructed to resemble a 17th-century Italian palace. Deemed the art-gallery hotel, the facility displays 2,000 pieces of art, some by the hotel's owner. Inside, guest rooms are surprisingly stark, although most have curving footboards and flowery spreads. The hotel is east of Port Antonio. **Pros:** lovely public areas, gorgeous pool area, good on-site dining options. **Cons:** not on beach, basic rooms, rather remote location. ⊠*Box 277, Rte. A4* ☎*876/993–7720* 🖷*876/993–7759* ⊕*www.jamaica-palace-hotel.com* ↝*34 rooms, 46 suites* ⌂*In-room: safe, dial-up. In-hotel: 2 restaurants, room service, bars, pool, no elevator, laundry service, public Internet, public Wi-Fi, parking (no fee)* ⊟*M, V* ⊚|*EP.*

$-$$ ⊺**Goblin Hill Villas at San San.** This lush 12-acre estate atop a hill overlooking San San Bay is best suited for travelers looking for a home-away-from-home atmosphere, not a bustling resort. Each attractively appointed villa comes with its own dramatic view, plus a staff member to do the grocery shopping, cleaning, and cooking for you. Villas come equipped with cable TV, ceiling fans (with air-conditioning in the bedrooms only), and tropical furnishings. The beach is a 10-minute walk away. Car-rental packages are available. **Pros:** hotel-quality facilities, nice bay views, spacious accommodations. **Cons:** not on beach, shared public areas, somewhat remote location. ☏*Box 26, San San* ☎*876/925–8108* 🖷*876/925–6248* ⊕*www.goblin-hill.com* ↝*28 1- and 2-bedroom villas* ⌂*In-room: no a/c (some), no phone, kitchen, refrigerator. In-hotel: bar, tennis courts, pool, no elevator* ⊟*AE, D, MC, V* ⊚|*EP.*

¢–$$ ⊺**Great Huts at Boston Beach.** Port Antonio's most unique accommodation is also its most basic, aimed solely at travelers who don't mind an experience that is, as Jamaicans would say, "rootsy." Great Huts, just minutes from the jerk stands of Boston Beach, is styled like an African village and celebrates African art and culture. Accommodations range from simple huts to two-story tree houses. None are air-conditioned, although all contain portable fans. The dedicated staff here can point you to out-of-the-way activities. **Pros:** good value, unique accommodations, friendly staff. **Cons:** some rooms are hot, sand floors in some rooms attract insects, remote location. ✉*Rte. A4, east of Port Antonio, Boston Beach* ☎*876/353–3388* ☎*876/993–8888* ⊕*www.greathuts.com* ✑*2 tree houses, 5 huts, 3 tents* ♿*In-room: no a/c, no phone, no TV. In-hotel: restaurant, bar, no elevator, public Internet, public Wi-Fi, parking (no fee)* ▭*MC, V* ⏐◯⏐*BP.*

$ ▧**Frenchman's Cove Resort.** This resort may be somewhat tired (a far cry from its heyday when Queen Elizabeth and her family stayed in Villa 18) but its location is pristine. Villas, definitely the best option in terms of surrounding beauty and space, are tucked back into the dense forest, and many lay just steps from one of Port Antonio's best beaches. The standard rooms, many of them fairly large, are in the main building known as the greathouse. **Pros:** excellent beach, lots of privacy, large accommodations. **Cons:** somewhat dated decor, long walk to public areas and beach, rather remote location. ✉*Rte. A4, 5 mi (8 km) east of Port Antonio* ☎*876/993–7270* ☎*876/993–7404* ⊕*www.frenchmans-cove-resort.com* ✑*9 rooms, 2 suites, 18 villas* ♿*In-room: no a/c (some), no phone (some), safe, kitchen (some), refrigerator (some), dial-up (some). In-hotel: restaurant, bar, beachfront, diving, water sports, bicycles, no elevator, laundry service, public Internet, parking (no fee)* ▭*MC, V* ⏐◯⏐*CP.*

PRIVATE VILLAS

▧**Belmont.** This luxury villa, surrounded by an acre of gardens, adjoins San San Beach. The air-conditioned master bedroom enjoys views of the beach and San San Bay as well as Pelleu Island; two other air-conditioned bedrooms feature twin beds and walk-in closets. The villa, with its airy feel and open floor plan, has a large living area with a raised wooden ceiling. For many guests, the focal point of the villa is the poolside gazebo. **Pros:** terrific views, beautiful landscaping, sizeable rooms. **Cons:** shared beach, small pool, need a car to get around. ✉*5 mi (8 km) east of Port Antonio* ☎ ⊕ ✑*3 bedrooms, 4 bathrooms* ♿*No a/c (some), dishwasher, VCR, dial-up, daily maid service, cook, on-site security, pool, water toys, laundry facilities* ▭ ⏐◯⏐*EP.*

▧**Tranquility Villa.** Furnishings from Jamaica and Bali give this hillside villa a tropical feel. From a poolside hammock you can enjoy a view of Port Antonio's harbor; balconies off the air-conditioned bedrooms look across to the Blue Mountains. This petite villa has many high-tech offerings, including unlimited overseas calling with Internet phone service. **Pros:** lovely views, nice pool area, nice amenities. **Cons:** not on beach, small rooms, rather remote location. ⊠*Richmond Hill, Port Antonio* ☎ ⊕ ⌂⌐2 *bedrooms, 1 bathrooms* ⚐*In-room: no a/c (some), dishwasher, DVD, VCR, Ethernet, Wi-Fi, daily maid service, cook, on-site security, pool, water toys, laundry facilities* ⊟ ⦿*EP.*

BEACHES

Boston Beach. Considered the birthplace of Jamaica's famous jerk-style cooking, this beach is where some locals come to buy dinner. You can get peppery jerk pork at any of the shacks spewing scented smoke—just follow your nose. While you're there, you can also enjoy the small beach for an after-lunch dip, although these waters are occasionally rough and much more popular for surfing. ⊠*11 mi (18 km) east of Port Antonio.*

Frenchman's Cove. This picturesque, somewhat secluded beach is petite perfection. Protected by two outcroppings that form the cove, the inlet's calm waters are a favorite with families. A small stream trickles into the cove. You can find a bar and restaurant serving fried chicken right on the beach. If this stretch of sand looks a little familiar, you just might have seen it in the movies; it has starred in *Club Paradise, Treasure Island* (the Charlton Heston version), and *The Mighty Quinn.* If you're not a guest of Frenchman's Cove, admission is $4.50. ⊠*Rte. A4, 5 mi (8 km) east of Port Antonio.*

San San Beach. This small beach has beautiful blue water. Just offshore, Monkey Island is a good place to snorkel (or even surf). ⊠*5 mi (8 km) east of Port Antonio.*

SPORTS & THE OUTDOORS

BIRD-WATCHING

The parish of Portland is, along with the Blue Mountains and Cockpit Country, one of the top birding destinations in Jamaica. Species including the Jamaican tody, black-billed streamtail, ringtail pigeon, and many others can be spotted in this sparsely-developed area.

Grand Valley Tours (☎*401/647–4730* ⊕*www.portanto-niojamaica.com*) offers four guided birding excursions of varying degrees of difficulty. The easy Golden Vale Tour travels through open fields to view ducks and other water birds. The easy Bourbon Trail travels along riverbanks in search of water birds. The moderately difficult Darley Trail, which winds along the Rio Grande and past three different waterfalls, is known for its wild parrots. The difficult Millbank/Macharidge Trail tour involves an overnight stay in the John Crow and Blue Mountains for the chance to spot giant swallowtail butterflies.

BOATING

With its long history of attracting an exclusive clientele, it's not surprising that Port Antonio is the island's top yacht port. The **Errol Flynn Marina** (✉*Ken Wright Dr.* ☎*876/715–6044* ⊕*www.errolflynnmarina.com*) is an official national port of entry, with 24-hour customs and immigrations services. The 32-berth marina, reached via a deepwater channel, includes 24-hour security, an Internet center, a swimming pool, and a 100-ton boatlift—the only one in the Western Caribbean.

DIVING & SNORKELING

Wall diving is especially popular in the Port Antonio area. For intermediate and advanced divers, a top spot is **Trident Wall,** lined with stunning black coral. Other top spots include **Alligator Hill,** a moderate to difficult dive known for its tubes and sponges. A beginner site, **Alligator West** is prized for its calm waters.

Lady G'Diver (✉*Errol Flynn Marina, Ken Wright Dr.* ☎*876/715–5957* ⊕*www.ladygdiver.com*) is the top dive operator in Port Antonio. Trips to interesting dive sites are offered most days except Tuesday, departing about 11 every morning for a two-tank dive.

FISHING

Port Antonio makes deep-sea-fishing headlines with its annual Blue Marlin Tournament. Licenses aren't required, and you can arrange to charter a boat at your hotel. A chartered boat (with captain, crew, and equipment) costs about $500 to $900 for a half-day or $900 to $1,500 for a full-day excursion, depending on the size of the boat.

Jamaica Deep Sea Adventures (✉*Errol Flynn Marina, Ken Wright Dr.* ☎*876/909–9552*) offers marlin, yellowfin tuna, and wahoo fishing in a 40-foot boat with an air-conditioned cabin.

HIKING

Hiking in Port Antonio ranges from very easy to extremely difficult, with everything from hour-long strolls along riverbanks to multiday sojourns through thick rain forests. A short hike to Scatter Falls followed by a rafting trip down the Rio Grande is a good choice for those looking for a short hike; the two- to three-hour hike to Nanny Falls near Moore Town is another good option. One the most difficult hikes is the two-day trip (and three days are generally recommended) to Nanny Town, where Nanny, Jamaica's only female national hero, led the Maroons against the British.

Grand Valley Tours (☎401/647–4730 ⊕*www.portantonio jamaica.com*) offers guided tours of varying lengths, such as a four-hour hike from the village of Maroon that leads to Nanny Falls.

Valley Hikes (✉*Harbour St.* ☎876/993–3881) offers 15 guided hikes ranging from one to four hours as well as longer hikes to Moore Town and Nanny Falls.

RAFTING

★ Fodor'sChoice A relaxing trip aboard a bamboo raft poled along by a local boatmen is a familiar symbol of Jamaica and represents the island's first tourist activity other than its beaches. Bamboo rafting in Jamaica originated on the **Rio Grande,** a river in the Port Antonio area. Jamaicans had long used the bamboo rafts to transport bananas downriver; decades ago actor and Port Antonio resident Errol Flynn saw the rafts and thought they'd make a good tourist attraction. Today the slow rides (taking about two and a half hours on a typical day; less time when the river's up) are a favorite with romantic travelers and anyone looking to get off the beach for a few hours. **Rio Grande Tours** (✉*St. Margaret's Bay* ☎876/993–5778 ⊕*www.jamaicatoursltd. com*) guides raft trips down the Rio Grande; the cost is $52 per raft. (Raftsmen expect a tip of about $5 to $10.) The last raft trips depart about 3 PM, a good time to observe locals fishing and washing clothes along the riverbanks.

SHOPPING

Shopping is not a major attraction in Port Antonio, compared to the duty-free shopping of Ocho Rios and Montego Bay. With the recent addition of the marina and cruise-ship port, there is some limited shopping to be had, but it still takes a back seat to other activities.

MARKETS

Musgrave Market (✉ *West St.* ☎ *876/993–2367*) is a traditional market that, unlike those in Ocho Rios and Montego Bay, is primarily aimed at locals. Although you can find some crafts here, look for luscious fruits and vegetables, household goods, and clothing in these stalls.

SPECIALTY ITEMS

HANDICRAFTS

Carricou Gallery (✉ *Hotel Mocking Bird Hill, off Rte. A4, 6 mi[9½ km] east of Port Antonio* ☎ *876/993–7267*) showcases local artists and also offers art classes.

As its name suggests, **Things Jamaican** (✉ *Errol Flynn Marina, Ken Wright Dr.* ☎ *876/715–5247*) sells an assortment of local items: books, music, crafts, spices, sauces, and more.

NIGHTLIFE & THE ARTS

ANNUAL EVENTS

For four decades, the **Port Antonio International Marlin Tournament** (✉ *Errol Flynn Marina, Ken Wright Dr.* ☎ *876/927–0145* ⊕ *www.errolflynnmarina.com*) has attracted anglers competing to see who can catch the biggest blue marlin. In addition to the fishing competition, a canoe race and lots of parties and receptions keep the action going for nonanglers.

The July **Portland Jerk Festival** (✉ *Village of St. George shopping center, Ft. George St.* ☎ *876/715–6553*) features the food for which Port Antonio is known: fiery jerk barbecue. The all-day festival includes jerk cookoffs (with plenty of opportunities for taste testing), live music, dominoes, and more.

BARS & CLUBS

Unlike the resort cities of Montego Bay and Ocho Rios, the hottest nightlife in town is not at the hotels, but at local joints such as the **Roof Club** (⊠*11 West St.* ☎*No phone*). Open Thursday to Sunday nights, the 2nd-floor club plays dancehall hits.

PORT ANTONIO ESSENTIALS   3

To research prices, get advice from other travelers, and book travel arrangements, visit www.fodors.com.

TRANSPORTATION

BY AIR

Limited domestic air service into the Port Antonio Aerodrome is available via charter companies.

Information **International Airlink** (☎*888/247-5465* ⊕*www. intlairlink.com*). **TimAir** (☎*876/952-2516* ⊕*www.timair.com*).

AIRPORTS & TRANSFERS

Port Antonio's small domestic airport west of the city only has charter service available.

Information **Port Antonio Ken Jones Aerodrome** (⊠*North Coast Hwy., Port Antonio* ☎*876/923-0222*).

BY CAR

Lighter traffic than the island's other resort areas makes driving in Port Antonio more reasonable—but incredibly rough road conditions mean a bouncy, detour-filled drive. If you rent a car, check on road conditions before heading anywhere off the beaten path. (A four-wheel-drive vehicle is recommended for many drives.)

Information **Eastern Car Rentals** (⊠*16 West St., Port Antonio* ☎*876/993-2562*).

BY CRUISE SHIP

Port Antonio's Ken Wright Pier accommodates small and medium-size ships, primarily from November to March. Most arrivals are European lines.

Information **Fred Olsen Cruises** (☎*01473/746175*). **Oceania** (☎*305/514-2300*).

BY TAXI

Taxi service is available in Port Antonio, but always hire a licensed taxi, indicated by the red PP license plate. The largest taxi operator is JUTA. Taxi service in the area is expensive, and be sure to agree on a price before departure, as most taxis are not metered.

Information **JUTA** (☎876/993–2684).

CONTACTS & RESOURCES

BANKS & EXCHANGE SERVICES

Due to Port Antonio's relative isolation, you'll see prices marked in Jamaican dollars more often than U.S. dollars. Although you can readily spend U.S. currency, your money will go further if you convert it to Jamaican dollars. Several local supermarkets contain exchange offices.

Information **Best Rate Cambio** (✉15 West St., Port Antonio). **Kamal's Supermarket & Cambio** (✉12 West St., Port Antonio). **Kamlyn's Super Center & Cambio** (✉19 Harbour St., Port Antonio). **National People's Co-Operative Bank of Jamaica** (✉19 W. Palm Ave., Port Antonio ✉4 Thompson Ave., Buff Bay). **Scotiabank** (✉3 Harbour St., Port Antonio).

EMERGENCIES

Emergency Services **Ambulance & Fire Emergencies** (☎110). **Police Emergencies & Air Rescue** (☎119). **Scuba-Diving Emergencies** (✉St. Ann's Bay Hospital, St. Ann's Bay ☎876/972–2272).

Hospitals **Port Antonio Hospital** (✉Naylors Hill, Port Antonio ☎876/993–2646).

Pharmacies **A&E Pharmacy** (✉3 West St., Port Antonio ☎876/993–9348). **City Plaza Pharmacy Ltd.** (✉City Centre Plaza, Port Antonio ☎876/993–2620). **Square Deal Gift Centre and Pharmacy Ltd.** (✉11 West St., Port Antonio ☎876/993–3629).

INTERNET, MAIL & SHIPPING

Internet access outside the hotels is fairly limited, especially as you travel beyond the boundaries of Port Antonio. Yachters will find high-speed access for $4 per hour at the Errol Flynn Marina. The Portland Parish Library is also a good option.

Due to Port Antonio's poor road conditions and lack of scheduled air service, if you purchase something bulky, the best way to send it home is to ship it from Kingston, Ocho Rios, or Montego Bay.

Internet Cafés **Errol Flynn Marina** (✉ *Ken Wright Dr., Port Antonio* ☎ *876/715–6044*). **Portland Parish Library** (✉ *Fort George St., Port Antonio* ☎ *876/993–2793*).

Post Offices **Port Antonio Post Office** (✉ *Harbour St., Port Antonio* ☎ *876/993–2158*).

TOUR OPTIONS

Along with hiking, birding, and river-rafting tours, guided sightseeing tours are a good way to get the lay of the land in Port Antonio, especially for first-time visitors. Joanna Hart of Port Antonio Tours leads a wide variety of guided tours. Prices range from $30 to $75 per person.

Information **Port Antonio Tours** (☎ *876/831–8434 or 876/859–3758* ⊕ *www.portantoniotours.netfirms.com*).

VISITOR INFORMATION

The best place for visitor information in Port Antonio is the downtown office of the Jamaica Tourist Board. The office, open weekends 8:30 to 4:30, offers brochures and maps as well as other kinds of assistance.

Information **Jamaica Tourist Board** (✉ *City Centre Plaza, Harbour St., Port Antonio* ☎ *876/993–3051* ⊕ *www.visitjamaica.com*). **Port Antonio Travel** (☎ *876/993–3051* ⊕ *www.portantoniotravel.com*).

Kingston & the Blue Mountains

WORD OF MOUTH

"If you are looking for a truly Jamaican experience (away from the AI beach resorts) that will figuratively transport you away from your worries and stresses back home (wherever that may be), I highly recommend Strawberry Hill."

—TomCayman

By Paris
Permenter
and John
Bigley

THE "HEART OF THE CARIBBEAN" is what they call Jamaica, so the beating heart of Jamaica surely must be Kingston. It's the epicenter of the political and cultural life of the country as well as the home of nearly one million inhabitants, making it by far the largest city on the island.

Kingston is a big city with big-city problems, so the reactions of some visitors to the capital are not always favorable. Yet, islanders themselves are always conscious of Kingston's influence on their lives. From the slums of Trenchtown, immortalized in Bob Marley's music, to the glittering high-rise towers in New Kingston, the city is an explosion of color and sound. Despite its problems, the capital is a source of pride for all Jamaicans.

For visitors, Kingston can be intimidating. Exploring some of its dicier neighborhoods without a licensed guide is foolhardy at best. Yet, with careful planning and the normal precautions, Kingston can reward the visitor with a greater appreciation for Jamaica's unique culture. True devotees of things Jamaican can ill afford to skip this metropolis entirely.

On a clear day, when beneficial breezes have shoved some of Kingston's motor-exhaust haze out to sea, you can admire the nearby Blue Mountains from many vantage points around the city. Following your gaze across the Kingston plain into the highlands is a study in contrasts as the gritty cityscape is gradually replaced by tropical splendor.

Leaving the city far below, the highway begins to twist and turn, narrowing to an unevenly paved road as it passes panoramas of lush vegetation and soaring peaks. Rounding hairpin turns, you encounter sudden views of tiny hamlets clinging to the hillsides, their inhabitants going about their daily chores in what seems to be luxuriously unhurried fashion. The view from the top is spectacular, with Kingston's sprawl spread out before you, bounded by the harbor, the ancient stones of Port Royal and, further out, the blue Caribbean Sea glittering in the sun. As the breeze shifts, a faint hum of the frenetic human activity below may reach your ears, but no louder than the buzz of a hummingbird's wing.

EXPLORING KINGSTON & THE BLUE MOUNTAINS

Few travelers—particularly Americans—take the time to visit Kingston, although organized day trips make the city accessible from Ocho Rios and Montego Bay. That's understandable, as Kingston is a tough city to love. It's big and, all too often, bad, with gang-controlled neighborhoods that are known to erupt into violence, especially near election time.

However, if you've seen other parts of the island and yearn to know more about the heart and soul of Jamaica, Kingston is worth a visit. This government and business center is also a cultural capital, home to numerous dance troupes, theaters, and museums. It's also home to the University of the West Indies, one of the Caribbean's largest universities. In many ways, Kingston reflects the true Jamaica—a wonderful cultural mix—more than the sunny havens of the North Coast. As one Jamaican put it, "You don't really know Jamaica until you know Kingston."

North of New Kingston, the city gives way to steep hills and magnificent homes. East of here, the views are even grander as the road winds into the Blue Mountains, one of the island's least developed yet most beautiful regions.

ABOUT THE RESTAURANTS

As home to foreign embassies and consulates, as well as many corporate headquarters, it's no surprise that Kingston offers a wide array of international cuisines, especially in the New Kingston area. Because some travelers are reluctant to venture out at night, hotel dining is often very good, although the city does have excellent independent restaurants, often with their own security. Dress is slightly more formal than at North Coast restaurants, and reservations for the more elegant eateries are a good idea.

ABOUT THE HOTELS

Although it sees relatively few vacationers, Kingston is a frequent destination for corporate travelers. The city boasts some of the island's finest business hotels, most of these in the New Kingston neighborhood. The hotels, primarily high-rise towers, offer exactly what on-the-go executives expect, from business centers to meeting rooms to concierge services. Skirting the city are the Blue Mountains, a completely different world from the urban frenzy of the capital city. Here you'll find mostly small, exclusive properties.

WHAT IT COSTS IN DOLLARS				
$$$$	$$$	$$	$	¢
RESTAURANTS				
Over $30	$20–$30	$12–$20	$8–$12	under $8
HOTELS*				
Over $350	$250–$350	$150–$250	$80–$150	under $80
HOTELS**				
Over $450	$350–$450	$250–$350	$125–$250	under $125

*EP, BP, CP; **AI, FAP, MAP; Restaurant prices are per person for a main course at dinner and do not include the 15% V.A.T. and 10% service charge. Hotel prices are per night for a double room in high season, excluding 15% V.A.T. and 10% service charge.

TIMING

As a business destination, the demand for rooms at New Kingston hotels peak Sunday to Thursday night. During Carnival celebrations, hotels are filled with former residents who return to the island to party. One time to avoid Kingston is the period immediately before and after a national election, when security becomes more of a concern.

In the Blue Mountains, demand is fairly steady through the year, although the rainy months of May to October see a diminished number of visitors.

WHAT TO SEE

Kingston sprawls in every direction. Most travelers head to New Kingston, the site of many upscale hotels and several historic sites. New Kingston is bordered by Old Hope Road on the east and Half Way Tree Road (which becomes Constant Spring Road) on the west. The area is sliced by Hope Road, a major thoroughfare that connects this region with the University of the West Indies, about 15 minutes east of New Kingston.

North of New Kingston, the city gives way to steep hills and magnificent homes. East of here, the views are even grander as the road winds into the Blue Mountains. Hope Road, just after the University of the West Indies, becomes

Gordon Town Road, and starts twisting up through the mountains—it's a route that leaves no room for error.

Approaching the city from the west you'll pass some of the city's worst slums in the neighborhoods of Six Miles and Riverton City. Farther south, Spanish Town Road skirts through a high-crime district that many Kingstonians avoid. In the heart of the business district, along the water, the pace is more relaxed, with lovely parks along Ocean Boulevard. From the waterfront you can look across Kingston Harbour to the Palisadoes Peninsula. This narrow strip is where you can find Norman Manley International Airport and, farther west, Port Royal, the island's former capital, which was destroyed by an earthquake.

Numbers in the margin correspond to points of interest on the Exploring Kingston and Exploring Kingston & Vicinity maps.

★ ⑮ **Blue Mountains.** Best known as the source of Blue Mountain coffee, these mountains rising out of the lush jungle north of Kingston are a favorite destination with adventure travelers, as well as hikers, birders, and anyone looking to see what lies beyond the beach. You can find guided tours to the mountains from the Ocho Rios and Port Antonio areas, as well as from Kingston. Unless you're traveling with a local, don't try to go on your own; the roads wind and dip without warning, and hand-lettered signs blow away, leaving you without a clue as to which way to go. It's best to hire a taxi (look for red PPV license plates to identify a licensed cab) or book a guided tour.

The site of Jamaica's government-owned coffee plant, the small town of Mavis Bank is northeast of Kingston on the main road to Blue Mountain Peak. An hour-long guided tour of **Mavis Bank Coffee Factory** (⊠*Gordon Town Rd., Mavis Bank* ☎*876/977–8528* ⊕*www.jablumonline.com* ☞*$8* ⊗*Weekdays 9–2*) takes you through the processing of coffee, from planting to distribution. Inquire about tours when you arrive at the main office. Funded by the Jamaica Conservation and Development Trust, **Holywell National Recreation Park** is in the Blue and John Crow Mountains National Park. Nature trails winding through the rugged terrain offer you the chance to spot some of the island's most reclusive creatures. Be on the lookout for the national bird, the streamer-tail hummingbird (known locally as the doctor bird) and the rare swallowtail butterfly. Rustic camping facilities are available, including showers and

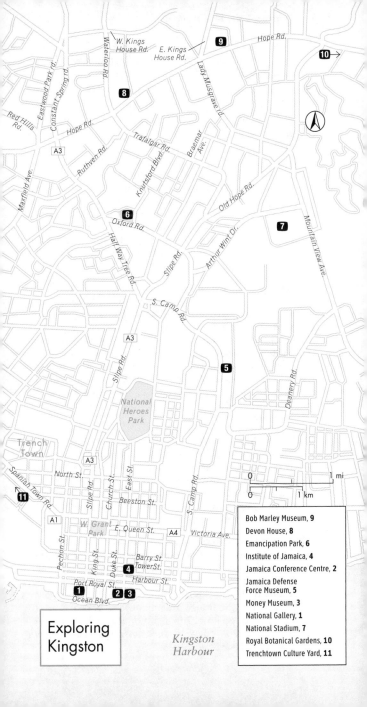

Exploring Kingston

Bob Marley Museum, **9**
Devon House, **8**
Emancipation Park, **6**
Institute of Jamaica, **4**
Jamaica Conference Centre, **2**
Jamaica Defense Force Museum, **5**
Money Museum, **3**
National Gallery, **1**
National Stadium, **7**
Royal Botanical Gardens, **10**
Trenchtown Culture Yard, **11**

Kingston Harbour

shelters. It's about 15 mi (25 km) north of Kingston on a very slow and winding road. ⊠*Rte. B1, northwest of Newcastle* ☎*876/960–2849* ▢*Free* ☉*Tues.–Sun. 10–5.*

★ **❾ Bob Marley Museum.** At the height of his career, Bob Marley built a recording studio—painted Rastafarian red, yellow, and green, of course. It now houses this museum, Kingston's best-known tourist site. The guided tour takes you through rooms wallpapered with magazine and newspaper articles that chronicle his rise to stardom. The tour includes a 20-minute biographical film on Marley's career; there's also a reference library if you want to learn more. A striking mural by Jah Bobby, *The Journey of Superstar Bob Marley,* depicts the hero's life from its beginnings, in a womb shaped like a coconut, to enshrinement in the hearts of the Jamaican people. ⊠*56 Hope Rd.* ☎*876/927–9152* ⊕*www.bobmarley-foundation.com* ▢*$10* ☉*Mon.–Sat. 9:30–4.*

❽ Devon House. Built in 1881 as the mansion of the island's first black millionaire, then bought and restored by the government in the 1960s, Devon House is filled with period furnishings, such as Venetian-crystal chandeliers and period reproductions. You can visit the two-story mansion (built with a South American gold miner's fortune) only on a guided tour. On the grounds you can find some of the island's best crafts shops, as well as one of the few mahogany trees to have survived Kingston's ambitious but not always careful development. ⊠*26 Hope Rd.* ☎*876/929–6602* ▢*$5* ☉*Mon.–Sat. 9:30–4:30.*

❻ Emancipation Park. A 7-acre swath of greenery in the St. Andrew district of New Kingston, Emancipation Park was created in 2002. The south entrance is graced by Redemption Song, a pair of monumental statues of slaves that serve as a reminder of the island's colonial past. The park contains jogging trails and quiet spots to relax away from the buzzing city streets. ⊠*Knutsford Blvd. at Oxford Rd.*

⓮ Guardsmen's Serenity Park. This retreat, 20 minutes from Kingston, offers a day of outdoor activity away from the hustle and bustle of the city. There's a zoo with animals ranging from birds to buffalo, canoeing, picnicking, and more. If you catch a fish in the pond, you can have it cooked at the nearby restaurant. The park is 4 mi (6 km) west of Spanish Town. ⊠*Off Rte. A2, Spring Village* ☎*876/708–5515* ⊕*www.serenityparkjamaica.com* ▢*$3.50* ☉*Thurs.–Sun. 10–6.*

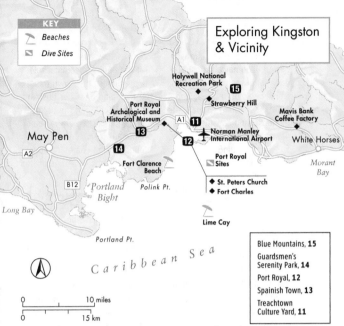

4 Institute of Jamaica. Dating back to 1879, this natural-history museum covers the island's past starting with its early Arawak residents and continuing to modern times. Collections span art, literature, and natural history, with exhibits that range from Jamaican furniture to a display on Marcus Garvey. ✉ *10–16 East St.* ☎ *876/922–0620* ⊕ *www.institu teofjamaica.org.jm* 🎫 *$2.20* ◷ *Mon.–Thurs. 9–4:30, Fri. 9–3:30.*

2 Jamaica Conference Centre. It's not often that a convention facility is also a tourist attraction, but that's the case with the Jamaica Conference Centre, which guides point out on most city tours. The facility, built in 1982, serves as headquarters for the International Seabed Authority, a division of the United Nations. The center is equipped with simultaneous translation facilities for six languages: English, Spanish, French, Chinese, Russian, and Arabic. Around-the-clock security protects the center, which includes delegates' lounges and a cafeteria and exhibition hall. ✉ *14–20 Port Royal St.* ☎ *876/922–9160* ⊕ *www. jamaicaconference.com* 🎫 *Free* ◷ *Weekdays 8–5.*

CLOSE UP

A Jamaican Treasure

A sculptor, educator, and wife of one of Jamaica's most influential prime ministers, Edna Manley was born in England in 1900. As a young woman, she demonstrated considerable artistic talent and was educated at several leading art institutes. She married her cousin, Jamaican-born Norman Washington Manley, in 1921, and the pair moved to Jamaica the following year. After giving birth to her first child, Michael (himself later to be elected prime minister), Manley returned to her art, finding new inspiration in the beauty of her adopted country.

Working in mostly native wood, Manley's sculptures sought to capture the struggles of Jamaicans as they attempted to cast off the bonds of colonial rule and establish their own nation. At the same time, her husband, who was entering the political arena, began to feel the same nationalistic spirit. In 1938, he founded the People's National Party, becoming prime minister in 1955.

Over a long career, Manley's art reflected the island's culture. Although English-born, she is considered one of the founders of modern Jamaican art. A replica of one of her most famous sculptures, the monumental *Negro Aroused*, now graces the Kingston waterfront. The original, as well as many more of her works, can be seen in Kingston's National Gallery.

❺ **Jamaica Defense Force Museum.** This museum is dedicated to Jamaica's military history. Exhibits include plans of the forts built around Kingston in the 18th century, as well as information, weapons, medals, and uniforms of the West Indies Regiment and the Jamaica Infantry Militia. It's north of Kingston's National Heroes Park at Arnold Road and South Camp Road. ⊠ *S. Camp Rd.* ☎ *876/754–9180* ⊕ *www.jdfmil.org* 🖅 *$2* ⊙ *Wed.–Sun. 10–4.*

❸ **Money Museum.** You don't have to be a numismatist to enjoy the exhibits at this museum. In the Bank of Jamaica building on Duke Street at Nethersole Place, the museum offers a fascinating look at Jamaica's history through its monetary system. It includes everything from glass beads used as currency by the Taino Indians to Spanish gold pieces to currency of the present day. There's also a parallel exhibit on the general history of currency through world history. ⊠ *Nethersole Pl.* ☎ *876/922–0750* ⊕ *www.boj.org. jm* 🖅 *Free* ⊙ *Weekdays 10–4.*

❶ **National Gallery.** The artists represented at the National Gallery may not be household names, but their paintings are sensitive and moving. You can find works by such Jamaican masters as painter John Dunkley and sculptor Edna Manley. Among other highlights from the 1920s through 1980s are works by the artist Kapo, a self-taught painter who specialized in religious images. Reggae fans should look for Christopher Gonzalez's controversial statue of Bob Marley. It was slated to be displayed near the National Arena, but was placed here because many Jamaicans felt it didn't resemble Marley. ✉*12 Ocean Blvd., Kingston* ☎*876/922–1561* 🎟️*$2* ⏲*Tues.–Thurs. 10–4:30, Fri. 10–4, Sat. 10–3.*

❼ **National Stadium.** Constructed in 1962, this 35,000-seat arena (nicknamed "the Office") hosts national and international soccer matches. It's the home of Jamaica's national team, dubbed the "Reggae Boyz," which made strong showings in world competitions in recent years. Surprisingly, one of the statues in front of the main entrance honors not a soccer star, but music legend Bob Marley. Marley's monument pays homage to an iconic moment in Jamaican history. During the 1970s, Jamaica was torn by political unrest when the ruling Jamaican Labor Party met a strong challenge by the rival People's National Party. Armed gangs representing the parties engaged in open warfare in the streets. On April 22, 1978, Bob Marley and the Wailers were performing at the packed stadium. During the song "Jammin'," Marley called for the leaders of both parties to join him on the stage. As the band continued playing the song, Marley made a spirited plea for peace and unity. For the night, at least, civility and harmony prevailed in the battered streets of Kingston. ✉*Independence Park, Arthur Wint Dr.* ☎*876/929–4970.*

⓬ **Port Royal.** Just south of Kingston, the Jamaican capital of Port Royal was once called "the wickedest city in Christendom." Jamaica's early English governors, eager to plunder treasure-laden Spanish ships, welcomed buccaneers. The city became more lawless—and more drunken. In one month alone, more than 40 new tavern licenses were issued. Rather than rein in the wild city, King Charles decided to create a royal monopoly on sales of brandy in Port Royal, using the profits to fortify and enlarge Fort Charles and to construct two smaller forts.

But brandy was not the downfall of Port Royal's residents; for most, rum was the drink of choice. A wicked drink called "kill-devil" was the pirate's preference. Jamaica's governor, Sir Thomas Modyford, wrote that "the Spaniards wondered much at the sickness of our people, until they knew of the strength of their drinks, but then they wondered more that they were not all dead."

The rollicking times came to an end on June 7, 1692, when an earthquake hit the town, plunging two-thirds of the buildings into the sea. Much of the surviving city collapsed or was hit by a tidal wave. Today this is now a small fishing village, its wild ways replaced by a handful of fish stands, a couple of outdoor restaurant, a few churches, and the occasional rum shop.

You can explore the remnants of **Fort Charles** ⊠*12 Long La., Port Royal* ☎*876/967–8438* ⊠*$4* ⊙*Weekdays 9–5*, once the city's largest garrison. Built in 1662, this is the oldest surviving structure from the British occupation. On the grounds you can find an old artillery storehouse, called Giddy House, which gained its name after being tilted by the earthquake of 1907. Locals say its slant makes you dizzy. The Fort Charles Maritime Museum is housed in what was once the headquarters for the British Royal Navy. Admiral Horatio Nelson served as a naval lieutenant here in 1779. The museum features a re-creation of Nelson's private quarters, as well as other artifacts from the era, including models of various sailing vessels. The **Port Royal Archaeological and Historical Museum** (⊠*End of Morgan Rd.* ☎*No phone* ⊕*www.jnht.com* ⊠*Free* ⊙*Weekdays 9–5*) displays items recovered from the ruins of Port Royal following its destruction in the 1692 earthquake. It's in the old British Naval Hospital. Built in 1725 after the previous church was swept into the sea, **St. Peter's Church** (⊠*Church St.* ☎*No phone* ⊠*Free* ⊙*Daily 9–5*) was constructed by Lewis Galdy, a survivor of the 1692 earthquake. His tombstone in the church cemetery describes how "he was swallowed up in the Great Earthquake in the year 1692 and by the providence of God was by another shock thrown into the sea and miraculously saved by swimming until a boat took him up. Beloved by all and much lamented at his Death." The modest church's other treasures include an ornate organ loft, a silver candelabra, and a silver communion service that was donated, according to legend, by the notorious pirate Henry Morgan. Visitors usually arrive at Port Royal by taxi, traveling via Norman Manley Highway

Pirate of the Caribbean

Politics and piracy had close connections in early Jamaica, thanks to one of the most notorious pirates of the Caribbean: Sir Henry Morgan. Most believe the Welshman came to the West Indies as an indentured servant, eventually becoming a licensed privateer. With the government's blessing, Morgan plundered Spanish ships—as well as Spanish towns of the Caribbean, for which he did not have the approval of the crown.

Morgan's raids took him to Cuba's Puerto Principe (today's Camagüey), then to Portobello, returning to Jamaica laden with gold and silver. His raids—including his famous attack on Panama in retaliation for raids on Jamaica—earned Morgan the favor of King Charles II.

Morgan was knighted and became Deputy Governor of Jamaica.

It was a job change for Morgan—in many ways. Soon Charles II decided that England should enjoy better relations with Spain. Morgan was asked to persuade the privateers of Jamaica—which some historians say made up a fifth of the island's population—to give up their marauding ways. Some of those who wouldn't stop their hunt for booty were caught and sent to trial, and often to the gallows.

Morgan himself died in Jamaica—not by the sword, but by the drink. Years of alcoholism caught up to the swashbuckler in 1688. The privateer turned knight was buried in Port Royal.

past the Norman Manley International Airport, where the highway becomes the Main Road. Driving from Kingston, you'll pass several other sights, including remains of old forts virtually hidden by vegetation, an old naval cemetery (with some intriguing headstones), and a monument commemorating Jamaica's first coconut tree, planted in 1863 (there's no tree there now, just plenty of cactus and scrub brush). Two small pubs remain in operation.

❿ **Royal Botanical Gardens at Hope.** The largest botanical garden in the Caribbean was originally called the Hope Estate, founded in the 1600s by an English army officer. Today it's often called Hope Gardens and features areas devoted to orchids, cacti, and palm trees. The gardens are also home to a somewhat dated zoo filled with local wildlife. ✉*Old Hope Rd.* ☎*876/927–1085* 🎟*Free* ⊙*Daily 8:30–6:30.*

⑬ Spanish Town. About 12 mi (19 km) west of Kingston on A1, Spanish Town was the island's capital when it was ruled by Spain. The original name was Santiago de la Vega, meaning St. James of the Plains. The town, which has been declared a national monument by the Jamaica National Heritage Trust, has a number of historic structures, including the Jamaican People's Museum of Crafts and Technology (in the Old King's House stables), and St. James Cathedral, the oldest Anglican cathedral in the Western Hemisphere. Other historic sites include the Old Barracks Building, built in 1791 to house military personnel. Although in disrepair, its facade of brick and native stone is still imposing. The Phillippo Baptist Church honors a local hero, the Reverend James Mursell Phillippo, a missionary who led the fight for emancipation of Jamaica's slaves. His grave is in the church's graveyard. An historic cast iron bridge dates from 1801 and is said to be the oldest such bridge in the Western Hemisphere. ⊠*Rte. A1, 13 mi (20 km) west of Kingston.*

⓫ Trenchtown Culture Yard. This restored tenement building is where Bob Marley spent much of his youth. Marley wrote frequently about life in the "government yard," and the area is credited with being the birthplace of reggae. The project was developed by the Trenchtown Development Association, a group dedicated to breathing new life into what had been one of Kingston's worst slums. The building contains a rudimentary museum of Marley and Wailer memorabilia. ⊠*6–10 1st St.* ☎*876/948–1455* ⊒*$10* ⊗*By appointment.*

WHERE TO EAT

Kingston's varied ethnic roots—and crowds of international visitors—are clearly demonstrated by its rich array of restaurants. Although local cuisine is well represented, this city boasts the island's largest variety of restaurants, from Chinese and Indian to French and Spanish.

CHINESE

$$ ✕ Jade Garden. On the 3rd floor of the Sovereign Centre mall, this place has great views of the Blue Mountains. Take a seat in one of the shiny black-lacquer chairs and settle in for rave-worthy Cantonese and Thai dishes. Favorites include steamed fish in black-bean sauce, black mushrooms stuffed with shrimp, and shrimp with lychee nuts. Dim sum is served every Sunday. ⊠*Sovereign Centre, 106 Hope Rd.* ☎*876/978–3476* ⊟*AE, MC, V.*

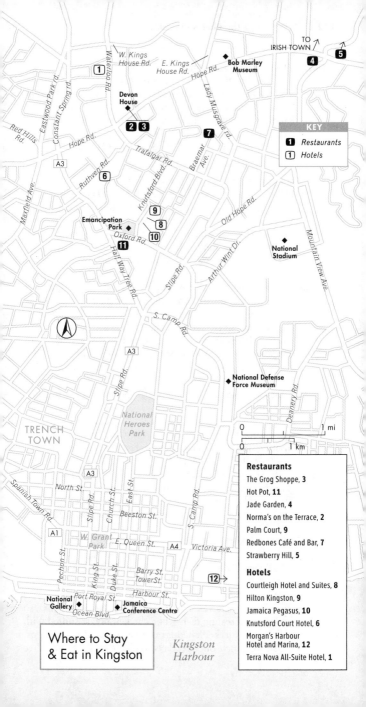

KEY

■1 *Restaurants*

□1 *Hotels*

Restaurants
The Grog Shoppe, **3**
Hot Pot, **11**
Jade Garden, **4**
Norma's on the Terrace, **2**
Palm Court, **9**
Redbones Café and Bar, **7**
Strawberry Hill, **5**

Hotels
Courtleigh Hotel and Suites, **8**
Hilton Kingston, **9**
Jamaica Pegasus, **10**
Knutsford Court Hotel, **6**
Morgan's Harbour
Hotel and Marina, **12**
Terra Nova All-Suite Hotel, **1**

Where to Stay
& Eat in Kingston

Kingston
Harbour

ECLECTIC

$$–$$$ ×**Palm Court.** On the mezzanine floor of the Hilton Kingston, the elegant Palm Court is open for lunch and dinner. The dining room is furnished in rich fabrics, and the subdued lighting creates a calm oasis in the hubbub of New Kingston. The menu includes such favorites as rack of lamb, snapper amandine, and grilled salmon. ⊠*Hilton Kingston, 77 Knutsford Blvd.* ☎876/926–5430 ⊟*AE, MC, V.*

JAMAICAN

$$$–$$$$ ×**Strawberry Hill.** A favorite with Kingstonians, Strawberry
★ Hill is well worth the drive from the city. The open-air terrace has a spectacular view of the surrounding countryside. Entrées range from steamed snapper with coconut-scented rice to jerk-marinated chicken with rice and peas. Stop by for the elegant Sunday brunch. ⊠*New Castle Rd., Irishtown* ☎876/944–8400 ⊛*Reservations essential* ⊟*AE, D, MC, V.*

$$–$$$ ×**Norma's on the Terrace.** Jamaican food with a gourmet touch (they call it fusion Jamaican) is the specialty of the day at this popular restaurant, the creation of Jamaica's best-known chef, Norma Shirley. Look for dishes like chicken thighs with guava cream and double-smoked pork chops marinated in Red Stripe beer. ⊠*Devon House, 26 Hope Rd.* ☎876/968–5488 ⊛*Reservations essential* ⊟*AE, D, MC, V* ⊙*Closed Sun.*

$–$$ ×**The Grog Shoppe.** At the historic Devon House, this restaurant is a bit of local history. Since 1961 it has been known for good local dishes (as well as assortment of international fare). It's pub atmosphere makes it a cool, inviting place to have a Red Stripe. ⊠*26 Hope Rd.* ☎876/929–7027 ⊟*MC, V.*

$–$$ × **Hot Pot.** Jamaicans love the Hot Pot for breakfast, lunch, and dinner. Fricassee chicken is the specialty, along with other local dishes like mackerel run-down (salted mackerel cooked with coconut milk and spices) and ackee and salted cod. The restaurant's freshly squeezed juices are the best—tamarind, sorrel, coconut water, soursop, and cucumber. ⊠*2 Altamont Terr.* ☎876/929–3906 ⊟*MC, V.*

$–$$ ×**Redbones Café & Bar.** In a colonial-era residence, this restaurant lets you choose between tables in two dining rooms or outdoors on the terrace or in the courtyard. The menu was created by Norma Shirley (of Norma's fame), so look for interesting dishes like chicken breast stuffed with callaloo and jerked cheddar or guava-glazed lamb chops. Open for lunch on weekdays, the café really comes alive during dinner when meals are accompanied by live jazz or events ranging from fashion shows to poetry readings. ✉*21 Braemar Ave.* ☎*876/978–8262* ⚑*Reservations essential* ▤*MC, V* ⊘*Closed Sun. No lunch Sat.*

WHERE TO STAY

$$$$ ⛾**Strawberry Hill.** A 45-minute drive from Kingston—but
★ worlds apart in terms of atmosphere—this exclusive resort was developed by Chris Blackwell, former head of Island Records. Perched in the Blue Mountains, it's where the rich and famous go to get away from it all. The resort has a pool, though this is one Jamaican property where fun in the sun is not a priority. Instead, people come here for gourmet dining, pampering spa treatments, and pure relaxation in Georgian-style villas. Views of the Blue Mountains can be seen from the expansive porches, most with oversize hammocks. Every bed has an electric mattress pad to warm things up on chilly evenings; mosquito nets surround you. (As there's no air-conditioning, guests usually prefer to keep windows open.) Rates include meals, beverages, and a minibar stocked with juices and bottled water. **Pros:** stylish accommodations, great mountain views, best spa in Jamaica. **Cons:** remote location, limited dining options, too quiet for some. ✉*New Castle Rd., Irishtown* ☎*876/944–8400* 🖷*876/944–8408* ⊕*www.islandoutpost.com* ⚑*12 villas* ⚐*In-room: no a/c, safe, kitchen (some), DVD. In-hotel: restaurant, room service, bar, pool, spa, bicycles, laundry service, airport shuttle, no elevator* ▤*AE, D, MC, V* ⍟*AI.*

$$–$$$$ ⛾**Morgan's Harbour Hotel and Marina.** Near the entrance to Port Royal, this hotel plays up the region's swashbuckling past in everything from its seafood restaurant to its slots-filled gaming room. The accommodations feature nice touches like mahogany four-poster beds and generously sized desks; some include private balconies overlooking the sea. Although the hotel is directly on the ocean, guests rely on the pool when they want to cool off. Another alterative is heading out to Lime Cay for a day of beach fun. **Pros:** easy airport access, leisurely pace, good water sports. **Cons:** limited dining, limited nightlife, long drive to Kingston. ✉*Queen St.* ☎*876/967–8040* 🖷*876/967–8873* ⊕*www.morgansharbour.com* ⚑*54 rooms, 7 suites* ⚐*In-room: refrigerator, Ethernet, dial-up. In-hotel: 2 restaurants, room service, bars, golf course, tennis courts, pool,*

4

beachfront, bicycles, no elevator, laundry facilities, laundry service, concierge, airport shuttle, parking (no fee), no-smoking rooms ⊟AE, D, DC, MC, V ⊺⊙⋀BP.

$–$$$ ⊞**Jamaica Pegasus.** In the heart of the financial district, this 17-story tower is popular with traveling executives because of its location and amenities like a full-service business center and 24-hour room service. All rooms have balconies and large windows that face the pool, the ocean, or the Blue Mountains. The hotel's restaurant offers plenty of local favorites, such as braised oxtail and grilled snapper. **Pros:** good business facilities, easy access to New Kingston business district, pretty pool area. **Cons:** limited activities, no wireless connections in rooms, long waits for elevators. ⊠81 Knutsford Blvd., Box 333 ☎876/926–3690 🖷876/929–5855 ⊕www.jamaicapegasus.com ⌁300 rooms, 19 suites ♿In-room: safe, refrigerator, Ethernet, dial-up. In-hotel: 3 restaurants, room service, bars, tennis courts, pool, gym, spa, laundry service, concierge, executive floor, public Internet, public Wi-Fi, airport shuttle, parking (no fee), no-smoking rooms ⊟AE, D, DC, MC, V ⊺⊙⋀EP.

$$ ⊞**Courtleigh Hotel and Suites.** This 10-story hotel is the newest of the "big three" business hotels in New Kingston. The property is aimed at business executives, but most travelers will find its rooms more than comfortable. The family-owned hotel, whose original location was a few blocks away, has one of the homiest atmospheres in the financial center. Activities range from poolside jerk buffets every Tuesday to Latin dance parties (complete with dance lessons) every Saturday. **Pros:** large rooms, lively nightlife, good business facilities. **Cons:** limited dining options, noisy location, most rooms lack balconies. ⊠85 Knutsford Blvd ☎876/929–9000 🖷876/926–7744 ⊕www.courtleigh.com ⌁88 rooms, 41 suites ♿In-room: safe, kitchens (some), refrigerator, Wi-Fi. In-hotel: 2 restaurants, bar, tennis courts, pools, gym, spa, laundry service, concierge, executive floor, public Internet, airport shuttle, parking (no fee), no-smoking rooms ⊟AE, D, DC, MC, V ⊺⊙⋀CP.

$$ ⊞**Terra Nova All-Suite Hotel.** Although it's in New Kingston, this graceful hotel, a former colonial mansion, is definitely Old Jamaica. You'll agree when you encounter the white-glove service in the dining room to the afternoon tea with freshly baked scones. Tucked in a quieter part of New Kingston, 1 mi (1½ km) from the commercial district, the hotel is within walking distance of the historic Devon House as well as designer boutiques and gourmet restaurants. Rooms are decked out with classic mahogany furniture and fresh flowers. Although the hotel claims to have only suites, the standard "suites" are closer in size to hotel rooms. Rates include a daily Jamaican buffet breakfast. **Pros:** elegant atmosphere, great outdoor dining, near shopping and dining. **Cons:** fills up quickly on weekends, small rooms, dated decor. ✉ *17 Waterloo Rd.* ☎*876/926–2211* 🖷*876/929–4933* ⊕*www.terranovajamaica.com* ⤳*43 suites* ⌂*In-room: safe, kitchen, refrigerator. Wi-Fi. In-hotel: 2 restaurants, bars, pool, gym, no elevator, laundry service, concierge, public Internet, public Wi-Fi, parking (no fee), no-smoking rooms* ☰*AE, D, DC, MC, V* ⦿*BP.*

$–$$ ⌷**Hilton Kingston.** With all the amenities you'd expect from a well-respected chain hotel, this property is a favorite with business travelers. The expansive marble lobby leads to attractive, well-appointed rooms. The concierge floors offer complimentary cocktails, hors d'oeuvres, and continental breakfast. Although the hotel offers wedding packages, don't get the idea this is a destination for lovers; like most of Kingston, this hotel is a place to relax between meetings. Kids under 18 stay free if they're in a room with parents. **Pros:** good variety of restaurants, central location, nightly entertainment. **Cons:** limited leisure activities, limited in-room amenities, no balconies. ✉ *77 Knutsford Blvd., Box 112* ☎*876/926–5430* 🖷*876/929–7439* ⊕*www. hiltoncaribbean.com* ⤳*290 rooms, 13 suites* ⌂*In-room: safe, kitchen (some), refrigerator, Ethernet, Wi-Fi, dial-up. In-hotel: 4 restaurants, room service, bars, pool, gym, spa, laundry service, concierge, executive floor, public Internet, public Wi-Fi, parking (no fee), no-smoking rooms* ☰*AE, D, DC, MC, V* ⦿*CP.*

$ ⌷**The Knutsford Court Hotel.** This hotel combines business services with the charm of a smaller property. Rooms are basic, most with white-tile floors and small bathrooms, but are enlivened with colorful walls or fabrics. The pool area and adjacent bar and restaurant are small but popular with the guests. **Pros:** good value, business amenities, friendly staff. **Cons:** drab decor, limited dining choices, small pool area. ✉ *16 Chelsea Ave.* ☎*876/929–1000* 🖷*876/960–7373* ⊕*www.knutsfordcourt.com* ⤳*143 rooms* ⌂*In-room: safe, kitchen (some), Ethernet. In-hotel: 2 restaurants, room service, bar, pool gym, laundry service, parking (no fee), no-smoking rooms* ☰*AE, D, DC, MC, V* ⦿*CP.*

BEACHES

Kingston's beaches can be packed, although rarely with tourists. The city, like much of the South Coast, doesn't boast the beautiful beaches of the north shore but instead has stretches of sand that serve as a gathering point for groups of families and friends, especially on the weekends. If you visit local beaches, be sure to talk with your concierge first, as crime is a problem on Kingston's beaches.

The best beach getaway in the Kingston area is at **Lime Cay,** a small island just off the peninsula leading out to Port Royal. You can reach the cay by boat from Morgan's Harbour Hotel. Once there, you can swim, snorkel, or picnic on the sandy beach. There are no real facilities here, so bring what you need for the day.

Southwest of the city are some of the best-known area beaches, including **Fort Clarence,** which offers changing facilities and live entertainment. About 32 mi (52 km) east of the city lies **Lyssons Beach,** another popular choice with Kingstonians.

SPORTS & THE OUTDOORS

BIRD-WATCHING

Some of Jamaica's best birding opportunities are found above Kingston in the misty Blue Mountains, especially in the **Blue and John Crow Mountains National Park.** You'll probably see the national bird, the streamer-tail hummingbird, a large hummingbird with a dramatic forked tail. Known locally as the "doctor bird," it's one of Jamaica's 28 endemic species. Other unique birds to watch for include the Jamaican woodpecker, Blue Mountain vireo, Rufous-tailed flycatcher, arrow-headed warbler, Jamaican stripe-headed tanager, and the yellow-shouldered grassquit. Another popular birding area is on **Lime Cay,** just offshore from Port Royal.

The Natural History Society of Jamaica (⊠*Department of Life Sciences, University of the West Indies Mona, Mona Rd.* ☎*876/977–6938*) organizes bird-watching trips into the Blue Mountains and nearby John Crow Mountains. Contact them directly for information on dates and prices.

Jiminy Cricket!

Jamaica played host to the World Cricket Cup in 2007, welcoming teams from around the world to newly built and newly renovated stadiums scattered across the island. Kingston's Sabina Park was one of the island's top venues for the competition. With a capacity of 20,000 fans, the stadium has been the scene for many dramatic matches over the years. The World Cricket Cup, however, brought a new level of excitement to the game.

Cricket has a long history in Jamaica, not surprising given the island's history as a British colony. The first matches were held in 1895, when locals played a series of matches against a touring English team. In those early days, it was a sport played only by society's elite, so players came mainly from the island's wealthy ruling families. Gradually, the sport became more egalitarian. Indeed, Jamaican cricket achieved its greatest success only after shedding much of its colonial trappings, selecting its players by talent rather than family influence.

At present, cricket is overshadowed only by soccer in its popularity among Jamaican fans. Former players, including George Headley, who wowed fans in the 1930s, are still remembered and revered by the Jamaican public.

Sun Venture Tours (✉ *30 Balmoral Ave., Kingston* ☎ *876/ 960–6685* ⊕ *www.sunventuretours.com*) specializes in ecotours.

DIVING & SNORKELING

With its murkier waters, the southern side of the island isn't as popular for diving. Near Morgan's Harbour Hotel and Marina, advanced divers can explore the wreck of the *Texas,* a World War II–era ship surrounded by cool coral formations. The ship's guns are easily recognizable. Another wreck in the area is the *Cayman Trader.* This merchant ship disabled by fire, the Trader was sunk intentionally to make a habitat for marine life. Another favorite spot is **Windward Edge,** beyond Kingston's small offshore cays. After a half-hour boat ride, divers are often able to spot large fish here.

Buccaneer Scuba Club (✉ *Morgan's Harbour Hotel and Marina, Queen St., Port Royal* ☎ *876/977–6938*) is home to Buccaneer divers. Here, scuba divers can have fun as they explore the Texas. Just offshore, the Edge offers great blue-water diving. Buccaneer Scuba Club offers dives for different skill levels, including trips to the wreck of the *Texas*. One-tank dives give you a chance to see many of the area's rare species, including manatees.

FISHING

The waters off Jamaica's southern coast are some of the richest fishing areas around. However, much of the fishing here is done by locals, rather than visitors. There are sport-fishing charters to be had from Port Royal and through local hotels such as Morgan's Harbour Hotel and Marina. Charters usually furnish bait and equipment, although typically not food and drinks. Most can be chartered for either half- or whole-day excursions. When chartering a fishing boat, be sure to discuss specifics with the captain before you set sail.

Buccaneer Scuba Club (✉*Morgan's Harbour Hotel and Marina, Queen St., Port Royal* ☎*876/977–6938*) charges $400 for half-day to $650 for full-day fishing trips. Evening drop-line fishing can also be arranged.

GOLF

Although golf isn't a major activity here, travelers will find two courses in the Kingston area. As in other parts of Jamaica, Kingston courses require that you hire the services of a caddy.

Caymanas Golf and Country Club (✉*Mandela Hwy., halfway between Kingston and Spanish Town* ☎*876/922–3388* ⊕*www.caymanasgolfclub.com*) is located about 8 mi (12 km) west of the city center. Jamaica's first major championship 18-hole course, Caymanas opened in 1957. Greens fees are $37 on weekdays, $45 on weekends.

Constant Spring Golf Club (✉*152 Constant Spring Rd.* ☎*876/924–1610*) dates back to 1920, when it was designed by Scotsman Stanley Thompson, mentor of Robert Trent Jones Sr. This short course, in one of Kingston's nicest downtown neighborhoods, charges $35 per round. Rentals are available. There's a clubhouse, restaurant, bar, and pro shop.

HORSE RACING

In Kingston, a trip to the track is a popular afternoon activity for many residents. Although the capital city has the island's only track, you'll see more than 60 off-track betting parlors scattered across the island.

Caymanas Park (✉*Caymanas Dr., Portmore* ☎*876/988–2523* ⊕*www.caymanasracetrack.com*) is a favorite with locals. Races are usually slated for Wednesday and Saturday afternoon. Admission to the air-conditioned lounge is $5 for adults. To enter the 3rd-floor lounges, don't show up wearing torn jeans, shorts, or sandals. Children are welcome.

MOUNTAIN BIKING

Although you should avoid Kingston, the placid Blue Mountains make a good outing for cyclists of all skill levels. The most popular outing is a downhill coast through Holywell National Park.

The Ocho Rios–based **Blue Mountain Bicycle Tours** (✉*121 Main St., Ocho Rios* ☎*876/974–7075* ⊕*www.bmtoursja.com*) takes travelers on guided rides in the spectacular Blue Mountains. The excursion, an all-day outing, starts high and glides downhill, so all levels of riders can enjoy the tour. The trip ends with a dip in a waterfall. Children age seven and up are welcome on the trip.

SHOPPING

Unlike the communities on the island's North Coast, Kingston isn't known for its duty-free stores. Shopping here is mostly limited to shops for residents. The city's Constant Spring Road and King Street are home to a growing roster of shopping malls offering fashions, housewares, and more.

The **Shops at Devon House** (✉*26 Hope Rd.* ☎*876/929–6602*) is a cluster of mostly upscale shops selling clothing, crafts, and other items. The location, at the historic Devon House, makes this a pleasant spot to spend a morning or afternoon. Prices are high, but bargains can be found.

MARKETS

Kingston Crafts Market (✉*Harbour St. and Ocean Blvd.* ☎*876/922–3015*) has a large assortment of Jamaican handicrafts. Paintings, sculptures, and inexpensive jewelry can be found in the stalls. Although pickpockets have been a problem in the past, it's much safer now. Some bargaining is tolerated, but don't expect many concessions.

Blue Mountain Coffee

CLOSE UP

Along the misty slopes of the Blue Mountains grow some of Jamaica's most valuable plants, flourishing in a perfect microclimate of altitude, temperature, rainfall, and soil type. It's not what you think, it's coffee—Blue Mountain coffee, to be exact. This Jamaican specialty is known throughout the world for its rich aroma and flavor.

Since 1973, the Jamaican government mandated that only coffee produced from Arabica beans grown in fields above 2,000 feet can be labeled Blue Mountain coffee. The coffee is graded by altitude, divided into lowland and high-mountain types, a distinction you'll find on every label. Most Blue Mountain coffee is exported and commands a high price. This is especially true in Japan, where the beans often sell for more than $60 per pound. On the island you'll find it for sale in many gift shops, but for the best prices, visit a local supermarket.

SPECIALTY ITEMS

The **Coffee Mill of Jamaica** (⊠*9 Barbados Ave.* ☎*876/929-2227*) sells Jamaica's famous Blue Mountain coffee. Enjoy a cup while shopping for herbs, spices, jellies, jams, teas, and condiments.

Starfish Essentials (⊠*26 Hope Rd.* ☎*876/926-1961* ⊕*www. starfishoils.com*) specializes in aromatherapy products such as fragrant oils. Some the most popular scents include cinnamon leaf, which aids digestion and bronchitis and is said to be an aphrodisiac. Another fragrance, tea tree, is said to combat dandruff, fungal infections, and age spots.

Things Jamaican (⊠*26 Hope Rd.* ☎*876/926-0815*) is a government-sponsored shop selling products made by Jamaican artisans. These items are usually of higher quality (and higher prices) than handicrafts sold in the street markets.

A recording studio, **Tuff Gong Studios** (⊠*220 Marcus Garvey Dr.* ☎*876/923-9380*) is also a retail music shop featuring Caribbean tunes, T-shirts, and memorabilia of the reggae scene.

NIGHTLIFE & THE ARTS

As the cultural hub of Jamaica, Kingston has the island's largest selection of nightlife options. Unlike the more tourist-oriented resort communities, nightlife here is aimed at locals, and varies from live music to discos. Because of Kingston's high crime rate, you should consult with your concierge before heading for the night's activities.

ANNUAL EVENTS

It's often said that Kingston is the heartbeat of Jamaica, and at no time does that heart beat any louder than during the annual **Carnival** (⊠*Liguanea Park, 89 King St.* ☎*No phone* ⊕*www.bacchanaljamaica.com*), held here in April. Parades for both children and adults fill the streets.

THE ARTS

Built in 1912, the **Ward Theatre** (⊠*North Parade, between King St. and Love La.,* ☎*876/922–0453*) was launched with the production of Gilbert and Sullivan's *Pirates of Penzance.* Over the years, the Ward Theatre has become one of Kingston's most cherished icons. Known not only for its prominent role in the city's cultural life, it has also hosted many important political events. Named a national monument in 2000, it continues to host year-around events ranging from classical concerts to theater.

NIGHTLIFE

Friday nights in Kingston bring on the Friday Night Jam, an impromptu street party that begins when office doors close and entrepreneurial chefs roll out oil drums transformed into jerk pits. Street corners sizzle with spicy fare, music blares, and the city launches into weekend mode.

Pick up a copy of the *Daily Gleaner,* the *Jamaica Observer,* or the *Star* (available at newsstands throughout the island) for listings on who's playing when and where.

At the Hilton Kingston, **Junkanoo Nightclub** (⊠*77 Knutsford Blvd.* ☎*876/926–5430*) shakes with the sounds of everything from reggae to rock Wednesday through Sunday night.

Peppers (⊠*31 Upper Waterloo Rd.* ☎*876/969–2421*) is a favorite with locals who start the evening with a plate of spicy jerk before working off that meal on the dance floor. The open-air restaurant and nightclub features many theme nights.

Redbones Café & Bar (⊠*21 Braemar Ave.* ☎*876/978–8262*) calls itself "the only juke joint in Jamaica." Although there might be plenty of other musical action in town, Redbones is well known for its live jazz as well as world music performances every Thursday night. Some events carry a cover charge ranging from $4 to $6.

KINGSTON ESSENTIALS

To research prices, get advice from other travelers, and book travel arrangements, visit www.fodors.com.

TRANSPORTATION

BY AIR

Jamaica is well served by major airlines. From the United States, Air Jamaica, American, Continental, Northwest, Spirit, and US Airways offer nonstop and connecting service. Air Canada offers service from major airports in Canada. Air Jamaica, Virgin Atlantic and British Airways offer service from the United Kingdom. Copa has flights between Miami and Kingston. Cayman Airways connects Jamaica to Grand Cayman and Cayman Brac.

Information **Air Canada** (☎*876/942-8211 in Kingston*). **Air Jamaica** (☎*888/359-2475 in Jamaica, 800/523-5585 in U.S.*). **AmericanAirlines** (☎*800/744-0006 in Jamaica*). **British Airways** (☎*876/929-9020 in Kingston*). **Caribbean Airlines** (☎*876/924-8364 or 800/744-2225*). **Delta** (☎*800/221-1212*). **Spirit Airlines** (☎*586/791-7300 or 800/772-7117*).

AIR TRAVEL AROUND JAMAICA

Domestic flights are available from Kingston's Tinson Pen Aerodome to Montego Bay, Negril, Runaway Bay, Ocho Rios, and, on a limited basis, Port Antonio. Except for International Airlink's flights to Montego Bay, most flights are operated on a charter basis.

Information **International Airlink** (☎*888/247-5465* ⊕*www.intlairlink.com*). **TimAir** (☎*876/952-2516* ⊕*www.timair.com*).

AIRPORTS & TRANSFERS

Jamaica's second-busiest airport is Kingston's Norman Manley International Airport, about 20 minutes from the city on the Palisadoes Peninsula. From the airport, the best way into the city is by taxi; a few hotels provide hotel transfers, although most do not. The Jamaica Union of

Travellers Association (JUTA) is the authorized taxi company at the Norman Manley International Airport; you'll find its desk just outside the Customs Hall in the Ground Transportation Hall.

Domestic charter flights within Jamaica depart from the Tinson Pen Aerodrome, the largest of the island's aerodromes.

Information **Norman Manley International Airport** (⊠*Palisadoes Peninsula, Kingston* ☎*876/924-8452* ⊕*www.manley-airport. com.jm*). **Tinson Pen Aerodrome** (⊠*Marcus Garvey Dr., Kingston* ☎*876/923-0022*).

BY CAR

Renting a car in Kingston is not recommended because of the city's high crime rate and its tremendous traffic problem. It's all too easy to find yourself in one of the neighborhoods that even taxi drivers refuse to visit. The best option for getting around town is to hire a licensed taxi driver.

BY TAXI

Some, but not all, of Jamaica's taxis are metered. If you accept a driver's offer to serve as a tour guide, be sure to agree on a price before the vehicle is put into gear. (Note that a one-day tour should run about $150 to $180, depending on distance traveled.)

All licensed taxis display red Public Passenger license plates. In Kingston, it's preferable to have a hotel call for a taxi rather than hailing one on the street. Rates are per car, not per passenger, and a 25% surcharge is added to the metered rate between midnight and 5 AM. Licensed minivans are also available and also bear the red PP plates. The Jamaica Union for Travellers Association (JUTA) is licensed by the Jamaica Tourist Board.

Information **JUTA** (☎*876/927-4534* ⊕*www.jutakingston.com*).

CONTACTS & RESOURCES

BANKS & EXCHANGE SERVICES

Currency exchange is available at Norman Manley International Airport, in larger hotels, and in local banks. However, few Americans bother to exchange money, since American dollars are widely accepted. Major credit cards are widely accepted, although cash is required at gas stations, in supermarkets, and in many small stores.

The official currency is the Jamaican dollar. At this writing the exchange rate was about J$68 to US$1. Prices quoted throughout this chapter are in U.S. dollars, unless otherwise noted.

Banks are generally open Monday through Thursday from 9 to 2, Friday 9 to 4. Post-office hours are weekdays from 9 to 5. Normal business hours for stores are weekdays from 8:30 to 4:30, Saturday 8 to 1.

Information **Bank of Nova Scotia Jamaica Limited** (⊠ *Port Royal St.*). **National Commercial Bank** (⊠ *32 Trafalgar Rd.*).

EMERGENCIES

Emergency Services **Ambulance & Fire Emergencies** (☎ *110*). **Police Emergencies & Air Rescue** (☎ *119*).

Hospitals **University Hospital of the West Indies** (⊠ *Aqueduct Rd. at Papine Rd., Kingston* ☎ *876/927–1620*).

Pharmacies **Jamaica Pegasus** (⊠ *81 Knutsford Blvd., Kingston* ☎ *876/926–3690*).

INTERNET, MAIL & SHIPPING

Internet service is becoming far more widespread, and most hotels offer at least limited service, either at public terminals or Wi-Fi. Most Internet cafés charge between $5 and $7.50 per hour.

Postcards may be mailed anywhere in the world for J$50. Letters cost J$60 to the United States and Canada, J$70 to Europe, J$90 to Australia and New Zealand. Due to costly and slow air-shipping service, most travelers carry home packages, even large wood carvings whenever possible.

A number of shipping companies, both international and domestic, operate within the Kingston area. Call around for the best rates and to confirm pickup options.

Internet Cafés **Cybervillage** (⊠ *Arawak Plaza, Half Way Tree Rd., Kingston* ☎ *876/920–5525*). **Kingston Bookshop** (⊠ *17 Constant Spring Rd., Kingston* ☎ *876/920–1529*). **Liguanea Cybercentre** (⊠ *89½ Half Way Tree Rd., Kingston* ☎ *876/968–0323*). **Logic Internet Café** (⊠ *32 Hagley Park Rd., Kingston* ☎ *876/920–3791*).

Post Offices **General Post Office** (⊠ *13 King St., Kingston* ☎ *876/922–2120*).

Shipping Companies **Airpac Express** (⊠ *Miel Plaza, 1 Molynes Rd., Kingston* ☎ *976/754–5298*). **DHL Jamaica** (⊠ *19 Haining Rd., Kingston* ☎ *976/920–0010*). **E-Biz Centre** (⊠ *14 Worthington Terrace,*

Kingston ☎*976/968–3251).* **FastPac Courier Service** (✉*70 Molynes Rd., Kingston* ☎*976/923–6992).* **Federal Express** (✉*75 Knutsford Blvd., Kingston* ☎*976/463–3339).* **Reliant Courier Services** (✉*56 Dumbarton Ave., Kingston* ☎*976/968–3518).*

TOUR OPTIONS

Numerous operators offer tours of the Kingston area, as well as excursions into the Blue Mountains. Professional tour operators provide a valuable service, as neither destination is particularly suited to exploration without a guide. In Kingston, certain areas can be dangerous; an organized tour provides a measure of security compared with going it alone. Think twice before roaming too freely in the Blue Mountains, as roads are narrow or in poor condition, and signs are few and far between.

Typical city tours include a city overview with stops at Devon House, the Bob Marley Museum, and Port Royal. Other tour options cover the Blue Mountains. Niche operators such as Olde Jamaica Heritage Tours provide theme tours, including a churches and museums tour.

Information **Caribisle Tours** (✉*80-C Spring Rd., Kingston* ☎*876/755–4108* ⊕*www.caribisletours.com).* **Jam Venture Tours and Services** (✉*Northside Plaza, Suite 3A, Haughton Ave., Kingston* ☎*876/702–2286).* **Olde Jamaica Heritage Tours** (✉*5 Cowper Dr., Kingston* ☎*876/371–3613 or 876/328–1385* ⊕*www.olde jamaicatours.com).* **Sun Island Tours** (✉*3 Healthshire Ave., Kingston* ☎*876/901–8826).* **Sun Venture Tours** (✉*30 Balmoral Ave., Kingston* ☎*876/960–6685* ⊕*www.sunventuretours.com).* **Tourmarks** (✉*7 Leighton Rd., Kingston* ☎*876/929–5078* ⊕*www.tourmarks.com).*

VISITOR INFORMATION

The Jamaica Tourist Board maintains two offices in Kingston, one in New Kingston, the other in Manley International Airport. Both are good sources for information on Kingston and Blue Mountains. They have maps and brochures, and can give recommendations for touring in the area.

Information **Jamaica Tourist Board** (✉*64 Knutsford Blvd., Kingston* ☎*876/929–9200* ⊕*www.visitjamaica.com).*

The South Coast

WORD OF MOUTH

"Go dolphin-watching in the waters from Treasure Beach to Parrottee Point, off which you'll find Pelican Bar, indeed 'the coolest bar' around."

—tivertonhouse

"We just loved Treasure Beach—how the tourism in the area took a backseat to the rest of the community, and how there seemed to be plenty of opportunities to interact with locals."

—ejcrowe

By Paris
Permenter
and John
Bigley

DURING THE 1970S, NEGRIL WAS Jamaica's most relaxed place to hang out. Now that Negril and the western end of the island have been discovered by developers, that distinction is now held by the South Coast. Many people who have visited for years consider the South Coast's Treasure Beach to be comparable to Negril Beach before the recent building boom changed it forever. Is the South Coast destined to follow Negril's pattern, trading its laid-back appeal for mass-market tourism? Only time will tell, but it's clear that change will come slowly to this region, traditionally one of island's least developed. Local business owners are keenly aware that much of the area's appeal lies in its remote feel and its lack of development.

The economy of the region is relatively diversified, with fishing and agriculture still important. You'll see small backyard gardens with clusters of banana trees and hillocks of beans and corn, as well as large commercially-grown fields of citrus fruit, papayas, melons, coconuts, corn, and sugarcane, which was once the island's prime moneymaker. Some valley fields will be filled to the horizon by banana trees, some wearing their "blue dresses," plastic bags placed over the maturing fruit to protect them from insects. (It's a concession to North American consumers, who insist on blemish-free produce.)

Industry also plays a big role in the local economy, especially the mining and refining of bauxite, or aluminum ore. Since the 1940s, when the metal was first discovered here, Jamaica's South Coast has become one of the world's largest producers. The Alcan Jamaica plant, known locally as the Kirkvine Works, has operated outside the city of Mandeville since the 1950s and has become one of the city's largest employers. Another plant that processes aluminum ore is in the small town of Nain in St. Elizabeth Parish.

All of which means that at least for now, the South Coast, with fishing villages dotting its pristine shoreline and small agricultural towns sprinkled around the interior, is a place to experience the day-to-day life of Jamaica. It's a friendly area where locals playing dominoes under the trees wave to passing cars. Small hotels (only one all-inclusive resort has entered the market here) cater to travelers seeking a peaceful place to unwind while exploring local communities and spending quiet evenings in local restaurants.

SOUTH COAST TOP 5

Getting Four for One:
Spread your towel out on
Treasure Beach, a series of
four pristine stretches of sand.

Meeting and Greeting: This
is one part of Jamaica where
you'll want to mingle with the
friendly welcoming locals.

Smiling at a Crocodile:
Take a boat trip on the Black
River, home to these amazing
creatures.

Sampling the Local Vintage:
This is Jamaica, so of course
we mean rum, and the best
place is at the Appleton
Estate.

Snapping Photos: There are
plenty of photo ops in this
region, including the canopy
of vegetation at Bamboo Avenue, between Middle Quarters
and Lacovia.

EXPLORING THE SOUTH COAST

Jamaica's South Coast spans the parishes of St. Elizabeth
and Manchester and the eastern portion of Westmoreland.
The terrain includes pockets of rich farmland, dry savannah, and several mountain ranges. The coastline is sparsely
populated, compared to the North Coast, with small fishing
villages scattered along Route A2, the coastal highway.

Another distinction of the South Coast is its ethnic diver-
sity, with descendents of German and Scottish settlers mix-
ing with those of Miskito Indians from Central America,
brought here during colonial days to help subdue the native
Maroon population. Until modern times, the South Coast
remained relatively isolated from the rest of the country,
contributing to the area's uniquely relaxed atmosphere.

The two major population centers in the region are
Mandeville, in the Don Figuerero Mountain Range, and
the coastal community of Black River. The latter is at the
mouth of the Black River, Jamaica's longest, which drains
one of Jamaica's most interesting natural environments, the
Black River Great Morass, with its resident crocodiles pad-
dling through mangrove thickets.

ABOUT THE RESTAURANTS

Dining on the South Coast is a casual affair, often enjoyed
on an outdoor terrace or beside the beach. With far less
hassling at than other parts of the island, visitors here enjoy
dining in small establishments ranging from neighborhood

hangouts to roadside eateries, all at prices far lower than found in the major resort areas.

With many mom-and-pop eateries in this area, ingredients are always fresh and usually local—sometimes right out of the backyard. Alligator Pond and Treasure Beach are both home to fishing communities offering the freshest catch of the day, whereas the area north of Whitehouse is considered Jamaica's breadbasket, filled with farms growing the fruits and vegetables that make their way to tables across the island.

ABOUT THE HOTELS

Until a few years ago, the South Coast was exclusively the home of a few small hotels and guesthouses, but then Sandals Whitehouse became the first all-inclusive resort in the south. Nonetheless, the South Coast is still known for its small, family-owned properties and laid-back charm, with prices generally lower than those found on the North Coast.

WHAT IT COSTS IN DOLLARS				
$$$$	$$$	$$	$	¢
RESTAURANTS				
Over $30	$20–$30	$12–$20	$8–$12	under $8
HOTELS*				
Over $350	$250–$350	$150–$250	$80–$150	under $80
HOTELS**				
Over $450	$350–$450	$250–$350	$125–$250	under $125

*EP, BP, CP; **AI, FAP, MAP; Restaurant prices are per person for a main course at dinner and do not include the 15% V.A.T. and 10% service charge. Hotel prices are per night for a double room in high season, excluding 15% V.A.T. and 10% service charge.

TIMING

The quiet South Coast doesn't have the spring-break crowds of Negril; this getaway is devoid of crowds whenever you choose to visit. As Jamaica's driest area, it's a good alternative from May to October, when the North Coast can be at its rainiest. Nevertheless, the South Coast, like the rest of Jamaica (and the whole Caribbean region) is vulnerable to adverse conditions during hurricane season, which runs from June to November.

SOUTH COAST ATTRACTIONS

Visitors to Jamaica's South Coast will normally fly into Montego Bay's Sangster International Airport, then drive overland, whether by rental car, taxi, or bus through Jamaica's interior. If the nearly two-hour hour drive is done during daylight hours, you can see much of Jamaica's "breadbasket," the agricultural region where much of the nation's foodstuffs are grown.

Numbers in the margin correspond to points of interest on the South Coast map.

WHAT TO SEE

5 ★ Fodor'sChoice **Appleton Estate.** Before the rise of tourism as Jamaica's main industry, the island was highly prized for its sugarcane production. Vast fortunes were made here during colonial times, and many of the island's historic greathouses remain as reminders of that time. Much of the sugarcane was processed into molasses, the main ingredient in the production of rum. At Appleton Estates, still one of the Caribbean's premier rum distillers, offers guided tours illustrating the history of rum making in the region. After a lively discussion of the days when sugarcane was crushed by donkey power, the tours move on to a behind-the-scenes tour of the modern facility. After the tour, samples flow freely, and every visitor receives a complimentary bottle of rum. There's a good restaurant here serving genuine Jamaican dishes. ⊠*Rte. B6, Siloah* ☎*876/963–9215* ⊕*www. appletonrum.com* ⌨*$12* ⊙*Mon.–Sat. 9–4.*

2 **High Mountain Coffee Factory.** Grown on nearby plantations, coffee beans are brought here for processing. Call ahead for tours, or just stop by the gift shop for a sample taste. In addition to coffee, the gift shop features other High Mountain products like spices, condiments, and scented candles. ⊠*Winston Jones Hwy., Williamsfield* ☎*876/963–4211* ⌨*Free* ⊙*Weekdays 10–4.*

DID YOU KNOW? **There's a lot of discussion in Jamaica about the origin of the name Y.S., the shortest place name on the island. Some believe it comes from the Gaelic word "wyess" (winding or twisting). Others say the name comes from a combination of the initials of the land's 1684 owners: John Yates and Lt. Col. Richard Scott.**

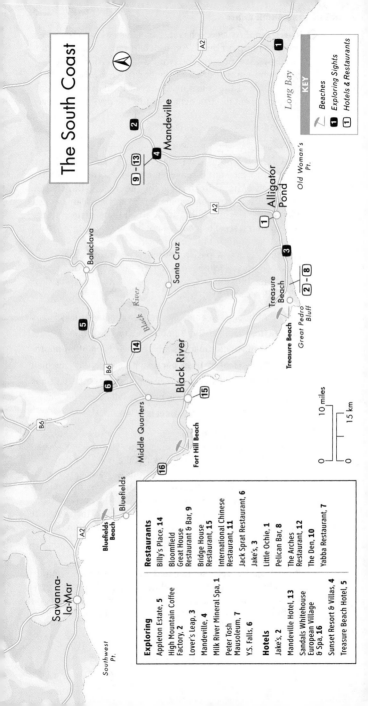

The South Coast

KEY

🏖️ Beaches
⬛ Exploring Sights
① Hotels & Restaurants

Exploring

Appleton Estate, **5**
High Mountain Coffee Factory, **2**
Lover's Leap, **3**
Mandeville, **4**
Milk River Mineral Spa, **1**
Peter Tosh Mausoleum, **7**
Y.S. Falls, **6**

Hotels

Jake's, **2**
Mandeville Hotel, **13**
Sandals Whitehouse European Village & Spa, **16**
Sunset Resort & Villas, **4**
Treasure Beach Hotel, **5**

Restaurants

Billy's Place, **14**
Bloomfield Great House Restaurant & Bar, **9**
Bridge House Restaurant, **15**
International Chinese Restaurant, **11**
Jack Sprat Restaurant, **6**
Jake's, **3**
Little Ochie, **1**
Pelican Bar, **8**
The Arches Restaurant, **12**
The Den, **10**
Yabba Restaurant, **7**

❸ **Lovers' Leap.** As legend has it, two slaves who were in love chose to jump off this 1,700-foot cliff rather than be recaptured by their master. Today it's a favorite stop with travelers, who enjoy a drink at the bar (try the lover's punch) and a view of the coastline. Tours of local cacti are available, and a small farm demonstrates the dry-farming technique used in this area. ⊠ Yardley Chase, Treasure Beach ☎ 876/965–6634 ☜ Free ☉Daily

❹ **Mandeville.** At 2,000-feet above sea level, Mandeville is considerably cooler than the coastal areas about 25 mi (40 km) to the south. Its vegetation is also lusher, thanks to the mists that drift through the mountains. But climate and flora aren't all that separate it from the steamy coast: Mandeville seems a hilly tribute to all that's genteel in the British character. The people here live in tidy cottages with gardens around a village green; there's even a Georgian courthouse and a parish church. The entire scene could be set down in Devonshire, were it not for the occasional poinciana blossom or citrus grove. ⊠*Rte. A2, between Black River and May Pen.*

EN ROUTE. **Although the constant roar of speeding trucks keeps the site from being idyllic, Bamboo Avenue, a section of Route A1 between Middle Quarters and Lacovia, is an often-photographed stretch of highway because it's completely canopied with tall bamboo. Here you can see innumerable COLD JELLY signs attached to small carts. These promise jelly coconuts, young coconuts that yield a clear, sweet jelly.**

❶ **Milk River Mineral Spa.** You can soak in natural springwater whose high levels of radioactivity are said to soothe aches and pains. The radioactivity here is higher than any other spa in the world—54 times more radioactive than the waters of Baden-Baden. The waters, which remain a constant temperature of 92°F, are enjoyed in a private bath, usually for a 15-minute dip. From Route B12, turn south at the small town of Rest and continue for about 3 mi (5 km). ⊠*Milk River at Clarendon* ☎876/902–4657 ☜*$4* ☉*Daily 7 AM–9 PM.*

❼ **Peter Tosh Mausoleum.** Located in the small community of Belmont, this simple white-concrete building contains the grave of reggae great Peter Tosh, (nee Winston Hubert McIntosh), who was murdered in Jamaica in 1987.

The Black River Great Morass

One of Jamaica's most unique environments, the Black River Great Morass, near the town of Black River, covers 80,000 acres of water, marsh, and low hammocks of land. Drained by the Black River, it's named for its water, which is stained dark by natural dyes released by rotting vegetation. Largely impenetrable except by boat, the Morass's ecosystem supports a wide assortment of Jamaica's flora and fauna.

While touring upriver on one of several tours offered in the town of Black River, you have the chance to spot some of the area's wildlife such as the American Crocodile as well as a wealth of birdlife including herons, ducks, and egrets. It's also common to pass small dugout canoes tied to overhanging mangrove branches while their inhabitants spearfish in the tea-color waters of the river, apparently unconcerned by sharing the river with crocodiles.

Venturing deeper into the Morass, you see other examples of Jamaica's plant life such as ackee trees, palms, and the logwood tree, a species whose dense, heavy wood was a valuable source of blue dye. The town of Black River was once an important port to export logwood, which was floated down the Black River on rafts made of more buoyant wood.

Together with Bob Marley and Bunny Wailer, Tosh formed the seminal reggae group the Wailers in 1967. In stark contrast to Jamaican memorials to Marley found in Kingston and Nine Mile, Tosh's burial place is quiet and uncrowded. ⊠Rte. A2, Belmont ☎No phone ⊕www.ptosh.com/mausoleum.html Donation suggested ⊙Daily 9–5

★ ❻ **Y.S. Falls.** This waterfall is a quiet alternative to Dunn's River Falls in Ocho Rios. Most often seen as a half-day trip from Negril, these spectacular falls are tucked away in a papaya plantation and reached via motorized jitney. Be sure to bring along your bathing suit for a dip in the pristine waters. ⊠Rte. A2, Middle Quarters ☎876/634–2454 ⊕www.ysfalls.com ☎$12 ⊙Tues.–Sun. 9:30–4.

WHERE TO EAT

TREASURE BEACH

CARIBBEAN

$–$$$ ✕**Jack Sprat.** It's no surprise that this restaurant, the beachside dining spot at Jake's, shares that resort's bohemian style. From the casual outdoor tables to the late-night dancehall rhythm, it's a place to come and hang loose. Jerk crab joins favorites like pizzas on the menu, all followed by Kingston's Devon House ice cream. (Try the coconut—you'll thank us.) ✉*Jake's, Calabash Bay, Treasure Beach* ☎*876/965–3583* ▭*AE, MC, V.*

$–$$$ ✕**Jake's.** The main restaurant at Jake's (there's also Jack Sprat, on the beach) offers an authentic local menu served outdoors in a casual seaside atmosphere. Dishes such as saltfish and ackee as well as escovitch fish join the fresh catch of the day prepared as you like. ✉*Calabash Bay, Treasure Beach* ☎*876/965–3583* ▭*AE, D, MC, V.*

$–$$ ✕**Pelican Bar.** One of the funkiest places in Jamaica to down a cold Red Stripe, this whimsical structure sits on stilts ½-mi (3/4-km) offshore from Treasure Beach, atop a small sandbar. It has become a local legend and a mandatory stop for bohemian visitors to the South Coast. The place serves fresh seafood for lunch and dinner, and will also cook your own catch for you. The hotels of Treasure Beach can arrange boat transportation to Pelican Bar, but these short rides can be pricey. ✉*Treasure Beach* ☎*No phone* ▭*No credit cards.*

JAMAICAN

$–$$$ ✕**Yabba.** Jamaican specialties—including plenty of fresh
★ seafood, jerk chicken, and lamb dishes—are on the menu at this poolside eatery. Many dishes are made with citrus and vegetables grown on the property at the Treasure Beach Hotel. ✉*Treasure Beach* ☎*876/965–4449* ▭*AE, MC, V.*

¢–$$ ✕**Little Ochie.** This casual beachside eatery is a favorite with
★ locals and travelers, favored for its genuine Jamaican dishes like fish tea, escoveitch fish, peppered shrimp, jerk chicken, and seapuss (octopus to the rest of us). Most of the seafood is brought in by fishermen who dock just yards away. For Treasure Beach guests, a favorite way to reach Little Ochie is by boat. ✉*About 7 mi (12 km) south of Rte. A2, Alligator Pond* ☎*876/965–4449* ⊕*www.littleochie.com* ▭*AE, MC, V.*

★ ¢ ✕**Billy's Place.** A true side-of-the-road stop on the South Coast Highway, Billy's Place serves fiery Jamaican food, including scorching peppered shrimp caught in the water just behind the kitchen. Dining's mostly a grab-and-go affair, although stands next door provide local desserts like fresh jelly coconut to cool the burn. ⊠*A2, about 30 mins east of Whitehouse, Middlequarters* ☏*876/366–4182* ⊟*No credit cards.*

BLACK RIVER

JAMAICAN

★ ¢–$ ✕**Bridge House.** A no-nonsense eatery, this is a popular spot with locals who come here for down-home meals of curried goat or chicken with trusty side dishes like rice and peas. It's also handy for tourists in town for the nearby Black River Safari tour. If you want to have a truly authentic Jamaican meal, skip the cola and ask for a glass of red punch. ⊠*14 Crane Rd., Black River* ☏*876/3965–2361* ⊟*MC, V.*

MANDEVILLE

CHINESE

$–$$$ ✕**International Chinese Restaurant.** If you're looking for an alternative to jerk, this unassuming place offers Chinese comfort food in a casual setting. You can find many of your traditional Asian favorites like cashew chicken and sweet and sour pork. Other specialties include seafood and egg rolls. ⊠*117 Manchester Rd., Mandeville* ☏*876/962–1252* ⌂*Reservations recommended* ⊟*MC, V.*

JAMAICAN

$$–$$$ ✕**Bloomfield Great House Restaurant & Bar.** International fare with a Caribbean twist is the order of the day at Mandeville's most lauded restaurant. It's in a plantation greathouse dating back more than two centuries. Dining in the antiques-filled main dining room is pleasant, but the open-air verandah offers a spectacular view of the twinkling lights of Mandeville. Entrées include filet mignon with a roasted garlic and guava sauce; seafood kebabs, shrimp Creole, and grilled pork chops stuffed with tropical fruits. ⊠*8 Perth Rd., Mandeville* ☏*876/962–7130* ⊟*AE, MC, V.*

$–$$$ ✕**The Arches.** Located poolside at the Mandeville Hotel, this eatery specializes in Jamaican favorites. Wednesday evenings, the chef prepares a barbecue feast including a variety of meat and fish dishes. The Sunday breakfast is a Mandeville tradition, serving a lavish buffet of local favorites such as ackee and saltfish, mackerel rundown, escoveitch fish, fried plantains, callaloo, bammy, dumplings, and boiled

CLOSE UP

A Helping Hand

Jason Henzell—coowner of Jake's, president of Island Outpost, and son of the legendary movie producer Perry Henzell (The Harder They Come)—is involved in a South Coast community program called **Breds** (⊕ www.breds.org). Launched by Henzell and Peace Corps volunteer Aaron Laufer in 1998, Breds (short for Brethren, a term used by local residents to greet each other) is a nonprofit association that promotes education, cultural heritage, and environmental awareness.

The organization has coordinated the construction of homes in the Treasure Beach community, brought in doctors to train local first responders, arranged for donations of fishing boats to needy families, and helped to expand the resources of a local elementary school.

Breds raises money through donations and fund-raisers. The largest moneymaker for the program is the annual Treasure Beach Off-Road Triathlon.

green bananas. ⊠ *4 Hotel St., Mandeville* ☎ *876/962–9764* ▤ *MC, V.*

¢–$ ✕ **The Den.** Dine on favorite local dishes in the dining room or outside in the garden at this Mandeville institution. Though the menu presents a range of sophisticated choices from steak kebab to chicken curry, the kitchen also makes some of the best jerk west of Boston Beach. ⊠ *35 Caledonia Rd., Mandeville* ☎ *876/962–3603* ⌂ *Reservations essential* ▤ *AE, MC, V* ⊗ *Closed Sun.*

WHERE TO STAY

$$$$ ★ Fodor'sChoice ⊞ **Sandals Whitehouse European Village & Spa.** The first all-inclusive resort on the South Coast, this property is one of the most upscale properties in the Sandals chain. The resort consists of several "villages" with Italian, Dutch, and French architectural flourishes; the theme is carried out in the resort's many restaurants as well. Guest rooms are all within an easy walk of the beach and cover a wide range of room categories including some with personal butler service. The resort is great for nature lovers—it's surrounded by a 500-acre nature preserve and lies on a 2-mi-long (3-km-long) beach. **Pros:** great beach, numerous dining options, stylish accommodations. **Cons:** kitschy version of European architecture, location can be hot

and buggy, no transportation to other Sandals properties. ⊠*Off Rte. A2, Whitehouse* ☎*876/957–5216* 🖷*876/957–5338* ⊕*www.sandals.com* ⚭*304 rooms, 54 suites* △*In-room: safe, refrigerator. In-hotel: 7 restaurants, bars, tennis courts, pools, gym, spa, beachfront, diving, water sports, concierge, airport shuttle, no kids under 18* ⚏*2-night minimum* ▭*AE, MC, V* ⏀*AI.*

$–$$$$ ⌦**Jake's.** The laid-back vibe of the South Coast is epitomized by Jake's, a place that's fun, funky, and friendly. Coowner Jason Henzell, now president of Island Outpost, is active in community development and encourages his guests to get out and mingle with the residents, whether that means fishing with a local captain or hitting a rum shop. Each villa here (designed by Jason's mother, a theatrical designer) is unique, but some are not especially roomy. **Pros:** unique accommodations, South Coast friendliness, personalized service. **Cons:** rooms can be cramped, few amenities, remote location. ⊠*Calabash Bay, Treasure Beach* ☎*876/965–3000* 🖷*876/965–0552* ⊕*www.jakeshotel.com* ⚭*8 rooms, 9 cottages, 2 villas* △*In-room: no a/c (some), no phone, safe, kitchen (some), refrigerator (some), no TV. In-hotel: 2 restaurants, pool, beachfront, water sports, bicycles, no elevator, public Wi-Fi, parking (no fee)* ▭*AE, D, MC, V* ⏀*EP.*

$–$$$ ⌦**Sunset Resort & Villas.** Next door to Jake's, this resort lacks the style of its attention-getting neighbor, but it still offers a friendly getaway that's lovingly overseen by its owners. Rooms are individually decorated and generously proportioned, although some of the decor is a bit too fussy. The owners are happy to advise guests about local activities. The open-air restaurant serves beside a large, Astroturf-covered pool area. **Pros:** friendly staff, large rooms, nice views of Calabash Bay. **Cons:** dated decor, remote location, pool area needs refurbishing. ⊠*Calabash Bay, Treasure Beach* ☎*876/965–0143* 🖷*876/965–0555* ⊕*www.sunsetresort.com* ⚭*14 rooms* △*In-room: no phone, refrigerator. In-hotel: restaurant, pool, beachfront, no elevator* ▭*AE, D, MC, V* ⏀*EP.*

$–$$ ⌦**Treasure Beach Hotel.** White-tile floors, rattan furniture, and four-poster beds add some romance to these sizeable yet modest rooms. Much of the activity at Treasure Beach centers around a large pool surrounded by tall coconut palms (there's a second, less appealing, pool in the rear) but the beach itself calls to guests who just want to chill out for a few hours. **Pros:** great beachfront location, friendly staff, nice pool area. **Cons:** limited dining options,

5

limited nightlife options, remote location. ✉*Treasure Beach* ☎*876/965–0110* 🖷*876/965–2544* ⊕*www.treasurebeachjamaica.com* ⇌*36 rooms* ⇔*In-room: safe (some), refrigerator (some), DVD, VCR. In-hotel: restaurant, room service, bar, pools, beachfront, bicycles, no elevator, laundry service, public Internet, public Wi-Fi, airport shuttle, parking (no fee), no kids under 12, no-smoking rooms* ⊟*AE, D, MC, V* �|◎|*EP.*

DID YOU KNOW? A fruit was developed in Mandeville: the ortanique. The combination orange and tangerine is unique to the island, hence the name.

$ 📺**Mandeville Hotel.** This historic building, used as officers' quarters before becoming a hotel in 1875, has a homey atmosphere. Family-owned and -operated, it has a friendly feel. Tropical gardens wrap around the main building, and flowers spill onto the terrace restaurant, where breakfast and lunch are served. Rooms are simple and breeze-cooled; suites have full kitchens. You'll need a car to get around town, go out for dinner, and get to the beach, which is an hour away. **Pros:** quaint colonial style, great views of surrounding hills, staff helps setting up tours. **Cons:** limited nightlife, some rooms are stuffy during summer months, dated decor. ✉*4 Hotel St., Mandeville* ☎*876/962–2460* 🖷*876/962–0700* ⊕*www.mandevillehoteljamaica.com* ⇌*60 rooms* ⇔*In-room: a/c (some), phone, safe, kitchen (some), refrigerator (some), dial-up. In-hotel: 2 restaurants, bar, pool, no elevator, parking (no fee)* ⊟*MC, V* �|◎|*EP.*

BEACHES

If you're looking for something off the beaten path, head for Jamaica's largely undeveloped southwest coast. Because it's a sparsely populated area, these isolated beaches are some of the island's safest, with hasslers practically nonexistent. You should, however, use common sense; never leave valuables unattended on the beach, even for a few minutes. Swimming isn't recommended along the beach in the Alligator Pond area, not because of alligators (although crocodiles are a concern in Black River) but because of strong currents.

Bluefields Beach Park. On the coastal road to Negril, you'll find this relatively narrow stretch of sand and rock in the town of Bluefields. A free beach, it's typically crowded only

CLOSE UP

Host Jamaica

In 2006 Jamaica launched a new bed-and-breakfast program called Host Jamaica. The program offers accommodations in private homes across the island, the South Coast as well as Montego Bay, Ocho Rios, Kingston, Negril, and Port Antonio. Room rates range from $30 to $70, with $10 for each additional person. The homes are inspected annually to ensure they meet cleanliness and security guidelines. Each home has its own rules, whether that means no liquor in the rooms, an evening curfew, or free use of the home's swimming pool. The program, which is a joint project of the Ministry of Tourism, Entertainment and Culture, and the Tourism Product Development Company, presently offers about 630 accommodations across the island. Rooms can be booked through **Unique Jamaica** (☎*876/929–7895 ⊕www.uniquejamaica.com*) or at the Jamaica Tourist Board desk in the immigration hall of Montego Bay's Sangster International Airport.

on weekends. The swimming here is good, although the sea is sometimes rough. There are some amenities, including restrooms, jerk stands, and an assortment of beach vendors. ⊠*Bluefields*.

Font Hill Beach. Located between Whitehouse and Black River, this beach is part of a nature reserve that's owned by the Petroleum Corporation of Jamaica. For about a $3 entry fee, you can enjoy the day at the beach that includes restrooms, picnic tables, and plenty of golden sand. There are usually few visitors. The beach park is open Tuesday through Sunday. ⊠*Route A2, near Luana Point*.

★ Fodor'sChoice **Treasure Beach.** The most atmospheric beach on the South Coast comprises four long stretches of sand as well as many small coves. Though it isn't as pretty as those to the west or north—it has more rocks and darker sand— the idea that you might be discovering a bit of the "real" Jamaica more than makes up for these small distractions. Both locals and visitors use the beaches, though you're just as likely to find it completely deserted except for a friendly beach dog. ⊠*Treasure Beach*.

SPORTS & THE OUTDOORS

BIRD-WATCHING

The South Coast is an excellent destination for birders who come in search of the mountain witch, jabbering crow, mango hummingbird, Jamaican oriole, and even the endangered yellow-billed parrot. The town of Bluefields was the home of the island's most famous naturalist, Englishman Philip Henry Gosse, who wrote several guides to Jamaica's birds.

Reliable Adventures Jamaica (☎876/955–8834 ⊕*www.reliableadventuresjamaica.com*) offers a guided birding tour on Monday, Wednesday, and Friday. It's aimed at serious birders with an interest in both birds and butterflies indigenous to Jamaica.

BOATING

The Black River, Jamaica's longest waterway, is named for the peat deposits that color its waters. This river is also known as the best place on the island to see crocodiles. Guided boat tours also spot local birds and point out native foliage.

South Coast Safaris (✉*1 Crane St., Black River* ☎876/965–2513) is the best of the Black River safaris, taking visitors on slow cruises up the river to see the birds and other animals, including crocodiles.

DIVING & SNORKELING

The South Coast is not one of the island's top diving destinations. There's less coral here, and the visibility is so-so. Consequently, there are no independent dive outfitters in the area. Sandals Whitehouse European Village & Spa maintains its own dive shop for guests. Other South Coast resorts are happy to book dive excursions through operators in Negril.

FISHING

The South Coast offers good deep-sea fishing opportunities. Half-day tours troll a few miles offshore for barracuda, kingfish, wahoo, tuna, dorado, and shark. Full-day tours can approach the Pedro Banks, where yellowtail, mutton, and redtail snapper are often caught.

At **Fi Reel Fishing Tours** (✉*Treasure Beach* ☎876/965–3433), Captain Paolo leads deep-sea fishing tours aboard *El Tazar,* a twin-engine cabin cruiser. Fishing tours are usually half-day trips, but longer trips to more distant locations can be arranged.

CLOSE UP

Birding in Jamaica

Jamaica has an amazing variety of birds—nearly 300 species at last count, with a full 10% of them endemic to the island. This high rate of endemism, true for some of Jamaica's native plants as well as its wildlife, has been attributed to a number of factors, including the island's relative isolation and its varied topography.

Jamaica has been a prime birding spot since the 1800s, when the celebrated British scientist and naturalist Philip Henry Gosse reported on his travels around the Bluefields area in several books: *The Birds of Jamaica, Illustrations of the Birds of Jamaica,* and *A Naturalist's Sojourn in Jamaica.* Gosse's popular volumes are still in print, as is *Birds of the West Indies,* by James Bond. Yes, James Bond. Author Ian Fleming, writing at his home on the North Coast, needed just the right name for his new British spy hero. His eye fell on his copy of *Birds of the West Indies,* and the world's most famous fictional spy was christened.

Endemic species include the streamer-tailed hummingbird,

popularly called the "doctor bird" by locals, which is also Jamaica's national bird. The yellow-billed parrot, black-billed parrot, rufous-tailed flycatcher, and Jamaican woodpecker are also species exclusive to Jamaica.

A number of tour operators, some on-island, others based in the United States, Canada, and the United Kingdom, host birding tours to Jamaica. In addition to the South Coast area, major birding hotspots include the Blue and John Crow Mountains near Kingston and the rugged Cockpit Country near Montego Bay.

There are a growing number of organizations, domestic and otherwise, dedicated to preserving and protecting Jamaica's native birds. The government, though typically slow to realize the potential value of Jamaica's birdlife, has responded in recent years by setting aside sizable areas for native flora and fauna, including the Blue and John Crow Mountains National Park, not established until 1990.

Based in Montego Bay, **Salty Angler Fishing Charters** (☎ 876/ 863–1599 ⊕ *www.flyfishingjamaica.com*) also serves the Treasure Beach area. Visitors can join Skipper Vic Shirley for half- or full-day fishing excursions. Both open-water and coastal fishing is available. Fishing lessons for beginners are available.

GOLF

The South Coast is not known as a golf destination—in fact, there's only one course in the region. Up in the hills, the South Coast's only golf course is the **Manchester Club** (⊠*Caledonia Rd., Mandeville* ☎*876/962–2403*). Established in the 1860s, the 9-hole course is the oldest in the Western Hemisphere. It charges greens fees of about $17, and caddies can be hired for around $10. No carts are offered.

HIKING

The terrain along the South Coast is incredibly varied, from savannah and rolling hills in the Whitehouse area to rugged mountains farther east near Mandeville. Thanks to the sparse population and light development, the area has many unspoiled hiking areas, although travelers are encouraged to hike with a local guide at all times. ⚠**Marijuana fields are hard to see until you wander upon one; these fields are closely controlled and guarded by ganja farmers.**

Reliable Adventures Jamaica (☎*876/955–8834* ⊕*www. reliableadventuresjamaica.com*) offers half- and full-day guided hikes with no more than 15 participants.

DID YOU KNOW? Janga, a type of crayfish, are marketed locally as hot peppered shrimp. They are sold by women along the side of the road in Middle Quarters, St. Elizabeth. They're salty, spicy, and as impossible as potato chips to stop eating.

HORSEBACK RIDING

One of the best ways to tour the South Coast's pastoral landscape is from horseback. In addition to riding along the beach, area stables offer trails through farm and pasture areas, allowing an up-close-and-personal look at some of the island's most rustic landscapes.

Font Hill Beach Park and Wildlife Sanctuary (⊠*Rte. A2, between Whitehouse and Black River* ☎*876/966–2222*) is a 3,000-acre park that offers horseback riding along the beach and through the dry upland plateaus. The park is open Tuesday through Sunday.

Paradise Park (⊠*Rte. A2, 1 mi [2 km] west of Ferris Cross* ☎*876/966–2222*) is a working farm that has been owned and operated by the same family for more than 100 years. Visitors can rent horses to explore the farm's fields and pastures and the beaches of Bluefields Bay.

MOUNTAIN BIKING

Much of the South Coast is made up of rolling plains, perfect even for beginning cyclists. This part of the island is also blessed with lighter traffic, which makes things easier than on the busy North Coast.

Ocho Rios–based **Blue Mountain Bicycle Tours** (✉ *121 Main St., Ocho Rios* ☎ *876/974–7075* ⊕ *www.bmtoursja.com*) takes travelers on guided rides across the Pedro Plains. The all-day excursion includes Bamboo Avenue as well as lunch at a jerk stand.

TENNIS

The **Manchester Club** (✉ *Caledonia Rd., at Ward Ave., Mandeville* ☎ *876/962–2403*) opens its tennis courts to visitors of the many small properties in the area that don't have their own facilities.

5

NIGHTLIFE & THE ARTS

The nightlife on the South Coast is among the island's quietest. With its many ecotourism activities, the South Coast is very much an early-to-bed, early-to-rise destination.

ANNUAL EVENTS

In April, the **Treasure Beach Off-Road Triathlon** (☎ *876/965–3000* ⊕ *www.breds.org*) is the region's biggest annual event. The race features a 500-meter ocean swim, a 13.7-mi (25-km) mountain-bike trek, and a 4.3-mi (7-km) country run. Participation is limited to 50 Jamaicans and 50 visitors.

The **Calabash International Literary Festival** (✉ *Treasure Beach* ☎ *876/965–3000* ⊕ *www.calabashfestival.org*) offers three days and nights of both literary and musical talent at Jake's. The May festival, which in past years has featured authors including Russell Banks, Andrea Levy, and Sonia Sanchez, is the only annual literary festival in the English-speaking Caribbean

The second Sunday in July is sure to be hot at the **Little Ochi Seafood Carnival** (✉ *7 mi [12 km] south of A2, Alligator Pond* ☎ *876/965–4449*) when several thousand hungry people enjoy the best Jamaican cooking on the South Coast. The **Treasure Beach Hook n' Line Canoe Tournament** (✉ *Treasure Beach* ☎ *876/965–0635*) takes place each October. This three-day tournament pairs local fishermen with visitors. The teams compete using traditional fishing techniques.

CLOSE UP

The Incredible Peter Tosh

Peter Tosh, born Winston Hubert McIntosh, left the South Coast and headed to Kingston at the age of 15. There he met (and taught guitar to) Bob Marley and Bunny Wailer. The trio played together until the early '70s when Tosh struck out on his own.

In 1978 Tosh performed at the One Love Peace Concert in Kingston, stopping his set to chastise the prime minister and opposition leader. A few months later, Tosh was attacked and severely beaten by local police. Although the authorities left him for dead, Tosh recovered and went on to perform with Mick Jagger and Eric Clapton and to later stage what became the longest reggae roadshow in history.

On September 11, 1987, gunmen broke into his Kingston home and killed Tosh. His funeral was held at the National Arena, where he had performed at the controversial One Love Peace Concert nearly a decade earlier.

SOUTH COAST ESSENTIALS

To research prices, get advice from other travelers, and book travel arrangements, visit www.fodors.com.

TRANSPORTATION

BY AIR

There are no major airports on the South Coast. Visitors to this region can fly into airports in Montego Bay, Negril, or Kingston.

BY CAR

As in the rest of Jamaica, we strongly advise against renting a vehicle to see the sights along Jamaica's South Coast. However, if you're determined to drive, this area is probably as safe as it gets, due to lighter traffic and fewer large towns. Be aware that many roads in the south are rough and narrow, and what traffic you do encounter will whiz along at high speed.

Information **Alicia Car Rental** (⊠ *44 High St., Black River* ☎ *876/965-2554*). **Hemisphere Car Rental** (⊠ *51 Manchester Rd., Mandeville* ☎ *876/962-1921*). **Mid Island Car Rental** (⊠ *1-B Caledonia Rd., Mandeville* ☎ *876/961-2363*). **Millinex Rental** (⊠ *3 Villa Rd., Mandeville* ☎ *876/962-3542*). **Moon Glow Car Rental** (⊠ *81-A Ward Ave., Mandeville* ☎ *876/962-9097*).

BY TAXI

Taxis are less common on the South Coast than in busier tourist areas, but are still an easy (albeit expensive) option. You'll want to call ahead for a taxi or arrange for a driver to pick you up at a designated time.

Information JUTA (☎876/957-9197). **Pat's Taxi** (☎876/918-0431 or 876/955-3335). **Treasure Tours** (☎876/965-0126).

CONTACTS & RESOURCES

BANKS & EXCHANGE SERVICES

Though converting U.S. dollars to Jamaican dollars may not be necessary in the tourist meccas along the North Coast, the situation is a little different on the South Coast. Here it's more likely that merchants and taxi drivers will charge Jamaican dollars, so it's handy to have some local currency on hand.

Bank of Nova Scotia (✉Ward Ave. and Caledonia Rd., Mandeville ✉6 High St., Black River). **Mandeville Cambio** (✉18 W. Park Crescent, Mandeville). **Shields Cambio** (✉Brumalia and Caledonia Rds., Mandeville). **Workers Bank** (✉13 Mandeville Plaza, Mandeville).

EMERGENCIES

Emergency Services **Ambulance & Fire Emergencies** (☎110). **Police Emergencies & Air Rescue** (☎119). **Scuba-Diving Emergencies** (✉St. Ann's Bay Hospital, St. Ann's Bay ☎876/972-2272).

Hospitals **Black River Hospital** (✉45 High St., Black River ☎876/965-2212). **Mandeville Hospital** (✉32 Hargreaves Ave., Mandeville ☎876/962-2067). **Savanna-La-Mar Hospital** (✉Barracks Rd., Savanna-La-Mar ☎876/955-2533).

Pharmacies **Daley's Pharmacy** (✉1 Wesley Rd., Mandeville ☎876/625-6309). **Maxi-Med Pharmacy** (✉95 Main St., Santa Cruz ☎876/966-9042). **Nuwalter's Pharmacy** (✉18 High St., Black River ☎876/965-2264). **South Sea Pharmacy** (✉Main St., White House ☎876/963-5489).

INTERNET, MAIL & SHIPPING

Far fewer visitors frequent the South Coast than either the North Coast or Kingston, so you'll find that Internet access is spotty. Larger hotels have connections, but smaller ones do not.

Internet Cafés **Cyber Lounge** (✉Shop 12, Empire Bldg., Mandeville ☎876/625-7084). **Internet Shop** (✉13 North St., Black River ☎876/965-2534). **Underground High Speed Cyber Café** (✉Shop 2, Willowgate Plaza, Mandeville ☎876/625-3490).

Post Offices **Black River Post Office** (✉*North St., Black River* ☎*876/965–2213*). **Mandeville Post Office** (✉*5 S. Race Course Rd., Mandeville* ☎*876/962–3229*).

Shipping Companies **Airpak Express** (✉*17 Caledonia Rd., Mandeville* ☎*876/962–4951*). **Mandeville Couriers** (✉*22 Ward Ave., Mandeville* ☎*876/625–8491*).

Tara Courier Service (✉*8 N. Race Course Rd., Mandeville* ☎*888/ 827–2226*).

TOUR OPTIONS

Visitors to the South Coast can experience more of the real Jamaica through Countrystyle Community Tours, a company that offers personalized tours of island communities.

Information **Countrystyle Peace Village** (✉*62 Ward Ave., Mandeville* ☎*876/962–7758 or 876/488–7207* ⊕*www.countystyle communitytourist.com*).

Negril

WORD OF MOUTH

"Negril is so cool because it seems that there really is something for everyone. You can be really really active (parasail, scuba, snorkel, jet ski, etc.), or you can be really really sedentary. We chose the latter and loved every minute of it!"
—laustic

By Paris
Permenter
and John
Bigley

ON A WINDING COAST ROAD about 55 mi (89 km) southwest of Montego Bay, Negril used to be Jamaica's best-kept secret. This community, long sheltered from development by the surrounding Great Morass swamp, was first introduced to tourism in the 1970s when it became a haven for hippies. At first residents rented them rooms (or hammocks), but slowly mom-and-pop hotels began to spring up on the cliffs and along the beach. But even then the place had a laid-back vibe.

Today, Negril is quickly (some say *too* quickly) catching up with the rest of Jamaica. Sprawling all-inclusive resorts have appeared, with more on the horizon. One good thing: the development so far is still of the low-rise variety, as local law mandates that no building here can be taller than a palm tree.

Despite it all, Negril hangs on to its reputation as a wild vacation destination. Nudity is still common on the beaches of Bloody Bay. The infamous Hedonism II, boasting the highest repeat guest rate in the Caribbean, has been the topic of plenty of stories involving late-night hot tub parties. Reggae clubs attract some of the island's best musicians to the cliffs that overlook spectacular sunsets. And, although not as popular as it was during the '70s, more than one establishment still sells hallucinogenic teas and freelance entrepreneurs still hawk ganja.

One thing that hasn't changed at this west-coast community (whose only true claim to fame is a 7-mi [11-km] beach) is its casual approach to life. As you wander from lunch in the sun to shopping in the sun to sports in the sun, you can find that swimsuits and cover-ups are common attire. Want to dress up for a special meal? Tie a pareo over your swimsuit.

EXPLORING NEGRIL

Negril stretches along the coast from horseshoe-shape Bloody Bay (named when it was a whale-processing center) along the calm waters of Long Bay to the Lighthouse. Nearby, divers spiral downward off 50-foot-high cliffs into the deep green depths as the sun turns into a ball of fire and sets the clouds ablaze with color. Sunset is also the time when Norman Manley Boulevard, which intersects West End Road, comes to life with bustling bistros and ear-splitting discos.

NEGRIL TOP 5

Soaking up the Sun: Stroll the chalky 7 mi (11 km) of sand along Negril Beach, one of the island's best beaches.

Dancing the Night Away: Negril is rocking all night long; catch some of the island's best nightlife at a beach bar like Alfred's Ocean Club.

Showing off your Birthday Suit: Cast off your cares—and your clothes—at one of the west coast's clothing optional beaches.

Looking for the Green Flash: People come from all over the island to watch the sun set from Negril's cliffs; the most popular spot is Rick's.

Getting close to nature: Watch birds—and crocodiles— at the Royal Palm Reserve, where you can stroll on meandering wooden walkways through the palms.

The real wildness in Negril lies just outside the city limits. Here, in an area known as the Great Morass, you can see a side of the country that most visitors never glimpse. Crocodiles, not vacationers, lie in the steamy afternoon sunshine. And spectacular birds, not parasailers, fill the air with dashes of color and a cacophony of exotic sounds.

ABOUT THE RESTAURANTS

They call Negril the "capital of casual," and nowhere is that more true than in its restaurants. Unlike the other destinations in Jamaica, where the occasional jacket is spotted especially during the winter months, Negril is about as laid-back as you can get. Most restaurants are right on the beach, and meals are more often than not enjoyed out on the sand. Shorts and T-shirts are appropriate at many restaurants, especially for lunch; sundresses and shirts with collars make an appearance for dinner at most properties (although you can find a few of the upscale properties, such as Sandals Negril, that insist on "casually elegant" clothes). Reservations are rarely required or even accepted at local restaurants.

ABOUT THE HOTELS

When it comes to hotels, there are almost two different Negrils: that of Norman Manley Boulevard and that of West End Road. Along Norman Manley, the road that leads to Negril from Montego Bay, you can find traditional hotels (including many smaller properties) as well as a growing number of all-inclusive resorts (especially along Bloody Bay).

At Norman Manley Boulevard, which becomes West End Road at the roundabout in town, has properties best described as small and funky. This road leads along Negril's famous cliffs, an area where the mom-and-pop properties that carry on the spirit of "old" Negril live alongside a handful of small boutique properties. These lodgings are especially favored by European travelers, who often stay several weeks.

For travelers who would like to get out and explore the region, both the main stretch of Negril Beach on Long Bay and the cliffs area are good options. The beach properties make it easy to get out and explore on foot; the walk is lined with hotels and restaurants and just a few undeveloped areas.

WHAT IT COSTS IN DOLLARS				
$$$$	$$$	$$	$	¢
RESTAURANTS				
Over $30	$20–$30	$12–$20	$8–$12	under $8
HOTELS·				
Over $350	$250–$350	$150–$250	$80–$150	under $80
HOTELS**				
Over $450	$350–$450	$250–$350	$125–$250	under $125

*EP, BP, CP; **AI, FAP, MAP; Restaurant prices are per person for a main course at dinner and do not include the 15% V.A.T. and 10% service charge. Hotel prices are per night for a double room in high season, excluding 15% V.A.T. and 10% service charge.

TIMING

Like other areas of Jamaica, Negril's high season extends from mid-December to mid-April. In late March and early April, the annual spring-break onslaught means thousands of college students, mostly from the United States and Canada, descend for days of foam parties and T-shirt contests and nights of reggae concerts and all-night disco music. The more expensive all-inclusive properties are generally devoid of the spring-break crowds because of their higher prices.

NEGRIL ATTRACTIONS

With lighter traffic than Montego Bay and Ocho Rios (and no cruise-ship port), Negril is fairly easy to get around in by taxi or, even better, on foot, strolling along the miles of sand on Negril Beach. This town's charms are found on its beaches, in its bars, and at its hotels—not really in area attractions, which are few and far between. The town is home to only one notable historic site, its lighthouse, and a few natural attractions such as the Royal Palm Reserve.

That said, it's an easy day trip from Negril to many attractions on the South Coast, from waterfalls to rivers, birding sites to horseback rides.

Numbers in the margin correspond to points of interest on the Negril map.

WHAT TO SEE

❸ **Kool Runnings Water Park.** Opened in 2007 across from Beaches Sandy Bay, this theme park makes a good beach alternative on days when the sea is rough or for those not staying at oceanfront properties. Admission to the park includes 10 waterslides and a lazy-river float ride; a go-kart track and climbing wall incur separate charges. The best bargain is the weekday twilight package, with half-price admission after 4. ⊠*Norman Manley Blvd.* ☎*876/957–5418* ⊕*www.koolrunnings.com* ☞*$28* ⊙*Oct.–Aug., Tues.– Sun. 11–7.*

DID YOU KNOW? Prostitution is a big problem in Negril. Along with female prostitution, male prostitution has becoming increasingly evident, especially during evening shows. Locally nicknamed Rent-A-Rasta, Rent-A-Dread, and Rasta-tutes, the young hustlers approach female tourists. (Middle-aged European women—thanks to their longer vacations—are favorite targets.) The practice is so common it became the subject of a recent London play called *Sugar Mommies.*

❶ **Negril Lighthouse.** Negril's only structure of historical significance is the Negril Lighthouse, which has guided ships past the island's rocky western coast since 1895. You can stop by the adjacent caretaker's cottage and, for a tip, climb the spiral steps to the best view in town. ⊠*West End Rd.* ☎*No phone* ☞*Free* ⊙*Wed.–Mon. 11–7.*

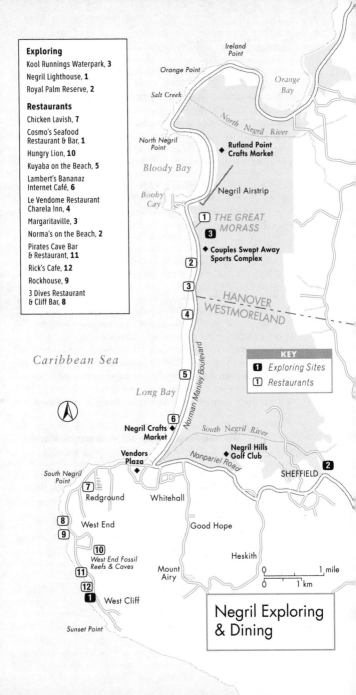

Exploring

Kool Runnings Waterpark, **3**
Negril Lighthouse, **1**
Royal Palm Reserve, **2**

Restaurants

Chicken Lavish, **7**
Cosmo's Seafood Restaurant & Bar, **1**
Hungry Lion, **10**
Kuyaba on the Beach, **5**
Lambert's Bananaz Internet Café, **6**
Le Vendome Restaurant Charela Inn, **4**
Margaritaville, **3**
Norma's on the Beach, **2**
Pirates Cave Bar & Restaurant, **11**
Rick's Cafe, **12**
Rockhouse, **9**
3 Dives Restaurant & Cliff Bar, **8**

Ireland Point
Orange Point
Orange Bay
Salt Creek
North Negril River
North Negril Point
◆ Rutland Point Crafts Market
Bloody Bay
Negril Airstrip
Booby Cay
1 THE GREAT MORASS
3
◆ Couples Swept Away Sports Complex
2
3
HANOVER
4
WESTMORELAND

Caribbean Sea

KEY
1 Exploring Sites
1 Restaurants

5
Long Bay
South Negril River
6
Negril Crafts ◆ Market
Norman Manley Boulevard
◆ Negril Hills Golf Club
Vendors Plaza ◆
Nonpariel Road
SHEFFIELD **2**
South Negril Point
7
Redground
Whitehall
8
West End
Good Hope
9
10
West End Fossil Reefs & Caves
Heskith
11
Mount Airy
12
1 West Cliff

Sunset Point

0   1 mile
0   1 km

Negril Exploring & Dining

CLOSE UP

Rasta for Beginners

Rastafarians, more commonly known as Rastas, are believers in the divinity of Haile Selassie, former ruler of Ethiopia. Rastafarianism remains a minority religion in Jamaica, but it is one of the most visible thanks to the popularity of Rastas such as the late reggae singer Bob Marley.

Rastafarians are usually seen wearing crocheted tams, beneath which are tucked their long dreadlocks. The Rastas do not believe in cutting their hair, citing Leviticus 21.5: "They shall not make baldness upon their head, neither shall they shave off the corner of their beard nor make any cuttings in their flesh." Rastafarian women generally wear dreadlocks as well, along with African-style clothing and headwraps.

When talking with a Rasta, you'll soon notice their distinc-

tion of speaking in the first person. "We" is substituted with "I and I," following the belief that God (known to the Rastas as Jah) is present in every person.

Rastas are also strict vegetarians, maintaining a salt-free diet of what is termed Ital food. Look for the red, green, and gold colors on restaurants as a clue to locating Ital eateries, which are often quite small.

Better known than their vegetarian diet is their use of *ganja*, or marijuana, as a part of their religion. They cite Psalm 104.14: "He causeth the grass to grow for the cattle, and herb for the service of man." Perhaps not coincidentally, Rastas are also renowned herbalists, using folk medicine and relying on the land's plants to heal many ills.

❷ **Royal Palm Reserve.** On the southern side of the Great Morass, this preserve protects the wetlands and the royal palms that thrive here. Along with plenty of majestic palms, these 300 acres are also home to 113 other plant species, including 10 kinds of fern and 18 types of climbing vine. Visitors stroll on the boardwalk winding through the grounds; along the way look for crocodiles and many bird species. The Negril Royal Palm Reserve Museum has displays about the Great Morass. ✉*Sheffield Rd., east of Negril* ☎*876/957–3736* ⊕*www.royalpalmreserve.com* 🖃*$10* ⊙*Daily 9–6.*

6

WHERE TO EAT

Dining in Negril is a casual affair, one most often enjoyed on the beach. Reservations aren't required and often aren't even accepted; many visitors just stroll down sand until they find an eatery that appeals to them.

ECLECTIC

$$–$$$ ×**Rick's Cafe.** It's hard to keep a good café down, even when a force like Hurricane Ivan blows through and sends much of it into the sea. Rick's has been rebuilt, and it's bigger than ever, with two floors of dining along with poolside cabanas for rent. As always, there are the cliff diving and eye-popping views the restaurant has been known for since 1974. Menu options range from escoveitch shrimp to jerk chicken to sizzling steak. Ricks is always busy, but it is most crowded at sunset. ⊠*Southern end of West End Rd.* ☎*876/957–4621* ⊕*www.rickscafejamaica.com* ▤*AE, D, MC, V.*

$–$$$ ×**Pirates Cave Bar & Restaurant.** If this place looks just a tad familiar, it might be because the cliffs and nearby sea cave were used as a setting in the *20,000 Leagues Under the Sea* and other movies. Steve McQueen leaped from the cliffs in *Papillon,* and cliff jumping continues to be the location's top draw. The menu is hardly the stuff of pirate lore: cheeseburgers, barbecue ribs, and fish sandwiches but you can find a tasty jerk chicken and rasta pasta with ackee and vegetables to remind you you're in Jamaica. ⊠*West End Rd.* ☎*876/957–0925* ▤*AE, MC, V.*

$–$$ ×**Kuyaba on the Beach.** This charming thatch-roof eatery has an international menu, including dishes like curried conch, kingfish steak, and grilled lamb with sautéed mushrooms. The place has lively ambience, especially at the bar. There's a crafts shop on the premises, and chaise lounges line the beach; come prepared to spend some time, and don't forget a towel and bathing suit. ⊠*Southern end of Norman Manley Blvd.* ☎*876/957–4318* ▤*AE, D, MC, V.*

$–$$ ×**Margaritaville.** Like its sister properties in Montego Bay and Ocho Rios, Margaritaville offers a very Americanized menu and fakish Caribbean experience—but with the added backdrop of Negril Beach. Burgers and are joined by a few Caribbean items like conch fritters. This restaurant–nightclub doesn't have the waterslides of the island's other outposts, but you can find a water trampoline and a rock-climbing wall to work off those calories. ⊠*Norman Manley Blvd.* ☎*876/957–4467* ▤*AE, D, MC, V.*

FRENCH

$–$$ ✕**Le Vendome.** At the middle-of-the-road Charela Inn, you might expect this place to be a simple eatery featuring standard beach fare. Le Vendome is fine dining at its best—with the added attraction of a beachside location. From fine wines to crusty bread baked fresh daily, this restaurant serves French cuisine with a hint of Jamaica (don't be surprised to see a dusting of jerk spice or ginger). The restaurant features a different five-course gourmet dinner every evening, but there are always dishes such as filet mignon in wine and mushroom sauce, canard à l'orange, and shrimp in garlic sauce. On Tuesday and Saturday night, the mood turns distinctly Jamaican with live performances. ✉*Norman Manley Blvd.* ☎*876/957–4277* ⚟*Reservations essential* ▭*AE, D, MC, V.*

JAMAICAN

★ $–$$$ ✕**Norma's on the Beach.** Although it's in the modest boutique hotel Sea Splash, make no mistake: this is Jamaican dining at its finest. Norma is Norma Shirley, one of the island's best-known culinary artists, often called the "Julia Child of the Caribbean." Her dressed-up Jamaican fare is prepared with a creative flair. Try callaloo-stuffed chicken breast or jerk chicken pasta. For a romantic meal, opt for terrace or candlelight dining. ✉*Sea Splash Hotel, Norman Manley Blvd.* ☎*876/957–4041* ▭*AE, MC, V.*

$–$$$ ✕**Rockhouse.** With its seaside perch, dining at Rockhouse would already be an evening to remember—but an incredible menu makes the experience that much more special. Serving what they've termed "new Jamaican cuisine," Rockhouse offers Jamaican fare prepared with a light touch. Top entrées include blackened mahimahi with mango chutney, Jamaican jambalaya with French bread, and even a Jamaican stir fry with callaloo, cho cho, carrot, cabbage, rice, and peas. ✉*West End Rd.* ☎*876/957–4373* ⚟*Reservations required* ▭*AE, MC, V.*

DID YOU KNOW? With its diagonal golden cross across a black and green background, the Jamaican flag is one of the most easily distinguishable Caribbean flags. In use since 1962, each part of the flag is symbolic. The black used for the left and right triangles represents the hardship of the people. The green of the upper and lower quadrants symbolizes hope and the fertile land of Jamaica, and the gold represents wealth and sunshine.

¢–$$$ ╳**3 Dives Restaurant and Cliff Bar.** This ultracasual restaurant, housed beneath a big roof and not much more, was featured on the *Amazing Race*. But before the television show, it was already tops for its amazing local cuisine. The restaurant is best known for its jerk (and its annual jerk festival), but it also serves a menu of traditional Jamaican dishes like curried goat, brown stew chicken, curried or steamed conch, and, in season, grilled lobsters. During the winter months, lunch is offered but dinner, thanks to the spectacular sunsets here, is the peak time when crowds forming well before the sun hits the horizon. ⊠ *West End Rd.* ☎*876/344–6850* ▭*AE, MC, V.*

$–$$ ╳**Lambert's Bananaz Internet Café.** With its brightly painted exterior, this place looks like a faux Caribbean restaurant. On the contrary, this eatery serves an authentic local menu, from ackee and saltfish to steam fish and bammy, curried goat, and roasted breadfruit. It's especially noted for its banana fritters, so don't pass those up. And don't miss the freshly made cane juice squeezed right on property. ⊠*Southern end of Norman Manley Blvd.* ☎*876/957–3249* ▭*MC, V.*

¢–$ ╳**Chicken Lavish.** This longtime West End eatery serves—you guessed it—chicken prepared the way locals like it: curried, fried, jerked, and grilled. The restaurant is in a simple, green-roofed house with a porch that serves as a dining room (takeout is also popular). If you've had enough chicken, you can find curried goat and fried fish on the menu as well. ⊠*Northern end of West End Rd.* ☎*876/957–4410* ▭*MC, V.*

SEAFOOD

★ $–$$$ ╳**Cosmo's Seafood Restaurant & Bar.** Owner Cosmo Brown has made this seaside open-air bistro a pleasant place to spend the afternoon—and maybe stay on for dinner. Fish is the main attraction, and the conch soup—a house specialty—is a meal in itself. You can also find lobster (grilled or curried), fish-and-chips, and the catch of the day served any way you like it. Customers often drop their cover-ups to take a dip in the sea before dessert, then return to lounge in chairs scattered under almond and sea grape trees. (There's an entrance fee of $1.50 for the beach.) ⊠*Norman Manley Blvd.* ☎*876/957–4330* ▭*AE, MC, V.*

Jamaican Patois

If you feel like you're hearing a foreign tongue, you're almost right. The language of the streets is patois, a colorful combination of English, Spanish, and Portuguese, with plenty of local slang all in one. Many words are African in origin. Most are believed to come from the Twi language and other Gold Coast languages. Other influences include the language of Mendi, Igbo, Efik, Yoruba, Kongo, Kimbundu, Ewe, Mandinka and, some say, Swahili.

Here's an example of some patois you might hear on the streets:

a go foreign: to leave Jamaica

bankra: a large basket

bendung maaket: a sidewalk market, a place where you would "bend down"

bendung: to shop

boonoonunus: wonderful, beautiful

bratta: something extra

bredda: brother

chaka-chaka: messy

craven: greedy

cuss-cuss: argument with cursing

dege-dege: skinny

duppy: ghost

irie (eye-ree): all's well, good

janga: crayfish

kiss teet: sucking teeth in disapproval

ku: look

kyaan: can't

laba-laba: gossip

labrish: gossip

lilly bit: tiny, small

mash up: destroy, wreck

nyam: eat

oht fi: about to

wa mek?: why?

wagga-wagga: bountiful

winjy: sickly

yard: home

6

VEGETARIAN

$-$$$ ✕**The Hungry Lion.** Whether you're a vegetarian, curious about the Rastafarian diet, or just looking for a good meal, the Hungry Lion has been a longtime favorite in the West End area. Traditional food is cooked to Rastafarian specifications (including no salt) means dishes like meatless shepherd's pie made with lentils. Seafood such as fried snapper is another top choice. You can also find a long list of freshly made juices, all enjoyed in an alfresco setting. ✉*Southern end of West End Rd.* ☎876/957–4486 ▤*AE, MC, V.*

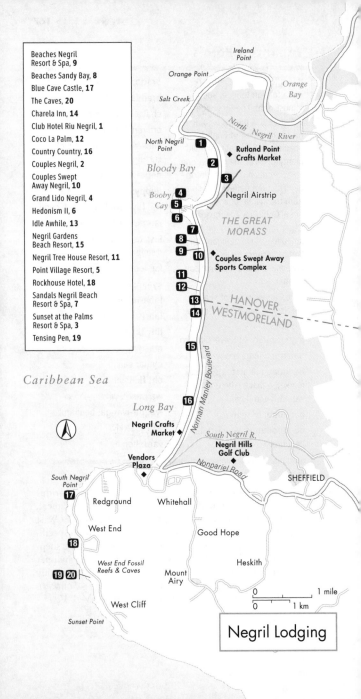

Beaches Negril
Resort & Spa, **9**

Beaches Sandy Bay, **8**

Blue Cave Castle, **17**

The Caves, **20**

Charela Inn, **14**

Club Hotel Riu Negril, **1**

Coco La Palm, **12**

Country Country, **16**

Couples Negril, **2**

Couples Swept
Away Negril, **10**

Grand Lido Negril, **4**

Hedonism II, **6**

Idle Awhile, **13**

Negril Gardens
Beach Resort, **15**

Negril Tree House Resort, **11**

Point Village Resort, **5**

Rockhouse Hotel, **18**

Sandals Negril Beach
Resort & Spa, **7**

Sunset at the Palms
Resort & Spa, **3**

Tensing Pen, **19**

Ireland
Point

Orange Point

Orange
Bay

Salt Creek

North Negril River

North Negril
Point

Rutland Point
Crafts Market

Bloody Bay

Negril Airstrip

Booby
Cay

THE GREAT
MORASS

Couples Swept Away
Sports Complex

HANOVER
WESTMORELAND

Caribbean Sea

Norman Manley Boulevard

Long Bay

Negril Crafts
Market

South Negril R.

Negril Hills
Golf Club

Vendors
Plaza

Nonpariel Road

SHEFFIELD

South Negril
Point

Redground

Whitehall

West End

Good Hope

West End Fossil
Reefs & Caves

Heskith

Mount
Airy

West Cliff

Sunset Point

0   1 mile
0   1 km

Negril Lodging

WHERE TO STAY

$$$$ ☷**Beaches Negril Resort & Spa.** This property's chief assets are its location on Negril Beach and its impressive water park. Pirates Island Water Park, an 18,000-square-foot theme park, is always popular. This resort also features an Xbox game room for kids (and plenty of adults, too). Sesame Street characters roam the grounds and interact with guests. Dining here can be enjoyed as a family or separately; two restaurants are for adults only and a supervised kids' program (and scheduled teen activities) keep everyone happy. **Pros:** great beach, extensive water park, friendly staff. **Cons:** on major road, children's programs cancelled if too few are enrolled, some activities have a surcharge. ✉*Norman Manley Blvd.* ☎*876/957–9270* 🖷*876/957–9269* ⊕*www.beaches.com* ⇆*210 rooms* ♿*In-room: safe, refrigerator (some), Ethernet, dial-up. In-hotel: 5 restaurants, room service (some), bars, tennis courts, pools, gym, spa, beachfront, diving, water sports, no elevator, children's programs (ages newborn–12), laundry service, concierge, public Internet, airport shuttle, parking (no fee), no-smoking rooms* ▭*AE, D, DC, MC, V* ⏹*AI.*

$$$$ ☷**Beaches Sandy Bay.** This family-friendly resort is not as extensive as its sister property, Beaches Negril Resort & Spa. But it's more economical and gives families full privileges—from the water parks to the restaurants—at the more expensive Beaches resorts. There's even a free shuttle between the properties. You can find a wide variety of rooms here, from two-level suites with kitchenettes and living rooms to standard rooms sized for a family of four. Like other Beaches, Sesame Street characters roam the grounds here and are available for special bookings such as breakfast and tuck-in service. **Pros:** moderate price, great location, extensive children's program. **Cons:** smallish pools can get crowded, rooms need a face-lift, meal option somewhat limited. ✉*Norman Manley Blvd.* ☎*876/957–5100* 🖷*876/957–5229* ⊕*www.beaches.com* ⇆*128 rooms* ♿*In-room: safe, kitchen (some), refrigerator (some), Ethernet. In-hotel: 3 restaurants, room service, bars, pools, gym, spa, beachfront, diving, water sports, no elevator, children's programs (ages newborn–12), laundry service, concierge, public Internet, airport shuttle, parking (no fee), no-smoking rooms* ▭*AE, D, DC, MC, V* ⏹*AI.*

$$$$ ★ Fodor'sChoice ☷**The Caves.** Although it's set on 2 tiny acres, this petite resort packs a lot of punch at its cliff-side location, drawing film stars as well as travelers looking for

6

boutique-style pampering. Thatch-roof cottages, all reno-vated in 2006, are individually designed with vivid colors and hand-carved furniture, every one offering spectacular sunset views. The cottages are built above the natural sea caves that line the cliffs, one of which is used for private romantic dinners. TVs are available, but only if you ask; some rooms offer outdoor showers. **Pros:** stylish rooms, personal service, quiet atmosphere. **Cons:** limited dining options, too quiet for some travelers, not on beach. ⊠ *West End Rd.* ☎*876/975–3354* ⊟*876/975–3620* ⊕*www.island-outpost.com* ⌖*6 suites, 3 cottages* ⌂*In-room: no a/c (some), refrigerator (some), dial-up. In-hotel: restaurant, pool, spa, beachfront, water sports, bicycles, no elevator, public Wi-Fi, no kids under 16* ⊟*AE, D, MC, V* ⦿*AI.*

$$$$ 🅣**Couples Negril.** This resort, which emphasizes rest and relaxation, is a more laid-back alternative to the nearby Sandals Negril. The resort has a good beachfront along Bloody Bay, north of the funkier Negril Beach, although Negril's bohemian nature is still reflected throughout the nine low-rise buildings. The property is decorated with a rainbow of colors, and lively art by local craftspeople peppers public spaces. Rooms are similarly bright and roomy, but are not luxurious. All land and water activi-ties, selected excursions, and weddings are included in the rates. **Pros:** plenty of dining options, bartender service on the beach, free weddings. **Cons:** restaurants can book up early, dated decor, social directors can be too insistent that guests join activities. ⊠*Norman Manley Blvd.* ☎*876/957–5960* ⊟*876/957–5858* ⊕*www.couples.com* ⌖*216 rooms, 18 suites* ⌂*In-room: safe, refrigerator (some). In-hotel: 4 restaurants, bars, tennis courts, pools, gym, spa, beach-front, diving, water sports, concierge, airport shuttle, no kids under 18, no elevator* ⌖*3-night minimum* ⊟*AE, D, MC, V* ⦿*AI.*

$$$$ ★ **Fodor'sChoice** 🅣**Couples Swept Away Negril.** Sports-minded couples are welcomed to this all-suites resort known for its expansive menu of sports offerings, top-notch facilities (the best in Jamaica, and among the best in the Caribbean), and emphasis on healthy cuisine. If you're looking for an active vacation that is still sprinkled with a hint of romance, this is your best option in Negril. The suites are in 26 two-story tropical villas—each with a private verandah overlooking the sea or a lush garden area—spread out along a ½-mi (¾-km) stretch of gorgeous beach. Across the road lies one of Jamaica's best sports complexes, with classes and first-rate equipment. A 2006 expansion added new restaurants and an Internet café. **Pros:** excellent fitness facilities, healthy choices at restaurants, free weddings. **Cons:** some facilities across the road, not a place for a relaxed vacation. ✉*Norman Manley Blvd., Long Bay* ☎*876/957–4061* 🖷*876/957–4060* ⊕*www.couples.com* ⬎*134 suites* ⚁*In-room: safe, refrigerator (some). In-hotel: 6 restaurants, bars, tennis courts, pools, gym, spa, beachfront, diving, water sports, concierge, public Internet, airport shuttle, no kids under 18, no elevator* ⚲*3-night minimum* ⊟*AE, D, DC, MC, V* ⎮◉⎮*AI.*

$$$$ 🖵**Grand Lido Negril.** A cursory look around the marble-clad lobby lined with elegant columns might give the impression that this upscale all-inclusive is a tad stuffy. But fancy touches are balanced by an expansive clothing-optional beach (including its own hot tub, bar, and grill). This is one of Negril's best resorts, where it's fun to dress for dinner but equally good to strip down for a day of fun in the sun. The non-nude beach is one of the best strips of sand in Negril. Appealing to an upscale crowd of all stripes, the mood here is quiet and relaxing—much different than at Hedonism II, which is next door. Low-rise rooms, both oceanfront and garden suites, are stylish; many offer glass doors just steps from the sand. **Pros:** excellent beaches, good dining, elegant setting. **Cons:** some rooms need updating, public area lacks view, clothing-optional pool is small. ✉*Norman Manley Blvd., Box 88* ☎*876/957–5010* 🖷*876/957–5517* ⊕*www.superclubs.com* ⬎*210 suites* ⚁*In-room: refrigerator, safe. In-hotel: 6 restaurants, room service, bars, tennis courts, pools, gym, spa, beachfront, diving, water sports, no elevator, concierge, public Internet, public Wi-Fi, laundry service, airport shuttle, no kids under 16, no-smoking rooms* ⚲*2-night minimum* ⊟*AE, D, DC, MC, V* ⎮◉⎮*AI.*

$$$$ 🖵**Sandals Negril Beach Resort & Spa.** Couples (no longer limited to male–female pairs) looking for an sports-oriented getaway and a casually elegant atmosphere (you can wear dressy shorts to dinner) flock to this resort on one of the best stretches of Negril Beach. Water sports, particularly scuba diving, are popular; the capable staff is happy to work with neophytes as well as certified veterans. Tennis, racquetball, squash, and other activities are included for landlubbers. There's a huge swim-up pool bar when you're through exerting yourself. The range of spacious accommodations includes some spacious two-story suites; personal butler service is available in top categories. Like other resorts in the Sandals chain, Sandals Negril offers guests the Stay at One, Dine at Six policy. If you venture into

Montego Bay or Ocho Rios for a day trip, you can dine at other Sandals resorts (transportation not included). **Pros:** excellent beach, good restaurants, private butler service. **Cons:** on-site nightlife options limited, no transportation to sister resorts. ⊠*Norman Manley Blvd.* ☎*876/957–5216* ⊟*876/957–5338* ⊕*www.sandals.com* ⌂*In-room: safe, refrigerator (some), Ethernet, dial-up. In-hotel: 6 restaurants, room service (some), bars, tennis courts, pools, gym, spa, beachfront, diving, water sports, bicycles, no elevator, laundry service, concierge, public Internet, airport shuttle, parking (no fee), no kids under 18, no-smoking rooms* ⊟*AE, D, DC, MC, V* ⦿*AI.*

$$$–$$$$ ▦**Hedonism II.** Promising a perpetual spring break for adults,
★ this resort gets a lot of repeat business. Although you can find "prude" activities ranging from a rock-climbing wall to an expansive new gym, it's the nude side that's perpetually sold out. Guest rooms don't match the opulence of those at Hedonism III, but they include sensual touches like multi-head showers and (of course) mirrors over the beds. Singles must allow the resort to match them with a same-sex roommate or pay a hefty supplement. Many nude travel groups plan vacations en masse here several times a year; another peak time is Halloween, when guests celebrate the resort's anniversary with wild costumes and decorated guest rooms. **Pros:** good beaches, numerous activities, less pricey than other all-inclusives. **Cons:** spring-break atmosphere not for everyone, nude beach and pool get crowded, basic rooms. ⊠*Norman Manley Blvd., Ruthland Point* ☎*876/957–5200* ⊟*876/957–5389* ⊕*www.superclubs.com* ⇖*280 rooms, 15 suites* ⌂*In-room: safe. In-hotel: 6 restaurants, bars, tennis courts, pools, gym, spa, beachfront, diving, water sports, bicycles, concierge, public Internet, no elevator, airport shuttle, no kids under 18* ⌖*2-night minimum* ⊟*AE, D, DC, MC, V* ⦿*AI.*

$$$–$$$$ ▦**Sunset at the Palms Resort & Spa.** This relaxed all-inclusive is a favorite with ecotourists. It was the world's first hotel to receive Green Globe Certification for environmentally-sustainable tourism, and the management works to maintain that status. The tree-house-like cottages are set amid towering royal palms. Open and airy, rooms have floral bedspreads, gauzy curtains, natural-wood floors, and high ceilings. The beach is across the street, along with activities including nonmotorized water sports. Nature enthusiasts can also take a walk with the resort's resident gardener. **Pros:** environmentally conscious, beautiful grounds, unique accommodations. **Cons:** beach across street, not walking

distance to attractions. ⊠*Norman Manley Blvd., Box 118* ☎*876/957–5350* 🖷*876/957–5381* ⊕*www.sunsetatthe palms.com* ⬅*65 rooms, 4 suites* 🗴*In-room: safe. In-hotel: 3 restaurants, bars, tennis court, pool, gym, spa, water sports, public Internet, no elevator, airport shuttle* ⊟*AE, D, MC, V* ⍩*AI.*

$$–$$$$ 🖵**ClubHotel Riu Negril.** This beautiful resort on Bloody Bay has a decent, sandy beachfront. Don't expect much personalized service at this massive place, but do expect to get your money's worth. There's good food and an extensive array of activities and facilities, and the prices are a bargain to boot. Rooms are attractive and offer the usual amenities, as well as a liquor dispenser, but those in the second and third blocks are a *very* long walk from everything, with no resort shuttle to help your weary feet. The programs for kids are slightly better here than at the neighboring Riu Tropical Bay, which is equally as large. **Pros:** good value for an all-inclusive resort, plenty of dining options, good children's program. **Cons:** pools get crowded, many rooms a long walk from public areas, not close to local attractions. ⊠*Norman Manley Blvd.* ☎*876/957–5700* 🖷*876/957–5020* ⊕*www.riu.com* ⬅*420 rooms, 18 junior suites* 🗴*In-room: refrigerator, safe. In-hotel: 4 restaurants, bars, tennis courts, pools, gym, spa, beachfront, diving, water sports, no elevator, children's programs (ages 4–12), laundry service, public Internet, airport shuttle* ⊟*AE, D, MC, V* ⍩*AI.*

$$–$$$ 🖵**Idle Awhile.** This boutique hotel is a far cry from the town's all-inclusives, which makes it even more surprising that Idle Awhile is owned by Lee Issa, who also owns Couples Resorts. Like its big sisters just up the beach, this property is skillfully decorated—green and brown tones with red accents provide almost a South Pacific feel. Sporting activities are limited, but all guests get complimentary access to the big sports complex at Couples Swept Away. If you book a one-bedroom suite, the resort will provide a cook for your meals for $20 per day plus groceries. **Pros:** personal service, unique accommodations, access to sports facilities. **Cons:** few on-site dining options, some rooms can be noisy at night. ⊠*Norman Manley Blvd.* ☎*876/957– 3302* 🖷*876/957–9567* ⊕*www.idleawhile.com* ⬅*8 rooms, 6 suites* 🗴*In-room: safe, kitchen (some), refrigerator, Wi-Fi. In-hotel: restaurant, room service, bar, beachfront, no elevator, public Wi-Fi, parking (no fee)* ⊟*AE, D, MC, V* ⍩*EP.*

$$–$$$ ☱**Point Village Resort.** Feeling more like an apartment com-
plex than a resort hotel, Point Village can make you feel as
if you're planting some roots in Negril. With both all-inclusive and room-only plans, you have the option of having it
all or not. Kitchens help out those keeping an eye on their
budget. Though it's at the north end of Negril, which is
mostly adults-only (Hedonism II and Grand Lido Negril
are neighbors), this resort is friendly to families. Rooms
have tile floors and basic furnishings, and each is individually decorated. The sprawling complex has two small crescent beaches, rocky grottoes to explore, and fine snorkeling
offshore. One child age 13 and under stays free when sharing a room with parents. **Pros:** good value for families,
large rooms, many on-site activities. **Cons:** public areas
packed with kids, small beaches, outdated décor. ✉*Manley
Blvd., Box 105* ☎*876/957–5170* 🖷*876/957–5113* ⊕*www.
pointvillage.com* ⇝*99 studios, 66 1-, 2-, and 3-bedroom
apartments* ⌂*In-room: safe, kitchen, refrigerator. In-hotel:
3 restaurants, bars, tennis court, pool, beachfront, water
sports, no elevator, children's programs (ages newborn–12)*
🖃*AE, D, MC, V* ❙◯❙*AI.*

$$–$$$ ☱**Tensing Pen.** Named for the inn's first dog (who was
named for a famed Sherpa), this hip and casual getaway is
a top choice for travelers who like to get out and explore.
Hammocks throughout the property promise lazy afternoons and cliffside perches tempt visitors to sit beneath
an umbrella and enjoy the sea view with a good book in
hand. Rooms, and the even more appealing cottages, have
a South-Seas-meets-the-Caribbean vibe, with rock accents,
handmade furnishings, and big glass doors that open to
the sea. The largest accommodations here are the three-
bedroom units in the Long House, but even the smaller
accommodations are roomy and comfortable. The resort
has some on-site activities including yoga classes. **Pros:**
unique accommodations, great snorkeling, spacious rooms.
Cons: not on beach, barking dogs and other noise, rooms
without air-conditioning can get buggy. ✉*West End Rd.*
☎*876/957–0387* 🖷*876/957–0161* ⊕*www.tensingpen.com*
⇝*6 cottages, 9 rooms* ⌂*In-room: no a/c (some), refrigerator. In-hotel: restaurant, bar, pool, beachfront, diving,
water sports, no elevator, parking (no fee)* 🖃*AE, D, DC,
MC, V* ❙◯❙*CP.*

$$ ☱**Charela Inn.** Directly on Negril beach, this quiet hotel is
understated but elegant, and has a widely praised French-
Jamaican restaurant. Each quiet room has a private balcony
or a covered patio. You can opt for a room-only plan if you

want to explore neighboring restaurants along the beach, but most guests go all-inclusive. Children up to 9 can stay in the parents' room for no additional charge; those 10 to 15 are charged $18 per night. The twice-weekly folkloric show draws guests from all over Negril. An all-inclusive meal plan is an option here, although with the many restaurants within walking distance it isn't a necessity. **Pros:** great dining, lovely beach, good value for families. **Cons:** dated decor, some rooms are small, not luxurious. ⊠*Norman Manley Blvd., Box 3033* ☎*876/957–4277* ⊟*876/957–4414* ⊕*www.charela.com* ⇨*49 rooms* ♿*In-room: safe. In-hotel: restaurant, bar, pool, beachfront, water sports, laundry service, no elevator* ☞*5-night minimum in high season, 3-night minimum in low season* ⊟*D, MC, V* ⊙*EP.*

$$ 🗆**Country Country.** Owned by Kevin and Joanne Robertson, who also own Montego Bay's Coyaba, this small hotel has the same home-away-from-home feel but with a distinct Negril charm. Rooms are housed in brightly painted cottages designed by Jamaican architect Ann Hodges (known for her work at Goldeneye and Strawberry Hill); the cottages come alive with quaint touches like gingerbread trim. The oversize rooms all have private patios. For an additional fee, you can add a meal plan, although most guests find plenty of restaurant choices within the area. **Pros:** charming decor, large rooms, good location on Negril Beach. **Cons:** noise from nearby bar, limited on-site dining options. ⊠*Norman Manley Blvd.* ☎*876/957–4273* ⊟*876/957–4342* ⊕*www.countryjamaica.com* ⇨*20 rooms* ♿*In-room: safe, refrigerator. In-hotel: restaurant, room service, bar, beachfront, no elevator* ⊟*AE, MC, V* ⊙*BP.*

$$ 🗆**Negril Gardens Beach Resort.** This low-rise resort epitomizes the relaxed and funky style for which Negril has long been known. Guests are always just a quick walk from Negril's 7-mi-long (11-km-long) beach. Rooms are fairly basic, but those beachside get some noise from nearby clubs until the wee hours. The resort is under Sandals management, but operates separately from the chain, welcoming couples, singles, and families. Children under two stay free, but each room has a maximum occupancy of three persons. **Pros:** good value, lovely beach, helpful staff. **Cons:** some rooms don't have balconies, nearby nightclubs can be noisy, limit of three to a room. ⊠*Norman Manley Blvd., Box 3058* ☎*876/957–4408* ⊟*876/957–4374* ⊕*www. negrilgardensresort.com* ⇨*65 rooms* ♿*In-room: safe. In-*

hotel: restaurant, bars, pool, beachfront, water sports, no elevator ☞*2-night minimum* ⊟*AE, D, MC, V* †◯†*AI.*

$$ ★ Fodor'sChoice ☷**Rockhouse Hotel.** With a spectacular cliffside location like that of the Caves—but without the high price tag—Rockhouse delivers both resort comfort and funky style. The accommodations are built from rough-hewn timber and quarry stone and filled with furniture that echoes the nature theme. Although double the price of a regular room, villas, with outdoor showers and private sundecks above the cliffs, are worth the splurge. Studios have outdoor showers but are otherwise like the regular rooms, which seem pleasantly rustic. You can ask for a TV—but only to watch videos. To be honest, you're far better off enjoying the sunset. There's a thatch-roof Jamaican restaurant, a pampering spa, and a cliff-top infinity pool and bar. **Pros:** excellent dining, unique accommodations, beautiful pool area. **Cons:** no beach, too quiet for some visitors. ⊠*West End Rd., Box 3024* ☎*876/957–4373* 🖷*876/957–0557* ⊕*www.rockhousehotel.com* ☞*14 rooms, 20 villas* ⚐*In-room: safe, no TV. In-hotel: restaurant, bars, pool, water sports, no kids under 12, no elevator* ⊟*AE, MC, V* †◯†*EP.*

$–$$ ☷**Coco La Palm.** This quiet, friendly hotel on the beach has oversize rooms (junior suites average 540 square feet) in octagonal buildings scattered around the pool. Some junior suites have private patios or terraces; most of these overlook the gardens (11 rooms have ocean views). The resort makes a good home base from which to explore Negril Beach, or you can just relax underneath one of the tall coconut palms. The beachside restaurant is open-air and casual. **Pros:** beautiful beach, large rooms, good on-site dining. **Cons:** small pools, dated decor. ⊠*Norman Manley Blvd.* ☎*876/957–4227* 🖷*876/957–3460* ⊕*www.cocolapalm.com* ☞*75 rooms* ⚐*In-room: safe, refrigerator, DVD, Ethernet. In-hotel: 2 restaurants, room service, bars, pools, spa, beachfront, no elevator, laundry facilities, laundry service, public Internet, parking (no fee)* ⊟*AE, DC, MC, V* †◯†*EP.*

$–$$ ☷**Negril Tree House Resort.** On a wide swatch of Negril Beach, this longtime resort draws many repeat visitors, especially during the winter months. Rooms are plain, but the beach can't be beat. At the center of the complex sits a two-story rondoval; upstairs an open-air restaurant serves breakfast (part of the room rate for all guests) as well as lunch and dinner. **Pros:** great beach, friendly staff, many nearby restaurants. **Cons:** basic rooms, dated decor, limited menu at restaurant. ✉*Norman Manley Blvd.* ☎*876/957–4287* 🖷*876/957–4386* 🌐*www.negril-treehouse.com* *58 rooms, 12 suites* *In-room: safe, kitchen (some), refrigerator (some), dial-up. In-hotel: restaurant, bars, pools, beachfront, diving, water sports, no elevator* *MC, V* *BP.*

$ **Blue Cave Castle.** One of Negril's most unique properties (and that's saying something in this land of one-of-a-kind boutique hotels), Blue Cave Castle is perched 50 feet over a pirate cave. A treasure is found within the walls of Blue Cave Castle, a keep towering over the cliffs of Negril. Each of the castle's rather basic rooms boasts a seaside view—the most elaborate is the Penthouse, with its three private sunning decks. Visitors can snorkel through the grotto into a secluded garden, or just descend the flight of stairs carved into the cliff face down to the seaside, where they can sit upon stone King and Queen thrones and watch the sun sink into the cobalt-blue water of the Caribbean ocean. **Pros:** unique accommodations, good snorkeling, friendly staff. **Cons:** basic rooms, no beach, some rooms lack of air-conditioning. ✉*West End Rd.* ☎*876/957-4845* 🌐*www.bluecavecastle.com* *14 rooms* *In-room: no a/c (some), no phone, refrigerator, (some), no TV (some). In-hotel: bar, beachfront, diving, water sports, no elevator* *No credit cards* *EP.*

6

VILLAS RENTALS

You won't find the luxurious villas of Ocho Rios and Discovery Bay, but Negril is slowly seeing more villas for those who would like a home-away-from-home experience. Since 1967, the **Jamaica Association of Villas and Apartments** (🌐*www.villasinjamaica.com*) has handled villas, cottages, apartments, and condos across the island. Membership requires inspection and adherence to a set of guidelines.

PRIVATE VILLAS

Negril Beach Villa. Booked through the reservations office at Hedonism II, this villa is on a pristine stretch of Negril Beach near Cosmo's. Staffed around the clock, the villa offers 2 floors of lemon-tinted rooms including a master bath with Jacuzzi tub and verandah leading out to the beach. All bedrooms are air-conditioned and include their own TVs. Pros: luxurious accommodations, great beach location, helpful and friendly staff. Cons: expensive, few on-site amenities, may be too quiet for some visitors. ✉*Norman Manley Blvd.* ☎*876/957–5200* 🌐*www.super-*

clubs.com ⬦3 bedrooms, 3 bathrooms ⬦In-villa: no a/c
(some), safe, kitchen, refrigerator, DVD, VCR, Wi-Fi, daily
maid service, cook, security on-site, fully staffed, pool,
beachfront, water toys, laundry service ⬛AE, DC, MC,
V ⬦EP.

BEACHES

★ Fodor'sChoice **Negril Beach.** Stretching for 7 mi (11 km), the
long, white-sand beach in Negril is arguably Jamaica's finest. It starts with the white sands of Bloody Bay north of
town and continues along Long Bay all the way to the cliffs
on the southern edge of town. Some stretches remain undeveloped, but not many. Along the main stretch of beach,
the sand is public to the high-water mark, so a nonstop
line of visitors and vendors parade from end to end. The
walk is sprinkled with many good beach bars and open-
air restaurants, some that charge a small fee to use their
beach facilities. Bloody Bay is lined with large all-inclusive
resorts, and these sections are mostly private. Jamaica's
best-known nude beach, at Hedonism II, is always among
the busiest; only resort guests or day-pass holders may sun
here. ✉*Norman Manley Blvd.*

DID YOU KNOW? **More than at any other Jamaican destination,
locals selling** *ganja* **(marijuana) are common throughout Negril.
On Negril Beach, any pretense drops and direct (and, sometimes,
frequent) offers occur. Remember, marijuana is strictly illegal
throughout Jamaica. Your status as a foreign traveler won't help
you. Roadblocks, undercover agents, and drug-sniffing dogs are
all used on the island.**

SPORTS & THE OUTDOORS

The North Coast is known for Dunn's River Falls, and the
South Coast for Y. S. Falls (both accessible from Negril on
a day tour), but the Negril area is home to some impressive
waterfalls. A top activity for travelers tired of the beach,
Mayfield Falls is tucked into the Dolphin Head Mountains
near Glenbrook. These falls have been the stuff of legend
since the 1700s, when locals swore a mermaid lived in
these mineral-rich pool. Today the "mermaids" are tourists from Negril and Montego Bay who come to enjoy the
waterfalls and underwater caves. Fifty-two varieties of fern

The Green Flash

CLOSE UP

Looking directly west, Negril's cliffs are Jamaica's best-loved sunset spot. Hundreds of visitors come every night to watch the end of another island day—and perhaps spot the rare green flash. Rick's Café has long been the island's favorite sunset spot, with a view that looks out over mile after mile of open water.

Just what is the green flash? Under the right conditions, as sunset cools into the sea, a momentary green sizzle appears on the horizon. Science explains it as the refraction of sunlight through the thick lens of the Earth's atmosphere. All agree that it's a rare sight, requiring just the right combination of sun, sky, and luck. The best chances of seeing a green flash come when the horizon is slightly below you, the water is warmer than the air, and the view is unobstructed by clouds or haze.

The practice of looking for the green flash came into vogue in the late 1800s with the publication of Jules Verne's novel *Le Rayon Vert* (*The Green Ray*). The author wrote of "a green which no artist could ever obtain on his palette, a green of which neither the varied tints of vegetation nor the shades of the most limpid sea could ever produce the like! If there is a green in Paradise, it cannot be but of this shade, which most surely is the true green of Hope."

And what happens if you are lucky enough to spot the green flash? Jules Verne claimed "he who has been fortunate enough once to behold it is enabled to see closely into his own heart and to read the thoughts of others." And according to island lore, couples that witness the flash are guaranteed true love.

6

are found here, as well as many types of tropical flowers. A visit here includes a guided hike up the river with a stop at a bar and grill along the way. Several operators offer tours here, usually with transportation from nearby hotels and lunch included.

Mayfield Falls and Mineral Springs (⊠*Dolphin Head, south of Lucea* ☎*876/953–3034 or 876/971–6580* ⊕*www.mayfieldfalls.com*) offers tours with round-trip transportation from Negril hotels, a free welcome drink, 90 minutes on the river and trail, lunch, free use of hammocks, and, twice weekly, a live heritage show. **River Walk** (⊠*Norman Manley Blvd.* ☎*876/957–3444* ⊕*www.riverwalkatmayfield.com*) offers transportation from Negril to Mayfield Falls.

BIRD-WATCHING

About 10 minutes from Negril, **Royal Palm Reserve** (⊠*Springfield Rd., Sheffield* ☎*876/957–3736* ⊕*www.roy-alpalmreserve.com*) is home to 50 bird species, including the West Indian whistling duck, which comes to feed at the park's Cotton Tree Lake. The park is also home to the Jamaican woodpecker, Jamaican oriole, Jamaican parakeet, and spectacular streamertail hummingbirds, which flit among the thick vegetation. Admission is $10.

BOATING

Negril doesn't have the marinas of Montego Bay or Port Antonio, but the larger resorts here do offer Sunfish and Hobie Cat sailing; you can also find sunset and catamaran cruises just about every day of the week.

Jamaica Rhino Safaris (⊠*Rhodes Hall, Green Island* ☎*876/877–0781 or 876/361–1326* ⊕*www.jamaicarhinosafaris. com*) offers one- and two-person excursions on rigid inflatable boats. An eastward route travels to Cousin's Cove and into Bulls Bay where you swim before heading out to Lucea to see the molasses pier. A westward itinerary travels around Booby Cay, then coast up the Negril River before turning back and continuing south along the Negril cliffs for a swimming stop at Pirates' Cave. Children 14 to 18 must be accompanied by an adult.

Wild Thing Watersports Negril (⊠*Norman Manley Blvd.* ☎*876/957–9930* ⊕*www.wildthingwatersportsnegril.com*) offers several different types of cruises aboard its catamaran. The three-hour sunset cruise ($50) stops at Rick's Café with time to swim and watch the cliff divers. It departs daily at 4 and costs $50. The Half Moon Beach Cruise ($60) includes a snorkel stop and lunch. The Rhodes Hall Plantation Cruise ($85) includes reef snorkeling in Orange Bay, a full buffet lunch, and a horseback ride at Rhodes Hall Plantation.

DIVING & SNORKELING

Thanks to its protected waters, Negril offers some of the best scuba diving on the island, although some sites damaged by Hurricane Ivan in 2004 still haven't recovered. There are a wide variety of dive sites to suit all levels, and you can see everything from unusual coral formations to forbidding caves to shipwrecks (and even some downed Cessna planes).

The **Negril Scuba Centre** (✉*Mariner's Negril Beach Club, Norman Manley Blvd.* ☎*876/957–0392* ✉*Sunset at the Palms, Norman Manley Blvd.* ☎*876/383–9533* ✉*Negril Escape Resort & Spa, West End Rd.* ☎*876/957–0392* ⊕*www.negrilscuba.com*) has three locations in Negril. The company offers numerous dive courses, including certification courses. **Wild Thing Water Sports** (✉*Norman Manley Blvd.* ☎*876/957–9930* ⊕*www.wildthingwatersportsnegril. com*) offers several cruises from their shop in the middle of Negril Beach. Cruises include snorkeling with full use of equipment and instruction for those new to the sport.

FISHING

For less serious anglers, Negril has several fishing parks. These offer lake fishing as well as nature trails, picnic facilities, and a family-friendly atmosphere. The easiest to reach is **Royal Palm Reserve** (✉*Springfield Rd., Sheffield* ☎*876/957–3736* ⊕*www.royalpalmreserve.com*), about 10 minutes from Negril. You can rent gear and try your luck at catching perch or tarpon in Cotton Tree Lake. There's an admission price of $10 to visit the park and a $5 charge for fishing.

GOLF

Great golf, rolling hills, and a "liquor mobile" go hand in hand at the 18-hole **Negril Hills Golf Club** (✉*Sheffield Rd., Negril* ☎*876/957–4638*), the only golf course in Negril. The greens fees are $28.75 for 9 holes or $57.50 for 18 holes.

HORSEBACK RIDING

Although it doesn't have the long history as the horseback riding options in Ocho Rios, Negril is home several good horseback options. Both beginning and experienced riders can be accommodated on guided rides.

Rhodes Hall Plantation (✉*Green Island, Hanover* ☎*876/929– 7895*) dates back to the 1700s, when it was a sugarcane plantation. Although the plantation continues to produce coconut, bananas, and mangoes, tourism is now the main draw, thanks to its location 5 mi (8 km) east of Negril. The property is home to 70 horses available for rides through a variety of terrains.

There's no better way to see the Great Morass than on horseback; you can take part in a guided ride at the **Royal Palm Reserve** (✉*Sheffield Rd., east of Negril* ☎*876/957–*

3736 ⊕*www.royalpalmreserve.com*). Be sure to reserve in advance; groups of up to 20 riders are welcome.

MOUNTAIN BIKING

Flanked by the marshy areas of the Great Morass, many of Negril's mountain-biking options lie along the South Coast. The fairly flat terrain makes mountain biking accessible for all levels of bikers.

The Ocho Rios–based **Blue Mountain Bicycle Tours** (✉*121 Main St., Ocho Rios* ☎*876/974–7075* ⊕*www.bmtoursja. com*) offers guided bike rides ($89) along the South Coast. The tour includes round-trip transportation from Negril hotels.

TENNIS

Couples Swept Away (✉*Norman Manley Blvd.* ☎*876/957–4061* ⊕*www.couples.com*) offers 10 tennis courts as well as squash, racquetball, and many other sports.

SHOPPING

Shopping isn't one of the top activities in Negril—you'll need to go to Montego Bay or Ocho Rios for that—but some excellent duty-free shops can be found at the top shopping destination in town: **Time Square** (✉*Norman Manley Blvd.* ☎*876/957–9263*). The mall is known for its luxury goods ranging from cigars to jewelry.

MARKETS

With its laid-back atmosphere, it's no surprise that most Negril shopping involves straw hats, woven baskets, and ★ T-shirts, all plentiful at the **Rutland Point** (✉*Norman Manley Blvd.* ☎*No phone*), a crafts market on the northern edge of town. The atmosphere is more laid-back than at similar establishments in Montego Bay and Ocho Rios.

SPECIALTY ITEMS

CIGARS

You can also buy Cuban cigars almost everywhere, even though they can't be brought legally back to the United States. **Cigar King** (✉*Time Square Mall, southern end of Norman Manley Blvd., Negril* ☎*876/957–3315*) has a wide selection of cigars stores in a walk-in humidor.

FOOD

The lowest coffee prices are found in local supermarkets. Check the **Hi-Lo Supermarket** (✉*West End Rd., Negril*

☎876/957–4546). But if the store is out of Blue Mountain, you may have to settle for High Mountain coffee, the second-favorite brand.

NIGHTLIFE & THE ARTS

With its many open-air beach bars and clubs, Negril has an active, if casual, nightlife scene. Most afternoons, cars with booming sound systems drive up and down Norman Manley Boulevard and West End Road, loudly promoting that night's main event. Typically every night brings a party or concert somewhere in Negril.

ANNUAL EVENTS

The **Reggae Marathon and Half Marathon Race Day** (✉*Long Bay Beach* ☎*876/922–8677* ⊕*www.reggaemarathon.com*) takes place in late November or early December. Runners can test themselves on a 13.1-mi (21.1-km) or 26.2-mi (42.1-km) run along the coast. This event, which draws competitors from more than 20 countries, grows every year.

BARS & CLUBS

Negril has some kind of event every evening, usually a beach party and live music. Some of the all-inclusive resorts offer a dinner and disco pass for $50 to $100; to buy a pass, call ahead to check availability, and be sure to bring a photo identification with you. In Negril, trucks with loudspeakers travel through the streets in the afternoon announcing the hot spot for the evening.

★ You can find Negril's best live music at **Alfred's Ocean Palace** (✉*Norman Manley Blvd., Negril* ☎*876/957–4735*), with live performances right on the beach. **Bourbon Beach** (✉*Norman Manley Blvd., Negril* ☎*876/957–4405*) is wildly popular for its live reggae music on Monday, Thursday, and Saturday night. Sunset brings the crowds to **Rick's Café** (✉*West End Rd., Negril* ☎*876/957–4621*) to watch live performances.

★ The always-packed disco at **Hedonism II** (✉*Norman Manley Blvd., Negril* ☎*876/957–5200*) is the wildest dance spot on the island. Tuesday pajama parties and Thursday toga night are tops. For nonguests, night passes are $75 and cover everything from 6 PM to 3 AM. **The Jungle** (✉*Norman Manley Blvd., Negril* ☎*876/957–4005*) is the hottest nightspot in Negril, with two raised bars and a circular dance floor. **Margaritaville** (✉*Norman Manley Blvd., Negril* ☎*876/957–4467*) is liveliest in the evening, especially for special theme nights such as the weekly Parrothead Sunset Beach Party. Call for complimentary hotel pickups.

NEGRIL ESSENTIALS

To research prices, get advice from other travelers, and book travel arrangements, visit www.fodors.com.

TRANSPORTATION

BY AIR

Negril has no international air service, but does have a small domestic airport across from Bloody Bay. The Negril Aerodrome has limited charter service from both Montego Bay and Kingston.

Information **International Airlink** (☎*888/247–5465* ⊕*www.intlairlink.com*).**TimAir** (☎*876/952–2516* ⊕*www.timair.com*).

Airports Most Negril travelers arrive from Montego Bay's Sangster International Airport. Many of the larger hotels (especially the all-inclusive resorts) offer shuttle service. Transportation is also available from JCAL Tours, Jamaica Tours, and Clive's Transport Service for about $50 to $60 per person round-trip.

Information **Clive's Transport Service** (✉*Box 4815, Lucea* ☎*876/956–2615 or 876/869–7571* ⊕*www.clivestransportservice-jamaica.com*). **Jamaica Tours** (✉*Providence Dr., Ironshore, Montego Bay* ☎*876/953–2107* ⊕*www.jamaicatoursltd.com*). **JCAL Tours** (✉*Claude Clarke Ave., Montego Bay* ☎*876/952–7574* ⊕*www.jcaltours.com*). **Negril Aerodrome** (✉*Norman Manley Blvd., Ocho Rios* ☎*876/957–5016*).

BY CAR

Driving in Negril is an easier task than in Montego Bay and Ocho Rios, but still a chore thanks to the very narrow roads (especially when the main road becomes West Bay Road along the cliffs). If you plan to spend the day exploring to the South Coast but don't want to travel with an organized tour, driving can be a good choice, although signage is poor on area roads.

Information **Rite Rate Car Rental** (✉*Norman Manley Blvd., Negril* ☎*876/957–4667*). **Vernon's Car & Jeep Rental** (✉*Plaza de Negril, Sheffield Rd., Negril* ☎*876/957–4354*).

BY TAXI

Taxis are the most popular mode of transportation (although not an inexpensive one). They can be caught at any hotel or on the road. Licensed taxis have a red license plate with a PP that indicates the taxi is a Public Passenger Vehicle. Very few taxis are metered, so be sure to agree on a price with the driver before departing. Hotel staffers can let you know how much to expect to pay before you begin your negotiations.

Information **JUTA** (☎876/957–9197 ⊕ *www.jutatoursnegrilltd. com*).

CONTACTS & RESOURCES

BANKS & EXCHANGE SERVICES

Most of the larger hotels in Negril can exchange money and cash traveler's checks; you can also find ATMs at some of the larger properties. Scotiabank has an ATM at its Negril Square location.

Information **Banmark Cambio** (✉*West End Rd., Negril*). **National Commercial Bank** (✉*Sunshine Village, northern end of West End Rd., Negril*). **Scotiabank** (✉*Negril Square, south of Sheffield Rd., Negril*).

EMERGENCIES

Medical care is fairly limited in Negril. All larger resorts have nurses on duty during work hours and a doctor on call and there's a medical clinic in town. The nearest hospitals are in Savannah-La-Mar and Lucea; the closest large hospitals are in Montego Bay.

Emergency Services **Ambulance & Fire** (☎*110*). **Hurricane Update** (☎*116*). **Police** (☎*119*).

Hospitals **Negril Beach Medical Center** (✉*Norman Manley Blvd., Negril* ☎*876/957–4888*).

Noel Holmes Hospital (✉*Fort Charlotte Dr., Lucea* ☎*876/956– 2733*).

Savannah-La-Mar Hospital (✉*Barracks Rd., Savannah-La-Mar* ☎*876/955–2533*).

Pharmacies **Negril Pharmacy** (✉*Shop 27, Plaza De Negril, Negril* ☎*876/957–4076*).

INTERNET, MAIL & SHIPPING

Internet access is somewhat limited in Negril, even in hotels you might expect to see high-speed or even wireless service, due to the lower number of business travelers, the lack of cruise-ship passengers, and the difficulty of obtaining even telephone lines in Negril. However, thanks in part to its large number of spring breakers, Negril does have some Internet cafés where you can hop on a high-speed connection and check your e-mail.

Internet Cafés **Bananaz Internet Café** (✉ *Norman Manley Blvd., Negril* ☎ *876/957–3249* ⊕ *www.bananazjamaica.com*). **Easy Rock Internet Café** (✉ *West End Rd., Negril* ☎ *876/957–0816 or 876/424–5481* ⊕ *www.negril.com/ezrock*). **Irie Vibes Cyber-Up Internet Café** (✉ *Norman Manley Blvd., Negril* ⊕ *irievibes.com*).

Post Offices **Negril Post Office** (✉ *West End Rd., Negril* ☎ *876/957–9654*).

Shipping Companies **Airpak Express** (✉ *Negril Aerodrome, Negril* ☎ *876/957–5051*).

TOUR OPTIONS

Although there are tours from Montego Bay that give day-trippers a chance to experience Negril, there are few tours available to those who are staying here. Tropical Tours, a Montego Bay–based company, offers Negril visitors a half-day highlights tour with a look at the Lighthouse and a stop at Rick's Café. The half-day tour is available Monday, Friday, and Saturday afternoons. Tropical Tours also offers a half-day shopping and sunset tour on Tuesday, Thursday, and Friday.

Information **Tropical Tours** (✉ *Norman Manley Blvd.* ☎ *876/957–4110 in Negril* ⊕ *www.tropicaltours-ja.com*).

VISITOR INFORMATION

The Negril Chamber of Commerce publishes the *Negril Guide,* a free brochure covering attractions, shopping, and dining. The organization also operates a visitor center just beyond the downtown roundabout on West End Road; you can find brochures and maps available as well as friendly assistance.

Information **Negril Chamber of Commerce** (✉ *West End Rd., Negril* ☎ *876/957–3463 or 957–4067* ⊕ *www.negrilchamberofcommerce.com*).

In Focus Jamaica Essentials

PLANNING TOOLS, EXPERT INSIGHT, GREAT CONTACTS

There are planners and there are those who, excuse the pun, fly by the seat of their pants. We happily place ourselves among the planners. Our writers and editors try to anticipate all the issues you may face before and during any journey, and then they do their research. This section is the product of their efforts. Use it to get excited about your trip to Jamaica, to inform your travel planning, or to guide you on the road should the seat of your pants start to feel threadbare.

GETTING STARTED

We're very proud of our Web site: Fodors.com is a great place to begin any journey. Scan "Travel Wire" for suggested itineraries, travel deals, restaurant and hotel openings, and other up-to-the-minute info. Check out "Booking" to research prices and book plane tickets, hotel rooms, rental cars, and vacation packages. Head to "Talk" for on-the-ground pointers from travelers who frequent our message boards. You can also link to loads of other travel-related resources.

▌ RESOURCES

ONLINE TRAVEL TOOLS

All About Jamaica **Jamaica Tourist Board** (⊕www.visitjamaica.com). **Association of Jamaica Attractions** (⊕www.attractions-jamaica.com). **Cruise Jamaica** (⊕www.cruisejamaica.com). **Government of Jamaica's Information Service** (⊕www.jis.gov.jm). **Jamaica Association of Villas and Apartments** (⊕www.villasinjamaica.com). **Jamaica Hotel and Tourist Association** (⊕www.jhta.org).

Currency Conversion **Google** (⊕www.google.com) does currency conversion. Just type in the amount you want to convert and an explanation of how you want it converted (e.g., "14 Swiss francs in dollars"), and then voilà. **Oanda.com** (⊕www.oanda.com) also allows you to print out a handy table with the current day's conversion rates. **XE.com** (⊕www.xe.com) is a good currency conversion Web site.

Safety **Transportation Security Administration** (TSA ⊕www.tsa.gov).

Time Zones **Timeanddate.com** (⊕www.timeanddate.com/worldclock) can help you figure out the correct time anywhere.

Weather **Accuweather.com** (⊕www.accuweather.com) is an independent weather-forecasting service with good coverage of hurricanes. **Weather.com** (⊕www.weather.com) is the Web site for the Weather Channel.

Other Resources **CIA World Factbook** (⊕www.odci.gov/cia/publications/factbook/index.html) has profiles of every country in the world. It's a good source if you need some quick facts and figures.

INSPIRATION

BOOKS

The Book of Jamaica: A novel by Russell Banks that begins in the shadowy footsteps of Errol Flynn in Port Antonio then moves to Cockpit

Country and an exploration of life with the Maroons.

Catch a Fire: The Life of Bob Marley: This biography traces the life of the reggae superstar from his birth at Nine Mile and childhood in Kingston to his rise in the music world.

The Real Taste of Jamaica: Enid Donaldson's classic cookbook covers Jamaican food from roadside stands to jerk huts to home kitchens.

Wide Sargasso Sea: This Jean Rhys novel was written as a prequel to Jane Eyre and explores plantation life in Jamaica. Also adapted into a movie.

MOVIES

Cool Runnings: This 1993 Disney film was based on the true story of the Jamaican bobsled team and its efforts in the Winter Olympic games.

The Harder They Come: This gritty look at life in Kingston was the first feature film produced in Jamaica.

How Stella Got Her Groove Back: This popular story of a successful stockbroker who finds love with a Jamaican man was shot on location at Round Hill.

VISITOR INFORMATION

At Montego Bay's Sangster International Airport, arriving passengers will find a Jamaica tourist Board booth in the customs hall. This desk can help with a limited number of brochures and maps and can also make hotel arrangements for travelers who arrive with reservations. The airport information desk is open 6 AM TO 10 PM daily.

Contacts **Jamaica Tourist Board** (☎800/233–4582 ⊕www.visit jamaica.com).

▌ THINGS TO CONSIDER

GOVERNMENT ADVISORIES

As different countries have different worldviews, look at travel advisories from a range of governments to get more of a sense of what's going on out there. And be sure to parse the language carefully. For example, a warning to "avoid all travel" carries more weight than one urging you to "avoid nonessential travel," and both are much stronger than a plea to "exercise caution." A U.S. government travel warning is more permanent (though not necessarily more serious) than a so-called public announcement, which carries an expiration date.

▬TIP➔ **Consider registering online with the State Department (https://travelregistration.state.gov/ibrs/), so the government will know to look for you should a crisis occur in the country you're visiting.**

The U.S. Department of State's Web site has more than just travel warnings and advisories. The consular information sheets issued for every country have general safety tips, entry requirements (though be sure to verify these with the country's embassy), and other useful details.

General Information & Warnings

Australian Department of Foreign Affairs & Trade (⊕www.smartraveller.gov.au). **Consular Affairs Bureau**

of Canada (⊕www.voyage.gc.ca). **U.K. Foreign & Commonwealth Office** (⊕www.fco.gov.uk/travel). **U.S. Department of State** (⊕www.travel.state.gov).

SHIPPING LUGGAGE AHEAD

Imagine globe-trotting with only a carry-on in tow. Shipping your luggage in advance via an air-freight service is a great way to cut down on backaches, hassles, and stress—especially if your packing list includes strollers, car seats, etc. There are some things to be aware of, though.

First, research carry-on restrictions; if you absolutely need something that isn't practical to ship and isn't allowed in carry-ons, this strategy isn't for you. Second, plan to send your bags several days in advance to U.S. destinations and as much as two weeks in advance to some international destinations. Third, plan to spend some money: it will cost at least $100 to send a small piece of luggage, a golf bag, or a pair of skis to a domestic destination, much more to places overseas.

Some people use Federal Express to ship their bags, but this can cost even more than air-freight services. All these services insure your bag (for most, the limit is $1,000, but you should verify that amount); you can, however, purchase additional insurance for about $1 per $100 of value.

Contacts **Luggage Concierge** (☎800/288-9818 ⊕www.luggageconcierge.com). **Luggage Express** (☎866/744-7224 ⊕www.usxpluggageexpress.com). **Luggage Free** (☎800/361-6871 ⊕www.luggagefree.com). **Sports Express** (☎800/357-4174 ⊕www.sportsexpress.com) specializes in shipping golf clubs and other sports equipment. **Virtual Bellhop** (☎877/235-5467 ⊕www.virtualbellhop.com).

PASSPORTS & VISAS

Proof of citizenship (valid U.S. passport or original government-issued birth certificate plus picture ID) is required to enter Jamaica. Further, the U.S. government requires all passengers traveling by air to the Caribbean (including Jamaica) to have a valid U.S. passport at this writing.

PASSPORTS

A passport verifies both your identity and nationality—a great reason to have one. Another reason is that you need a passport now more than ever. At this writing, U.S. citizens must have a passport when traveling by air between the United States and several destinations for which other forms of identification (e.g., a driver's license and a birth certificate) were once sufficient. These destinations include Mexico, Canada, Bermuda, and all countries in Central America and the Caribbean (except the territories of Puerto Rico and the U.S. Virgin Islands). Soon enough you'll need a passport when traveling between the United States and such destinations by land and sea, too.

U.S. passports are valid for 10 years. You must apply in person if you're getting a passport for the first time; if your previous passport was lost, stolen, or damaged; or if your previous passport has expired and was issued more than 15 years ago or when you were under 16. All children under 18 must appear in person to apply for or renew a passport. Both parents must accompany any child under 14 (or send a notarized statement with their permission) and provide proof of their relationship to the child.

■TIP→ Before your trip, make two copies of your passport's data page (one for someone at home and another for you to carry separately). Or scan the page and e-mail it to someone at home and/or yourself.

There are 13 regional passport offices, as well as 7,000 passport acceptance facilities in post offices, public libraries, and other governmental offices. If you're renewing a passport, you can do so by mail. Forms are available at passport acceptance facilities and online.

The cost to apply for a new passport is $97 for adults, $82 for children under 16; renewals are $67. Allow six weeks for processing, both for first-time passports and renewals. For an expediting fee of $60 you can reduce this time to about two weeks. If your trip is less than two weeks away, you can get a passport even more rapidly by going to a passport office with the necessary documentation. Private expediters can get things done in as little as 48 hours, but charge hefty fees for their services.

VISAS

A visa is essentially formal permission to enter a country. Visas allow countries to keep track of you and other visitors—and generate revenue (from application fees). You *always* need a visa to enter a foreign country; however, many countries routinely issue tourist visas on arrival, particularly to U.S. citizens. When your passport is stamped or scanned in the immigration line, you're actually being issued a visa. Sometimes you have to stand in a separate line and pay a small fee to get your stamp before going through immigration, but you can still do this at the airport on arrival.

Getting a visa isn't always that easy. Some countries require that you arrange for one in advance of your trip. There's usually—but not always—a fee involved, and said fee may be nominal ($10 or less) or substantial ($100 or more).

If you must apply for a visa in advance, you can usually do it in person or by mail. When you apply by mail, you send your passport to a designated consulate, where your passport will be examined and the visa issued. Expediters—usually the same ones who handle expedited passport applications—can do all the work of obtaining your visa for you; however, there's always an additional cost (often more than $50 per visa).

Most visas limit you to a single trip—basically during the actual dates of your planned vacation. Other visas allow you to visit as many times as you wish for a specific period of time. Remember that requirements change, sometimes at the drop of a hat, and the burden is on you to make sure that you have the appropriate visas. Otherwise, you'll be turned away at the airport or, worse, deported after you arrive in the country. No company or travel insurer gives refunds if your travel plans are disrupted because you didn't have the correct visa.

U.S. Passport Information U.S. Department of State (☎877/487–2778 ⊕http://travel.state.gov/passport).

U.S. Passport & Visa Expediters A. Briggs Passport & Visa Expediters (☎800/806–0581 or 202/338–0111 ⊕www.abriggs.com). American Passport Express (☎800/455–5166 or 800/841–6778 ⊕www.americanpassport.com). Passport Express (☎800/362–8196 ⊕www.passportexpress.com). Travel Document Systems (☎800/874–5100 or 202/638–3800 ⊕www.traveldocs.com). Travel the World Visas (☎866/886–8472 or 301/495–7700 ⊕www.world-visa.com).

SHOTS & MEDICATIONS

Jamaica reported a small outbreak of malaria in 2006, almost all of the cases in the Kingston area. The outbreak subsided almost immediately, but it's still a good idea to be on your guard. If you use mosquito repellent (particularly at dusk and after dark, when malarial mosquitoes are more active), you'll greatly reduce your risk of being bitten. Dengue fever is still present and a more realistic threat; these mosquitoes bite during the daylight hours. *For more information see Health under On the Ground in Jamaica, below.*

■TIP→ **If you travel a lot internationally—particularly to developing nations—refer to the CDC's** *Health Information for International Travel* **(aka Traveler's Health Yellow Book). Info from it is posted on the CDC Web site (wwwn.cdc.gov/travel/default.aspx), or you can buy a copy from your local bookstore for $24.95.**

Health Warnings National Centers for Disease Control & Prevention (CDC ☎877/394–8747 international travelers' health line ⊕www.cdc.gov/travel). World Health Organization (WHO ⊕www.who.int).

TRIP INSURANCE

We believe that comprehensive trip insurance is especially valuable if you're booking a very expensive or complicated trip (particularly to an isolated region) or if you're booking far in advance. Who knows what could happen six months down the road? But whether you get insurance has more to do with how comfortable you are assuming all that risk yourself.

Comprehensive travel policies typically cover trip-cancellation and interruption, letting you cancel or cut your trip short because of a personal emergency, illness, or, in some cases, acts of terrorism in your destination. Such policies also cover evacuation and medical care. Some also cover you for trip delays because of bad weather or mechanical problems as well as for lost or delayed baggage. Another type of coverage to look for is financial default—that is, when your trip is disrupted because a tour operator, airline, or cruise line goes out of business. Generally you must buy this when you book your trip or shortly thereafter, and it's only available to you if your operator isn't on a list of excluded companies.

If you're going abroad, consider buying medical-only coverage at the very least. Neither Medicare nor some private insurers cover medical expenses anywhere outside of the United States (including time aboard a cruise ship, even if it leaves from a U.S. port). Medical-only policies typically reimburse you for medical care (excluding that related to preexisting conditions) and hospitalization abroad, and provide for evacuation. You still have to pay the bills and await reimbursement from the insurer, though.

Expect comprehensive travel insurance policies to cost about 4% to 7% or 8% of the total price of your trip (it's more like 8% to 12% if you're over age 70). A medical-only policy may or may not be cheaper than a comprehensive policy. Always read the fine print of your policy to make sure that you're cov-

ered for the risks that are of most concern to you.

TRIP-INSURANCE RESOURCES

INSURANCE-COMPARISON SITES

Insure My Trip.com (☎800/487–4722 ⊕www.insuremytrip.com).

Square Mouth.com (☎800/240–0369 or 727/490–5803 ⊕www.squaremouth.com).

COMPREHENSIVE TRAVEL INSURERS

Access America (☎800/729–6021 ⊕www.accessamerica.com).

CSA Travel Protection (☎800/873–9855 ⊕www.csatravelprotection.com).

HTH Worldwide (☎610/254–8700 or 888/243–2358 ⊕www.hthworldwide.com).

Travelex Insurance (☎800/228–9792 ⊕www.travelex-insurance.com).

Travel Guard International (☎715/345–0505 or 800/826–4919 ⊕www.travelguard.com).

Travel Insured International (☎800/243–3174 ⊕www.travelinsured.com).

MEDICAL-ONLY INSURERS

International Medical Group (☎800/628–4664 ⊕www.imglobal.com).

International SOS (⊕www.internationalsos.com).

Wallach & Company (☎800/237–6615 or 540/687–3166 ⊕www.wallach.com).

BOOKING YOUR TRIP

Unless your cousin is a travel agent, you're probably among the millions of people who make most of their travel arrangements online.

But have you ever wondered just what the differences are between an online travel agent (a Web site through which you make reservations instead of going directly to the airline, hotel, or car-rental company), a discounter (a firm that does a high volume of business with a hotel chain or airline and accordingly gets good prices), a wholesaler (one that makes cheap reservations in bulk and then resells them to people like you), and an aggregator (one that compares all the offerings so you don't have to)?

Is it truly better to book directly on an airline or hotel Web site? And when does a real live travel agent come in handy?

▌ ONLINE

You really have to shop around. A travel wholesaler such as Hotels.com or HotelClub.net can be a source of good rates, as can discounters such as Hotwire or Priceline, particularly if you can bid for your hotel room or airfare. Indeed, such sites sometimes have deals that are unavailable elsewhere. They do, however, tend to work only with hotel chains (which makes them just plain useless for getting hotel reservations outside of major cities) or big airlines (so that often leaves out upstarts like jetBlue and some foreign carriers like Air India).

Also, with discounters and wholesalers you must generally prepay, and everything is nonrefundable. And before you fork over the dough, be sure to check the terms and conditions, so you know what a given company will do for you if there's a problem and what you'll have to deal with on your own.

■TIP→ **To be absolutely sure everything was processed correctly, confirm reservations made through online travel agents, discounters, and wholesalers directly with your hotel before leaving home.**

Booking engines like Expedia, Travelocity, and Orbitz are actually travel agents, albeit high-volume, online ones. And airline travel packagers like AmericanAirlines Vacations and Virgin Vacations—well, they're travel agents, too. But they may still not work with all the world's hotels.

An aggregator site will search many sites and pull the best prices for airfares, hotels, and rental cars from them. Most aggregators compare the major travel-booking sites such as Expedia, Travelocity, and Orbitz; some also look at airline Web sites, though rarely the sites of smaller budget airlines. Some aggregators also compare other travel products, including complex packages—a good thing, as you can sometimes get the best overall deal by booking an air-and-hotel package.

ONLINE-BOOKING RESOURCES

AGGREGATORS

Kayak (⊕www.kayak.com) looks at cruises and vacation packages.

Mobissimo (⊕www.mobissimo.com) examines airfare, hotels, cars, and tons of activities.

Qixo (⊕www.qixo.com) compares cruises, vacation packages, and even travel insurance.

Sidestep (⊕www.sidestep.com) compares vacation packages and lists travel deals and some activities.

Travelgrove (⊕www.travelgrove.com) compares cruises and vacation packages and lets you search by themes.

BOOKING ENGINES

Cheap Tickets (⊕www.cheaptickets.com) discounter.

Expedia (⊕www.expedia.com) large online agency that charges a booking fee for airline tickets.

Hotwire (⊕www.hotwire.com) discounter.

lastminute.com (⊕www.lastminute.com) specializes in last-minute travel; the main site is for the U.K., but it has a link to a U.S. site.

Luxury Link (⊕www.luxurylink.com) has auctions (surprisingly good

deals) as well as offers on the high-end side of travel.

Onetravel.com (⊕www.onetravel.com) discounter for hotels, car rentals, airfares, and packages.

Orbitz (⊕www.orbitz.com) charges a booking fee for airline tickets, but gives a clear breakdown of fees and taxes before you book.

Priceline.com (⊕www.priceline.com)discounter that also allows bidding.

Travel.com (⊕www.travel.com) allows you to compare its rates with those of other booking engines.

Travelocity (⊕www.travelocity.com) charges a booking fee for airline tickets, but promises good problem resolution.

ONLINE ACCOMMODATIONS

Hotelbook.com (⊕www.hotelbook.com) focuses on independent hotels worldwide.

Hotel Club (⊕www.hotelclub.net) good for major cities and some resort areas.

Hotels.com (⊕www.hotels.com) big Expedia-owned wholesaler that offers rooms in hotels all over the world.

Quikbook (⊕www.quikbook.com) offers "pay when you stay" reservations that allow you to settle your bill when you check out, not when you book; best for trips to U.S. and Canadian cities.

OTHER RESOURCES

Bidding For Travel (⊕www.biddingfortravel.com) good place to figure out what you can get and for how much before you start bidding on, say, Priceline.

▌ WITH A TRAVEL AGENT

If you use an agent—brick-and-mortar or virtual—you'll pay a fee for the service. And know that the service you get from some online agents isn't comprehensive. For example Expedia and Travelocity don't search for prices on budget airlines like jetBlue, Southwest, or small foreign carriers. That said, some agents (online or not) *do* have access to fares that are difficult to find otherwise, and the savings can more than make up for any surcharge.

A knowledgeable brick-and-mortar travel agent can be a godsend if you're booking a cruise, a package trip that's not available to you directly, an air pass, or a complicated itinerary including several overseas flights. What's more, travel agents that specialize in a destination may have exclusive access to certain deals and insider information on things such as charter flights. Agents who specialize in types of travelers (senior citizens, gays and lesbians, naturists) or types of trips (cruises, luxury travel, safaris) can also be invaluable.

▌TIP→ Remember that Expedia, Travelocity, and Orbitz are travel agents, not just booking engines. To resolve any problems with a reservation made through these companies, contact them first.

A top-notch agent planning your trip to Russia will make sure you get the correct visa application and complete it on time; the one booking your cruise may get you a cabin upgrade or arrange to have bottle of champagne chilling in your cabin when you embark. And complain about the surcharges all you like, but when things don't work out the way you'd hoped, it's nice to have an agent to put things right.

Certain package trips that are available only through travel agents can save you money in Jamaica by bundling the cost of your airfare, hotel room, and airport transfers into a single, affordable sum. *For more information on Jamaica travel packages, see* ⇨ *Vacations Packages, below.*

Agent Resources **American Society of Travel Agents** (☎703/739–2782 ⊕www.travelsense.org).

▌ ACCOMMODATIONS

Jamaica was the birthplace of the all-inclusive beach resort, and many people still choose to stay in these large resorts, which provide all lodging, dining, drinks, activities, and entertainment for a single rate. Some of these hotels are open only to couples (and some of these only to male-female couples), so that is always a consideration when choosing an all-inclusive. But Jamaica also has many small inns and independent hotels and resorts in all price ranges—from super-budget to expensive, luxurious properties as well as business hotels. Villas, especially luxury villas, are a growing market as well with many extended families and multiple couples opting to share a villa for a home away from home experience.

Most hotels and other lodgings require you to give your credit-card details before they will confirm your reservation. If you don't feel comfortable e-mailing this information, ask if you can fax it (some places even prefer faxes). However you book, get confirmation in writing and have a copy of it handy when you check in.

Be sure you understand the hotel's cancellation policy. Some places allow you to cancel without any kind of penalty—even if you prepaid to secure a discounted rate—if you cancel at least 24 hours in advance. Others require you to cancel a week in advance or penalize you the cost of one night. Small inns and B&Bs are most likely to require you to cancel far in advance. Most hotels allow children under a certain age to stay in their parents' room at no extra charge, but others charge for them as extra adults; find out the cutoff age for discounts.

∎TIP➔ Assume that hotels operate on the European Plan (EP, no meals) unless we specify that they use the Breakfast Plan (BP, with full breakfast), Continental Plan (CP, continental breakfast), Full American Plan (FAP, all meals), Modified American Plan (MAP, breakfast

and dinner), or are all-inclusive (AI, all meals and most activities).

∎ AIRLINE TICKETS

Most domestic airline tickets are electronic; international tickets may be either electronic or paper. With an e-ticket the only thing you receive is an e-mailed receipt citing your itinerary and reservation and ticket numbers.

The greatest advantage of an e-ticket is that if you lose your receipt, you can simply print out another copy or ask the airline to do it for you at check-in. You usually pay a surcharge (up to $50) to get a paper ticket, if you can get one at all.

The sole advantage of a paper ticket is that it may be easier to endorse over to another airline if your flight is canceled and the airline with which you booked can't accommodate you on another flight.

CHARTER FLIGHTS

Charter companies rent aircraft and offer regularly scheduled flights (usually nonstops). Charter flights are generally cheaper than flights on regular airlines, and they often leave from and travel to a wider variety of airports. For example, you could have a nonstop flight from Columbus, Ohio, to Punta Cana, Dominican Republic, or from Chicago to Dubrovnik, Croatia.

You don't, however, have the same protections as with regular airlines. If a charter can't take off for mechanical or other reasons, there usually isn't another plane to take its place. If not enough seats are sold, the flight may be canceled. And if a company goes out of business, you're out of luck (unless, of course, you have insurance with financial default coverage; see ⇨ *Trip Insurance under Things to Consider in Getting Started, above*).

Montego Bay's Sangster International Airport is served by many seasonal charter companies—most are from the United States and Canada, but there's an increasing number from Europe. From Minneapolis, Sun Country offers weekly direct charter service to Montego Bay. From Pittsburgh and Chicago, USA 3000 offers direct service to Montego Bay.

Charter Companies **Sun Country** (☎800/359-6786 ⊕www.suncountry.com). **USA 3000** (☎877/872-3000 ⊕www.usa3000airlines.com).

▌ RENTAL CARS

When you reserve a car, ask about cancellation penalties, taxes, drop-off charges (if you're planning to pick up the car in one city and leave it in another), and surcharges (for being under or over a certain age, for additional drivers, or for driving across state or country borders or beyond a specific distance from your point of rental). All these things can add substantially to your costs. Request car seats and extras such as GPS when you book.

Rates are sometimes—but not always—better if you book in advance or reserve through a rental agency's Web site. There are other reasons to book ahead, though: for popular destinations, during busy times of the year, or to ensure that you get certain types of cars (vans, SUVs, exotic sports cars).

■ TIP→ Make sure that a confirmed reservation guarantees you a car. Agencies sometimes overbook, particularly for busy weekends and holiday periods.

Because many car renters are returning Jamaicans, the breakdown between high season and low season for car rentals is different than the high and low hotel seasons. Car-rental prices are highest over the winter holidays, Easter (when Carnival brings in many former residents), and July and August.

To rent a car you must be between the ages of 23 (with at

least one year possessing a valid driver's license) and 70. Many car-rental companies also offer cell-phone rentals, and that's a very good idea if your phone doesn't have service in Jamaica.

Your driver's license may not be recognized outside your home country. You may not be able to rent a car without an International Driving Permit (IDP), which can be used only in conjunction with a valid driver's license and which translates your license into 10 languages. Check the AAA Web site for more info as well as for IDPs ($15) themselves.

CAR-RENTAL RESOURCES

AUTOMOBILE ASSOCIATIONS

U.S.: American Automobile Association (AAA ☎315/797–5000 ⊕www.aaa.com); most contact with the organization is through state and regional members.

National Automobile Club (☎650/294–7000 ⊕www.thenac.com); membership is open to California residents only.

Local Agencies **Alex's Car Rentals and Tours** (☎876/971–2615). **Fiesta Car Rentals** (☎876/953–9444 ⊕www.fiestacarrentals.com). **Island Car Rentals** (☎876/952–7225 ⊕www.islandcarrentals.com). **Jamaica Car Rental** (☎876/952–5586).

MAJOR AGENCIES

Alamo (☎800/522–9696 ⊕www.alamo.com).

Avis (☎800/331–1084 ⊕www.avis.com).

Budget (☎800/472–3325 ⊕www.budget.com).

Hertz (☎800/654–3001 ⊕www.hertz.com).

National Car Rental (☎800/227–7368 ⊕www.nationalcar.com).

CAR-RENTAL INSURANCE

Everyone who rents a car wonders whether the insurance that the rental companies offer is worth the expense. No one—including us—has a simple answer. It all depends on how much regular insurance you have, how comfortable you are with risk, and whether money is an issue.

If you own a car, your personal auto insurance may cover a rental to some degree, though not all policies protect you abroad; always read your policy's fine print. If you don't have auto insurance, then seriously consider buying the collision- or loss-damage waiver (CDW or LDW) from the car-rental company, which eliminates your liability for damage to the car.

Some credit cards offer CDW coverage, but it's usually supplemental to your own insurance and rarely covers SUVs, minivans, luxury models, and the like. If your coverage is secondary, you may still be liable for loss-of-use costs from the car-rental company. But no credit-card insurance is valid unless you use that card for *all* transactions, from reserving to paying the final bill. All companies exclude car rental in some countries, so be sure to find out about the destination to which you are traveling.

■TIP➔ **Diners Club offers primary CDW coverage on all rentals reserved and paid for with the card. This means that Diners Club's company—not your own car insurance—pays in case of an accident. It** *doesn't* **mean your car-insurance company won't raise your rates once it discovers you had an accident.**

Some rental agencies require you to purchase CDW coverage; many will even include it in quoted rates. All will strongly encourage you to buy CDW—possibly implying that it's required—so be sure to ask about such things before renting. In most cases it's cheaper to add a supplemental CDW plan to your comprehensive travel-insurance policy (see ⇨Trip Insurance, under Things to Consider in Getting Started, above) than to purchase it from a rental company. That said, you don't want to pay for a supplement if you're required to buy insurance from the rental company.

If you rent a car in Jamaica, you will probably have to purchase CDW coverage, since most credit-card policies and private policies do not cover renters in Jamaica. We strongly urge you to purchase full insurance if you do rent a car in Jamaica.

■TIP➔ **You can decline the insurance from the rental company and purchase it through a third-party provider such as Travel Guard** (www.travelguard.com)—$9   per day for $35,000 of coverage. That's sometimes just under half the price of the CDW offered by some car-rental companies.

▌VACATION PACKAGES

Packages *are not* guided excursions. Packages combine airfare, accommodations, and perhaps a rental car or other extras (theater tickets, guided excursions, boat trips, reserved entry to popular museums, transit passes), but they let you do your own thing. During busy periods packages may be your only option, as flights and rooms may be sold out otherwise.

Packages will definitely save you time. They can also save you money, particularly in peak seasons, but—and this is a really big "but"—you should price each part of the package separately to be sure. And be aware that prices advertised on Web sites and in newspapers rarely include service charges or taxes, which can up your costs by hundreds of dollars.

■TIP➔ **Some packages and cruises are sold only through travel agents. Don't always assume that you can get the best deal by booking everything yourself.**

Each year consumers are stranded or lose their money when packagers—even large ones with excellent reputations—go out of business. How can you protect yourself?

First, always pay with a credit card; if you have a problem, your credit-card company may help you resolve it. Second, buy trip insurance that covers default. Third, choose a company that belongs to the United States Tour Operators Association, whose members must set aside funds to cover defaults. Finally, choose a company that also participates in the Tour Operator Program of the American Society of Travel Agents (ASTA), which will act as mediator in any disputes.

You can also check on the tour operator's reputation among travelers by posting an inquiry on one of the Fodors.com forums.

Organizations American Society of Travel Agents (ASTA ☎703/739–2782 or 800/965–2782 ⊕www.astanet.com). **United States Tour Operators Association** (USTOA ☎212/599–6599 ⊕www. ustoa.com).

■TIP→ Local tourism boards can provide information about lesser-known and small-niche operators that sell packages to only a few destinations.

❚ AIR & HOTEL PACKAGES

Package vacations that include air and hotel are offered by several companies, including Air Jamaica Vacations and Apple Vacations. Depending on the company, these packages may use charter flights for transportation. Vacationers traveling on a package tour will most likely find company representatives at the airport with directions to the hotel. Once you arrive at the hotel, on-site package desks keep you posted on departure times.

Recommended Companies **Air Jamaica Vacations** (☎800/568–3247 ⊕www.airjamaica vacations.com). **Apple Vacations** (☎800/517–2000 ⊕www.apple vacations.com). **FunJet Vacations** (☎888/558–6654 ⊕www.funjet. com). **Vacations by Adventure Tours** (☎800/642–8872 ⊕www. vacationsbyadventuretours.com). **Worry Free Vacations** (☎888/225–5658 ⊕www.worry freevacations.com).

TRANSPORTATION

▌ BY AIR

Frequently scheduled air service links Jamaica to major hub cities with the most frequent service into Montego Bay's Sangster International Airport. Flight times from Miami to Montego Bay are approximately 1 hour and 25 minutes; from Atlanta, plan on 2 hours and 40 minutes; from Chicago 3 hours; and from Los Angeles 5 hours and 30 minutes. Flights to Kingston take just minutes longer. **■ TIP→ If you travel frequently, look into the TSA's Registered Traveler program. The program, which is still being tested in several U.S. airports, is designed to cut down on gridlock at security checkpoints by allowing prescreened travelers to pass quickly through kiosks that scan an iris and/or a fingerprint. How sci-fi is that?**

Airlines & Airports **Airline and Airport Links.com** (⊕www.airlineandairportlinks.com) has links to many of the world's airlines and airports.

Airline-Security Issues **Transportation Security Administration** (⊕www.tsa.gov) has answers for almost every question that might come up.

AIRPORTS

Most travelers will fly into Sangster International Airport in Montego Bay (MBJ); this airport offers the best access to Montego Bay, Ocho Rios, Runaway Bay, and Negril. The island's other major airport is Norman Manley International Airport in Kingston (KIN); fly into Kingston to more easily reach the Blue Mountains, the southwest coast, and Port Antonio. Negril has no international air service, but does have a small domestic airport across from Bloody Bay. Limited domestic air service into the Port Antonio Aerodrome is available via charter companies.

Montego Bay's Sangster International Airport has made it increasingly easy to spend your waiting time. The airport is now home to the country's largest shopping mall, with stores specializing in everything from Jamaican crafts to coffees to beachwear. Air Margaritaville, a slightly scaled-down version of the popular chain restaurant, and Jamaican Bobsled Café are both top choices for meals. Just across from the Jamaican Bobsled Café, you can also find a free exhibit featuring Jamaican art through the years including some works by Edna Manley.

Major Airports **Norman Manley International Airport** (✉Kingston ☎876/924–8452 ⊕www.manley-airport.com.jm). **Sangster International Airport** (✉Montego Bay ☎876/952–3124 ⊕www.mbjairport.com).

Secondary Airports Negril Aerodrome (⊠Norman Manley Blvd., Negril ☎876/957–5016). **Port Antonio Ken Jones Aerodrome** (⊠North Coast Hwy., Port Antonio ☎876/923–0222).

GROUND TRANSPORTATION

Many hotels offer shuttles to pick you up at the airport, or airport transfers may be included in the cost of a travel package. If your hotel does not offer a shuttle, the best way to your destination is by taxi, but the costs can be substantial. It's a long and expensive drive, for instance, from Norman Manley Airport in Kingston to Port Antonio.

In Montego Bay, the airport's new arrivals hall is home to hotel lounges for Sandals, Beaches, SuperClubs, Ritz-Carlton, Couples, Sunset, and Half Moon resorts; check-in at the desk and relax until the bus departs. The authorized airport taxi desk is just beyond the exit past Customs.

Hotel shuttles are less likely to be provided for Kingston hotels. The Jamaica Union of Travellers Association (JUTA) is the authorized taxi company at the Norman Manley International Airport; you'll find its desk just outside the Customs Hall in the Ground Transportation Hall.

TRANSFERS BETWEEN AIRPORTS

TimAir and International Airlink offer charter service between Montego Bay's Sangster International Airport and airports in Port Antonio, Ocho Rios, Runaway Bay, Kingston, and Negril. Scheduled service is available on International Airlink between Montego Bay and Kingston. Charter helicopter service is provided by Island Hoppers to Ocho Rios.

Contacts **International Airlink** (☎888/247–5465 ⊕www.intlairlink. com). **Island Hoppers** (☎876/974–1285 ⊕www.jamaicahelicoptertours. com). **TimAir** (☎876/952–2516 ⊕www.timair.com).

FLIGHTS

Jamaica is well served by major airlines. From the United States, Air Jamaica, American, Continental, Delta, Northwest, Spirit, United, and US Airways offer nonstop and connecting service.

Airline Contacts **Air Jamaica** (☎800/523–5585). **AmericanAirlines** (☎800/433–7300 ⊕www. aa.com). **Continental Airlines** (☎800/523—3273 for U.S. and Mexico reservations, 800/231–0856 for international reservations ⊕www.continental.com). **Delta Airlines** (☎800/221–1212 for U.S. reservations, 800/241–4141 for international reservations ⊕www. delta.com). **Northwest Airlines** (☎800/225–2525 ⊕www.nwa.com). **Spirit Airlines** (☎800/772–7117 or 586/791–7300 ⊕www.spiritair.com). **United Airlines** (☎800/864–8331 for U.S. reservations, 800/538–2929 for international reservations ⊕www.united.com). **US Airways** (☎800/428–4322 for U.S. and Canada reservations, 800/622–1015 for international reservations ⊕www. usairways.com).

▌ BY CAR

We don't recommend renting a car in Jamaica. Driving on the island can be extremely frustrating. You must constantly be on guard—for enormous potholes, people and animals darting out into the street. With a narrow road encircling the island, local drivers are quick to pass other cars. Sometimes two cars will pass simultaneously, inspiring the UNDERTAKERS LOVE OVERTAKERS signs seen throughout the island. Gas stations are open daily, but many accept only cash. Gas costs are roughly double that in the United States. Driving in Jamaica is on the left, British-style.

To rent a car you must be between the ages of 23 (with at least one year possessing a valid driver's license) and 70. Many car-rental companies also offer cell-phone rentals.

GASOLINE
Gas stations are open daily, but many accept only cash. Gas costs are roughly double that in the United States.

ROAD CONDITIONS
Many roads in Jamaica are in very poor condition, so you have to be on the lookout for enormous potholes. Be sure to budget extra time on the roads; in general, you can expect to spend just about twice as long to cover a distance as you would back home. The North Coast Highway from Ocho Rios to Port Antonio is undergoing a major construction project; expect long delays and rough driving conditions for the next several years on this road.

FROM	TO	RTE./
Montego Bay	Negril	48 mi (77 km); 1 hr 30 min
Montego Bay	Runaway Bay	45 mi (74 km); 1 hr 15 min
Montego Bay	Ocho Rios	63 mi (101 km); 1 hr 45 min
Kingston	Strawberry Hill	19 mi (30 km); 45 min
Kingston	Port Antonio	58 mi (93 km); 3 hrs
Kingston	Montego Bay	117 mi (189 km); 3 hr 15 min
Ocho Rios	Kingston	55 mi (89 km); 1 hr 30 min

ROADSIDE EMERGENCIES
In case of an accident, dial 119. On the major roads such as the North Coast Highway, you can call a garage in one of the larger towns. In rural areas, you'll probably have to rely on the help of locals to get your car up and running as far as one of the larger towns.

To report a car theft, call 119. You also need to call your rental-car agency.

Emergency Services **119**

RULES OF THE ROAD

Driving in Jamaica is on the left, British-style. Drivers and passengers in the front seat are required to wear seat belts, and motorcycle drivers are required to wear helmets. Children under age 4 must be in a car seat. The speed limit is 30 mph in town and 50 mph on the highways (although you'll see many local drivers going faster). Bad road conditions make it fairly easy for most drivers to remain below the speed limit, however.

Jamaica has strict drunk driving laws; drivers are prosecuted if they are found to have a blood level alcohol of more than .08%.

For U.S. drivers, Jamaica's many roundabouts or traffic circles are particularly perplexing. The rule of the road is the traffic entering the roundabout must yield to those already in it.

ON THE GROUND

▌ COMMUNICATIONS

INTERNET

Internet service is becoming far more common across Jamaica, and most hotels offer at least limited service, either at public terminals (sometimes free at the all-inclusive resorts) or in-room connections. High-speed cable and broadband connections are becoming more and more common at the larger resorts; expect to pay $15 to $20 per day for this option. A growing number of resorts are adding wireless service for a comparable price; some offer it only in public areas (including poolside), whereas others offer it in guest rooms as well.

PHONES

The good news is that you can now make a direct-dial telephone call from virtually any point on earth. The bad news? You can't always do so cheaply. Calling from a hotel is almost always the most expensive option; hotels usually add huge surcharges to all calls, particularly international ones. In some countries you can phone from call centers or even the post office. Calling cards usually keep costs to a minimum, but only if you purchase them locally. And then there are mobile phones (⇨ below), which are sometimes more prevalent—particularly in the developing world—than land lines; as expensive as mobile-phone calls can be, they are still usually a much cheaper option than calling from your hotel.

Public phones are common in Jamaica but you'll generally need to use a Cable & Wireless phone card; these are available across the island at hotels and retail stores. Cellular service is good in the resort areas although service is spotty in the hills.

CALLING WITHIN JAMAICA

Jamaica has an efficient telephone system with direct dialing; local telephone numbers are all seven digits. All calls in Jamaica are within the 876 area code. All calls, however, are not local calls; dialing between parishes generally involves long-distance charges. To reach directory assistance on the island, dial 114.

CALLING OUTSIDE JAMAICA

Long-distance calls outside Jamaica can be made directly from hotels; however, calling from the hotel is the most expensive option. Some long-distance telephone companies provide calling-card service to Jamaica; others, such as MCI, provide limited availability at only some hotels due to the high rate of fraud.

CALLING CARDS

Although used less often by visitors than cell phones and long-distance services, phone cards are very common in Jamaica, sold at the airports, retail stores, and hotels. Cable & Wireless sells phone cards in varying denominations up to $500; Cable & Wireless also sells WorldTalk cards, which can be used for international calls.

MOBILE PHONES

If you have a multiband phone (some countries use different frequencies than what's used in the United States) and your service provider uses the world-standard GSM network (as do T-Mobile, Cingular, and Verizon), you can probably use your phone abroad. Roaming fees can be steep, however: 99¢ a minute is considered reasonable. And overseas you normally pay the toll charges for incoming calls. It's almost always cheaper to send a text message than to make a call, since text messages have a very low set fee (often less than 5¢).

If you just want to make local calls, consider buying a new SIM card (note that your provider may have to unlock your phone for you to use a different SIM card) and a prepaid service plan in the destination. You'll then have a local number and can make local calls at local rates. If your trip is extensive, you could also simply buy a new cell phone in your destination, as the initial cost will be offset over time.

■ TIP→ **If you travel internationally frequently, save one of your old mobile phones or buy a cheap one on the Internet; ask your cell-phone company to unlock it for you, and take it with you as a travel phone, buying a new SIM card with pay-as-you-go service in each destination.**

Good mobile-phone coverage is available in the resort areas although coverage can be spotty in rural areas. Jamaica's cellular system uses TDMA and GSM technologies; phones that are TDMA or GSM compatible will work if your provider has a roaming agreement with Cable & Wireless Mobile or Digicel Jamaica. Cell phone rates are expensive, however; rates range about $1.50 to $2 per minute for calls from Jamaica to the United States or Canada.

Cell-phone rental is available at both the Montego Bay and Kingston airports as well as from some car-rental companies. Expect to pay about $50 for a one-week rental; this includes a Jamaican SIM card. With a Jamaican SIM card, expect to pay about 14 cents per minute for local calls within Jamaica and 30 cents per minute for calls to the United States.

Contacts Cellular Abroad (☎800/287-5072 ⊕www.cellular abroad.com) rents and sells GMS phones and sells SIM cards that work in many countries. **Mobal** (☎888/888-9162 ⊕www.mobal rental.com) rents mobiles and sells GSM phones (starting at $49) that will operate in 140 countries. Per-call rates vary throughout the world. **Planet Fone** (☎888/988-4777 ⊕www.planetfone.com) rents cell phones, but the per-minute rates are expensive.

CUSTOMS & DUTIES

You're always allowed to bring goods of a certain value back home without having to pay any duty or import tax. But there's a limit on the amount of tobacco and liquor you can bring back duty-free, and some countries have separate limits for perfumes; for exact figures, check with your customs department. The values of so-called "duty-free" goods are included in these amounts. When you shop abroad, save all your receipts, as customs inspectors may ask to see them as well as the items you purchased. If the total value of your goods is more than the duty-free limit, you'll have to pay a tax (most often a flat percentage) on the value of everything beyond that limit.

Clearing customs is generally a fast process at both the Montego Bay and Kingston airports. You are provided a customs form (often on the airplane) that you hand to customs officials. Arriving passengers are permitted to bring a ½ pound of tobacco, 1 quart of spirits, 6 fluid ounces of perfume, and 12 fluid ounces of cologne. Prohibited items include coffee, fruits, vegetables, fresh flowers, honey, firearms, explosives, and illegal drugs. Pet lovers should note that it is prohibited to bring any animals into Jamaica.

U.S. Information **U.S. Customs and Border Protection** (⊕www. cbp.gov).

EATING OUT

Although a lot of people stay at all-inclusive resorts, there is still a good selection of independent restaurants scattered around Jamaica, particularly in the Montego Bay and Negril resort areas. From beach bars that serve spicy jerk barbecue to seafood shacks serving the catch of the day to international eateries with white-glove service, there are plenty of dining options. Vegetarians will favor the meatless food at Rastafarian restaurants. As the capital, Kingston has a very lively dining scene.

For information on food-related health issues, see Health, below.

MEALS & MEALTIMES

Jamaica maintains much the same meals times as found in the United States. Larger hotels serve American-style breakfasts; away from the resort areas, look for a traditional breakfast of ackee (a fruit that, when prepared properly, resembles scrambled eggs) alongside saltfish, boiled bananas, fritters, and fresh fruit. Lunch, served around noon, consists of patties (turnovers stuffed with spicy beef or chicken) or other local dishes such as jerk chicken or pork, often accompanied by fruit punch. Dinner is typically served at 7 or later and may includes offerings such as escovitch fish served with a vinegary sauce and a variety of soups such as pumpkin or callaloo. In larger towns (especially in Kingston), it's traditional for many families to eat out on Friday night; restaurants away from resorts will be busiest that night.

Unless otherwise noted, the restaurants listed in this guide are open daily for lunch and dinner.

PAYING

Credit cards are accepted at most restaurants, but not at the more modest local spots. But you can usually pay in U.S. dollars at even the simplest establishment, though your change may be given in Jamaican currency.

For guidelines on tipping see Tipping, below.

RESERVATIONS & DRESS

Although bathing suits are never appropriate for anywhere except the beach and the pool, casual dress is expected at most restaurants. In the nicest restaurants (including some hotel restaurants), long pants and collared shirt are appreciated and, at a few establishments, jackets.

In this book, we mention dress only when men are required to wear a jacket or a jacket and tie.

WINES, BEER & SPIRITS

There's no shortage of spirits in Jamaica; the island produces many excellent rums and beers. Local liquors are always the least expensive option (and, in some limited all-inclusives, the only options available without a surcharge). Wine is one spirit that's not made locally in Jamaica so it often demands a premium.

WORD OF MOUTH

Was the service stellar or not up to snuff? Did the food give you shivers of delight or leave you cold? Did the prices and portions make you happy or sad? Rate restaurants and write your own reviews in "Travel Ratings" or start a discussion about your favorite places in "Travel Talk" on www.fodors.com. Your comments might even appear in our books. Yes, you, too, can be a correspondent!

Bars, particularly at the all-inclusives, generally open at 10 AM and remain hopping into the early morning hours. Away from the resorts, rum shops, usually open-air bars, are very common; inquire at your hotel as to which are safe to visit.

▍ELECTRICITY

As in North America, the current in Jamaica is 110 volts with 50 cycles, and outlets that take two flat prongs. Some hotels provide 220-volt plugs for electric shavers. If you plan to bring electrical appliances with you, it's best to ask when making your reservation.

Consider making a small investment in a universal adapter, which has several types of plugs in one lightweight, compact unit. Most laptops and mobile-phone chargers are dual voltage (i.e., they operate equally well on 110 and 220 volts), so require only an adapter. These days the same is true of small appliances such as hair dryers. Always check labels and manufacturer instructions to be sure. Don't use 110-volt outlets marked FOR SHAVERS ONLY for high-wattage appliances such as hair dryers.

Contacts **Steve Kropla's Help for World Traveler's** (⊕www.kropla. com) has information on electrical and telephone plugs around the world. **Walkabout Travel Gear** (⊕www.walkabouttravelgear.com) has a good coverage of electricity under "adapters."

EMERGENCIES

Emergency Services **Ambulance & Fire Emergencies** (☎110). **Police Emergencies & Air Rescue** (☎119).

▌ HEALTH

The most common types of illnesses are caused by contaminated food and water. Especially in developing countries, drink only bottled, boiled, or purified water and drinks; don't drink from public fountains or use ice. You should even consider using bottled water to brush your teeth. Make sure food has been thoroughly cooked and is served to you fresh and hot; avoid vegetables and fruits that you haven't washed (in bottled or purified water) or peeled yourself. If you have problems, mild cases of traveler's diarrhea may respond to Imodium (known generically as loperamide) or Pepto-Bismol. Be sure to drink plenty of fluids; if you can't keep fluids down, seek medical help immediately.

Infectious diseases can be airborne or passed via mosquitoes and ticks and through direct or indirect physical contact with animals or people. Some, including Norwalk-like viruses that affect your digestive tract, can be passed along through contaminated food. If you're traveling in an area where malaria is prevalent, use a repellent containing DEET and take malaria-prevention medication before, during, and after your trip as directed by your physician. Condoms can help prevent most sexually-transmitted diseases, but they aren't absolutely reliable and their quality varies from country to country. Speak with your physician and/or check the CDC or World Health Organization Web sites for health alerts, particularly if you're pregnant, traveling with children, or have a chronic illness.

For information on travel insurance, shots and medications, and medical-assistance companies see Shots & Medications under Things to Consider in Before You Go, above.

SPECIFIC ISSUES IN JAMAICA

Heat exhaustion and sunburn are the most common tourist ailments in Jamaica. Sunscreen is widely available in drug stores (and hotel gift stores), but is priced much higher than what you'd pay at home. Insect repellent is another handy item to pack both for mosquitoes and sand flies that generally come out at sunset.

Malaria was reported in the Kingston area in 2006. The outbreak quickly subsided, however. Another mosquito-borne disease is dengue. This disease, which causes fever and aches, is transmitted by a mosquito that, unlike malarial mosquitoes, bites during the daytime hours. A good-quality insect repellent is the best defense. Most hotels are air-conditioned, so mosquitoes are not a problem in the rooms; those that are not generally provide both mosquito netting for the bed and mosquito coils to burn to repel the insects. Also, hotel gift shops as well as local supermarkets sell mosquito repellents, although at higher prices than in the United States.

Although Jamaica has no poisonous snakes, swimmers should take care to avoid sea urchins, jellyfish, and fire coral. Wearing water shoes is the easiest way to avoid the needles of the sea urchin in shallow water.

OVER-THE-COUNTER REMEDIES

Familiar brands of pain relievers, stomach medicines, and other over-the-counter medications will be found in the resort areas, although less commonly in the small towns. All will be priced higher than in the United States.

▌ HOURS OF OPERATION

Banks are generally open Monday through Thursday 9 to 2, Friday 9 to 4. Post offices are open weekdays 9 to 5. Normal business hours for stores are weekdays from 8:30 to 4:30, Saturday 8 to 1. In the cruise ports

of Montego Bay and Ocho Rios, stores often have extended hours to accommodate cruise-ship passengers. Expect most shops to be closed on Sunday unless a cruise ship is in port. Many bars and nightclubs close at 2 AM, but some stay open much later depending on the crowds.

HOLIDAYS

Public holidays include New Year's Day, Ash Wednesday (6 weeks before Easter), Good Friday, Easter Monday, Labor Day (May 23), Independence Day (1st Monday in August), National Heroes Day (October 15), Christmas, and Boxing Day (December 26). Along with the closure of many attractions, numerous tours do not operate on these days.

▌ MAIL

Postcards may be mailed anywhere in the world for J$50. Letters cost J$60 to the United States and Canada, J$70 to Europe, J$90 to Australia and New Zealand. Due to costly and slow air-shipping service, most travelers carry home packages, even bulky wooden carvings. As home of the island's busiest international airport, you can find international courier services in Montego Bay for shipping extremely large purchases. A number of shipping companies, both international and domestic, also operate out of Kingston. Call around for the best rates and to confirm pickup options.

▌ MONEY

The official currency is the Jamaican dollar. At this writing the exchange rate was about J$66.27 to US$1. Prices quoted throughout this chapter are in U.S. dollars, unless otherwise noted. The U.S. dollar is widely accepted, and few Americans bother to exchange money—especially if they stay in an all-inclusive resort for their entire trip. As long as you're in a resort area, you can almost be assured of being able to pay in U.S. dollars (though your change may be given in Jamaican currency). You can exchange money at the airport or your hotel, and you'll get a fairly good exchange rate regardless of where you go.

Prices throughout this guide are given for adults. Substantially reduced fees are almost always available for children, students, and senior citizens.

ATMS & BANKS

Your own bank will probably charge a fee for using ATMs abroad; the foreign bank you use may also charge a fee. Nevertheless, you'll usually get a better rate of exchange at an ATM than you will at a currency-exchange office or even when changing money in a bank. And extracting funds as you need them is a safer option than carrying around a large amount of cash.

■TIP→ **PIN numbers with more than four digits are not recognized at ATMs in many countries. If yours has five or more, remember to change it before you leave.**

Not all ATMs in Jamaica accept American cards, although a growing number in the resort areas do. Travelers often find themselves having to try more than one machine. Some ATMs dispense either Jamaican or U.S. dollars. NCB ATMs offer U.S. dollars using debit or credit cards.

CREDIT CARDS

Throughout this guide, the following abbreviations are used: **AE**, American Express; **D**, Discover; **DC**, Diners Club; **MC**, MasterCard; and **V**, Visa.

It's a good idea to inform your credit-card company before you travel, especially if you're going abroad and don't travel internationally very often. Otherwise, the credit-card company might put a hold on your card owing to unusual activity—not a good thing halfway through your trip. Record all your credit-card numbers—as well as the phone numbers to call if your cards are lost or stolen—in a safe place, so you're prepared should something go wrong. Both MasterCard and Visa have general numbers you can call (collect if you're abroad) if your card is lost, but you're better off calling the number of your issuing bank, since MasterCard and Visa usually just transfer you to your bank; your bank's number is usually printed on your card.

If you plan to use your credit card for cash advances, you'll need to apply for a PIN at least two weeks before your trip.

Although it's usually cheaper (and safer) to use a credit card abroad for large purchases (so you can cancel payments or be reimbursed if there's a problem), note that some credit-card companies *and* the banks that issue them add substantial percentages to all foreign transactions, whether they're in a foreign currency or not. Check on these fees before leaving home, so there won't be any surprises when you get the bill.

Major credit cards are accepted throughout the island, although cash is required at most gas stations, supermarkets, and drug stores. Cash advances at ATMs and banks can be made using credit cards—provided that you have a PIN.

Reporting Lost Cards **American Express** (☎800/528–4800 in U.S., 336/393–1111 collect from abroad ⊕www.americanexpress.com). **Diners Club** (☎800/234–6377 in U.S., 303/799–1504 collect from abroad ⊕www.dinersclub.com). **Discover** (☎800/347–2683 in U.S., 801/902–3100 collect from abroad ⊕www.discovercard.com). **MasterCard** (☎800/627–8372 in U.S., 636/722–7111 collect from abroad ⊕www.mastercard.com). **Visa** (☎800/847–2911 in U.S., 410/581–9994 collect from abroad ⊕www.visa.com).

█ SAFETY

Jamaica has a reputation as a dangerous destination thanks to a murder rate that consistently ranks among the world's highest. Much of the violence is centered around gang conflicts in Kingston, but it does occasionally spill over into other communities. The weeks before and after general elections are particular hazardous, as political tensions have been known to spark gunfire and killings.

Beyond murder, road safety is another prime concern. Jamaica is also plagued by one of the world's highest auto fatality rates. Excessive speed and reckless driving are commonplace, so travelers should always be conscientious about taking licensed taxi cabs.

Theft is also a problem, everything from wallets left on beach blankets to items from parked cars. Most hotels provide in-room safes, so be sure to use them for all valuables that aren't necessary during the day. It's best to leave jewelry at home, although costume jewelry is generally fine. Pickpocketing and snatch-and-run thefts are not much as problem in the resort areas, but are concerns in Kingston.

█TIP→ **Distribute your cash, credit cards, IDs, and other valuables between a deep front pocket, an inside jacket or vest pocket, and a hidden money pouch. Don't reach for the money pouch once you're in public.**

█ TAXES

A departure tax of $27 must be paid in cash if it's not added to the cost of your airline tickets; this policy varies by carrier, although most tickets now include the departure tax. Jamaica has replaced the room occupancy tax with a V.A.T. of 15% on most goods and services, which is already incorporated into the prices of taxable goods. Since 2005, incoming air passengers are charged a $10 tourism enhancement fee; incoming cruise passengers pay a $2 fee. Both these fees are almost always included in the price of your ticket.

TIME

Jamaica is in the eastern time zone (GMT-5). The island does not observe daylight savings time.

TIPPING

Most hotels and restaurants add a 10% service charge to your bill. When a service charge isn't included, a 10% to 20% tip is expected. Tips of 10% to 20% are customary for taxi drivers as well. However, many all-inclusives have a strict no-tipping policy.

INDEX

NOTES

NOTES

NOTES

NOTES

ABOUT OUR WRITERS

John Bigley and Paris Permenter fell in love with the Caribbean two decades ago and have turned their extensive knowledge of the region into an occupation. As professional travel writers and photographers, the husband-wife team contributes to many consumer and trade publications. From their home base in the Hill Country near Austin, Texas, Paris and John also edit Lovetripper.com, an online romantic travel guide for honeymooners and romantic travelers. Both Paris and John are members of the Society of American Travel Writers.